GET RICH
BLOGGING

Zoe is the founder of the celebrity news and fashion blog www.livelikeavip.com.

Prior to establishing this online hub of celebrity information, Zoe had print columns in the *Sunday Mirror* and the *London Paper*, and she was a staff reporter at the *Mail on Sunday*. Zoe also wrote freelance celebrity articles for glossy magazines, including *Grazia*, *Cosmopolitan*, *Company*, *Now*, *Heat* and *Look*.

She became a full-time blogger in 2009, and her remuneration has rocketed. Zoe's revenue is from a mixture of advertising, guest-blogging, public speaking engagements and consultancy projects. Brands she's worked with include Very.co.uk, the Arcadia Group, Medichem International, British Airways, Cadburys, Kenco Coffee and Charnos.

A *Cosmopolitan Magazine* Blog Award for Best Celebrity Blog and a London Lifestyle Award for London Personality of the Year take pride of place in Zoe's east London office, alongside a photograph taken with Brad Pitt in Cannes and a pair of Armani pants signed by David Beckham.

GET RICH BLOGGING

Zoe Griffin

JOHN BLAKE

Published by John Blake Publishing Ltd,
3 Bramber Court, 2 Bramber Road,
London W14 9PB, England

www.johnblakepublishing.co.uk

www.facebook.com/Johnblakepub   facebook

twitter.com/johnblakepub   **twitter**

First published in paperback in 2013

ISBN: 978 1 78219 011 0

British Library Cataloguing-in-Publication Data:

A catalogue record for this book is available from the British Library.

Design by www.envydesign.co.uk

Printed and bound in Great Britain by CPI Group (UK) Ltd

1 3 5 7 9 10 8 6 4 2

© Text copyright Zoe Griffin 2013

Papers used by John Blake Publishing are natural, recyclable products made
from wood grown in sustainable forests. The manufacturing processes
conform to the environmental regulations of the country of origin.

Every attempt has been made to contact the relevant copyright-holders,
but some were unobtainable. We would be grateful if the
appropriate people could contact us.

It is nevertheless intended that the work is interesting, entertaining and as accurate as possible taking into account all the circumstances prevailing at the time of going to press.

CONTENTS

PART I

CHAPTER 1

BLOGS – THE WHAT, WHEN, WHO AND MORE

WHAT I WISH I'D KNOWN BEFORE I STARTED

Do you know what a blog is? Are you sure? Do you know what you're meant to put on a blog? These are not trick questions. Before you can expect to earn an income from any business, you need to know the fundamentals.

I've learned from experience that making money from a blog requires a strategic approach. I have a celebrity news and gossip blog called *Live Like A VIP* (livelikeavip.com). It's entertaining, it's gossipy and we sometimes talk about superficial subjects like fit men and cupcakes, but I didn't wake up one morning to discover a website wizard had waved his magic wand and granted me high levels of traffic. There's no fairy dust and there's no quick fix. I worked my way up and made mistakes on the way. I may not blog about the most intellectually stimulating subject in the world – but it sells!

You, too, could make a living from what you love writing about, as long as you take a businesslike approach to your blog.

Growing a blog is a step-by-step process and if you set one up in haste and try to run before you can walk, it's guaranteed to end in tears.

Right now, I am smiling. In fact, I am grinning like I have just won the jackpot on the EuroMillions lottery. I am lucky. After three years of full-time blogging, I am able to set my own hours. I can work from wherever I want in the world, and I can write about what I want to write about. I've won awards that are proudly displayed on my mantelpiece such as a *Cosmopolitan Magazine* Blog Award for Best Celebrity Blog and a London Lifestyle Award for London Personality Of The Year. I can talk about my favourite subjects all day long with like-minded people, and I make excellent money. Sometimes I get paid to write about events for which many people fight for invites, such as the London 2012 Olympics, where British Airways picked me as an influential ambassador, gave me tickets and asked me to blog about it. Sometimes I get to try revolutionary hair and beauty treatments before anyone else. I was one of the first to try the world's most popular hair dye remover, Colour B4, and I was one of a few brave bloggers involved in testing the UK's first Garra Rufa fish pedicure treatment – where fish eat the soles of your feet – before it became a nationwide phenomenon. I am delighted with how it has all turned out because I made some stupid mistakes along the way.

I decided to set up an independent celebrity news and gossip website three years ago, at a time when there was nothing quite like it in the UK. Many people thought I was crazy because I had a good job at a national newspaper. The *Sunday Mirror* sent me around the world to interview celebrities and write about lavish showbiz events, and my face appeared at the top of a double-page column. But it was while I was on an assignment in LA that I found out more about the world of blogging. In Los Angeles, bloggers are treated like kings and queens. Publicists realise these bloggers have the power to send albums to Number One and conversely, the power to destroy entire careers with one push of the publish button. I'm talking about the likes of *TMZ* (tmz.com), *The Huffington Post* (huffingtonpost.com), *Gawker* (gawker.com), *Deadline Hollywood* (deadlinehollywood.com) and *Perez Hilton* (perezhilton.com).

These bloggers are their own bosses, with no screaming editors ordering what to cover or telling them their writing isn't good enough. They're able to pick and choose what events they attend without justifying their decisions to a line manager. If they want to take a day off, they simply schedule a blog post to go up and head for the beach. There's no need to put in a holiday request form or arrange cover. How amazing is that?

I set up a blog as soon as I got back to the UK. Initially I tried to run it at the same time as working for the *Sunday Mirror* and ended up surviving on four hours' sleep a night. While I loved contributing to a national newspaper, I was working long hours and I was often trying to write my blog at 3am. The blogging suffered as I was writing when I was tired and it soon became clear that I would have to make a decision – column or blog? And so I resigned.

With the benefit of hindsight, I acted in haste. I didn't know what it truly meant to be a blogger and therefore traffic growth was slow. Ultimately, I didn't have a strategy. I truly expected that if I wrote some posts about celebrity-related subjects, then readers would miraculously find me. They didn't and I'd quit my job! What on earth was I going to do? If I wanted to continue blogging, I'd need to learn how to do it better. If I didn't improve, I wouldn't be able to pay my mortgage, I wouldn't be able to afford cupcakes, and I certainly wouldn't be able to buy new clothes and shoes. Trauma! I needed a plan.

If you want to make money in any field, then a plan is vital. When a new company prepares to launch, they tend to draw up a five-year business plan. The company directors work out where they want the company to be in five years' time and set long-term goals. With that vision in mind, they work backwards and set goals for year one and year two. If the goal after five years is a profit of £10 million, then they might plan to achieve £1 million in year one, £2 million in year two, £5 million in year three and so on. They might also jot down ways to raise that money – will they achieve a revenue of £10 million through selling a product or a service, or both? How much do they need to sell to make £10 million?

If you hope to make money from your blog, you need a plan. You need to know the ways blogs generate revenue and the conditions that must be in place to generate the most money possible. Then you can set yourself targets, and work through a step-by-step process to lay down the foundations for a blog that will make you money.

This book is divided into two parts. In Part I, I talk you through the steps needed to ensure your blog becomes a profit-making business. Most chapters end with a checklist, and every time you tick off the targets on these lists, you are one step closer to getting rich from your blog. In Part II, I delve deeper into popular blogging subject areas, from fashion and beauty to business and technology, and give you some industry-specific points for your checklists. When a business starts out, often its directors will consult similar business models to copy the success stories. What they learn depends on what type of industry they're in, so each blogging subject area gets its own chapter. Fashion bloggers will be taking a different route to tech bloggers – simply pick the chapter that's most relevant to you.

Now I'm business-like and methodical about it, I'm earning more than I ever thought possible and it's all because I have a plan. I wish I'd known this before I quit my job. So, there is no better place to start than with the basics!

WHAT IS A BLOG?

If you want your blog to make you rich, you need to know what a blog is. Businesses that make money do so because they meet their customers' expectations. If a fashion store didn't know what customers expected and started stocking TVs or cakes then people entering the store hoping to find clothing would be disappointed and would not return. To avoid disappointing prospective readers, you need to know what they expect from a blog. You need to know what elements make up a blog so that when people search the Internet looking for a blog they're not surprised by what they see on yours.

To understand what a blog is, we must first understand the difference between a blog and a website. The dictionary definition of 'website' is that it's a set of web pages containing content that is hosted on a web server and accessible via the Internet. Surely the so-called 'blogs' *TMZ*, *Gawker* and *Perez Hilton* fall into that category? Indeed they do, but they also fall into a sub-category of that term. There are features *Perez Hilton* and *TMZ* have in common that other static websites don't have, which I'll explain in more detail below. On a basic level, they have common traits like regular updates, RSS (really simple syndication) feeds and date-based archives and they are regularly updated with fresh content, but not all websites have these features.

To put it simply, a blog is a type of website and all blogs have common characteristics. Whether you're looking at a blog about food and drink, a blog about fashion or a blog about technology, you'll always find it's updated often and the freshest content is at the top. In contrast, the design features of most websites never change.

For example, if I go to the website of my favourite online retailer and look for shoes (something I spend far too much time doing), then I'll probably see it hasn't changed much in the past year. New stock may have come in, but the overall design will have stayed consistent. Products will always be displayed with thumbnail images and the retailer's logo is always at the top of the site. But if I look at my favourite fashion blogs, I will see they're constantly changing and evolving. Each day, a new post is published and the top area of the blog completely changes.

Blogs are dynamic and constantly changing, whereas other websites tend to be fixed and solid.

EXERCISE

Look at the website Very.co.uk and make a list of how it is similar to and how it is different from the blog *Style Bubble* (stylebubble.typepad.com). Look out for things like:

• How often are they updated?

- How old is the information in the top third of the website?
- How much content is there?
- Is the new content presented in a chronological order or organically?
- What tone is the website written in?

To make sure you get it exactly right, here are all the key features of blogs:

REGULAR UPDATES

Remember that 'blog' is short for 'web log' and that's the whole point: most people update their blog a few times a week, some update a few times a day. It all depends on how much a blogger feels moved to comment about a particular subject. And remember, if one blogger doesn't update regularly, you'll always be able to find one who does.

CHRONOLOGICAL UPDATES

When a blogger writes a new blog post, that blog post appears at the top of the blog's homepage. Other recent posts move down the page to make room for the newest content at the top. This makes it easy for people to join in with the newest part of the conversation.

DATE-BASED ARCHIVES

A lot of blogs contain an archive section in their sidebar, allowing readers to see all the information that was written in a particular month. We want to be able to find information easily so we can engage with a subject. If bloggers didn't archive their subjects, then searching for a particular post would be almost impossible. Who has time to scroll through pages and pages of a blog to find something that was written months ago?

CATEGORY-BASED ARCHIVES

Some bloggers choose to label their content with keywords that describe what an article is about. For example, a celebrity blogger might categorise their blog by subjects like music, film, fashion and TV, and some others go even further and categorise with celebrity names and list this on their sidebar in an A to Z format. At the time of posting a blogger will include some information as to what categories a post is relevant to. This allows readers to navigate the blog by category as opposed to the usual chronological way. For example, if readers are specifically interested in music they can click on the music category and all the posts that have been labelled 'music' will show up. This makes life a lot easier for readers than scrolling down through all the posts to find the music ones.

PERMALINKS

Each time someone writes a blog post, it comes up at the top of the blog's homepage. In addition to this, the blog software automatically creates a separate page of your blog containing nothing else but that article and your sidebar links and any comments that people make under the post. The URL (uniform resource locator) at the top of that page is your permalink, short for 'permanent link'. This adds another page to your website and it's a brilliant way to get a blog noticed. Each new page is another chance a blog will be picked up by search engines so new people discover you and join in the conversation. Thankfully bloggers don't need to do anything or have any knowledge to create a permalink. If the blog is designed in the right way, it just happens.

HEADER LOGO

Most blogs differentiate themselves from others with a logo or an image alongside the title of the blog in the top bar. (The words *Live Like A VIP* are in the header of my blog and there's an image of me.) This header is visible on every page of the blog, even the individual posts, so readers can identify the blogger at all times. It's particularly useful if they visit the blog through a permalink without going through your homepage. If the header wasn't on every page then permalinks would be floating through cyberspace at random without a clear way of tracing what websites they belong to.

COMMENTS AND FEEDBACK

Most blogs allow readers to leave comments underneath blog posts. A lot of websites don't want people to spoil the design by commenting and interacting on top of a carefully designed page. Imagine if the shops Asos or Very.co.uk allowed readers to write what they thought all over the thumbnail images on the homepage. There would be so many comments that you wouldn't be able to see the clothes. Websites, in general, don't allow people to give their feedback, whereas blogs actively encourage this.

DATE AND AUTHOR INFORMATION

Often – but not always – a blogger will display information such as who wrote the post, as some blogs have multiple authors.

They normally display the date and time so you can see how relevant it is.

LINKS

The aim of a blog is to encourage conversation; so many bloggers have introduced buttons at the end of posts like 'Send to a friend' or 'Post this blog to Facebook'. It's all part of a blog's design so that whenever a blogger writes a new post, these buttons come up automatically.

BLOGROLL

If a blogger lists other blogs they find interesting or useful, then readers are grateful that they have another relevant place to visit if they're looking for a certain piece of information. By admitting you don't have all the answers, people pay attention to what you do have to offer. Also, the blogs you link to may repay the favour and link to your blog, thus giving you new traffic.

RSS FEED

Readers can use RSS to subscribe to your blog. They can link this to a newsletter or embed it in their own site so they can read the latest updates without visiting your blog. If another blog is using your RSS feed, then it's massively increasing your profile.

If you design your blog with all these elements in mind, you'll fit right into the blogging community. Your blog will be easy to use and people will keep coming back. I'll explain the design process in more detail in Chapter 3. For now, we still need to work on the general plan.

HOW CAN YOU MAKE MONEY BLOGGING?

You can't put together a five-year plan and set yourself financial goals without having an idea of how to achieve these targets. Imagine I said I wanted to make £1 million in year one, sat back, did nothing and then wondered why I hadn't got anywhere!

When a business formulates a plan, it will know what it can sell or provide to bring in money. The sportswear brand Nike makes a large proportion of its profits by selling trainers. However, the company also sells sports clothing with tracksuits and jogging vests and yoga gear as well as accessories, including watches, sunglasses and hats. There's even a Nike training app on the iPhone for sports enthusiasts around the world to download workouts formulated by fitness instructors sponsored by Nike. All of those revenue streams mean Nike can realistically set a multi-million target because the company has identified several different ways it can generate funds. So, how can a blog make you money?

DIRECT REVENUE

Google AdSense This program will match ads to your blog's content without you having to lift a finger. Simply visit google.com/adsense and answer some questions about the content of your blog. If you blog about celebrity and fashion, you may get advertisers from a clothing store. If your readers click on these ads then the clothing label pays Google and in turn Google pays you. What you earn is closely related to how many people click through, which is related to how much traffic you have.

Ad networks A number of advertising middlemen can help bloggers place ads on their sites. Bloggers choose between text and graphic, set the size, tell the advertising agency how much space is available and the agencies negotiate a suitable deal. The proportion of revenue is spilt between the blogger and the network that negotiated the deal. Ads on my blog are sold with Glam Media, and these are targeted towards my fashion and beauty content. If someone clicks on one of these ads, Glam Media and I will each get 50 per cent of the revenue.

Affiliates Affiliate advertising involves taking a commission by referring a customer to a product. For example, if I write about an album by a new artist and link to where my readers can buy the track on Amazon, I will receive money every time one of my readers buys it. Through what's known as a cookie, the retailer is able to track where the customer came from to realise that it was my blog which referred them to the sale. There are lots of affiliate programs and you can do deals with individual retailers like Argos or Amazon, or do them all at once by signing up to affiliate networks. The network Affiliate Window manages deals with clothing chains, and Buy.AT specialises in gadget firms. If you get it right, this can be a lucrative way to make money, especially if you receive high levels of traffic. However, some bloggers find if they recommend products too often or recommend products that its readers do not need, they're in danger of losing traffic as the community of readers starts to feel that the blogger is selling out and trying to cash in.

Link-based ads You can make the links in your posts earn money by signing up to a link-based advertising program such as Skim Links (skimlinks.com) or Link Share (linkshare.com). Using links to other websites within your copy is a way to improve search engine optimisation (SEO) and the link-based programs make it even more beneficial by negotiating deals with advertisers that will pay your per link click. You register for the program, pick the brands you want to promote, install some tracking code into your website and count the cash! It's a more discreet way to advertise than putting banner ads all over your blog, and people are more likely to click through if you encourage them through the words you've written in that blog post.

INDIRECT REVENUE

Collaborations A successful blog has the ability to influence hundreds of thousands if not millions of people – it's a very powerful tool. Many bloggers make a good living by doing consultancy projects, acting as the middle ground between all their readers and a manufacturer or brand with a product. This could range from being asked to be part of a focus group testing out a product-in-development to a hands-on role in actually designing the item. The blogger behind *Fashion Foie Gras* (fashionfoiegras.com) has her own handbag, and blogger Bip Ling (bipling.com) has worked with clothing brand Forever 21 to such an extent that she is now a model for the fashion chain.

Speaking engagements Your blog is an online showcase, better than any CV, showing you are an expert in a particular field. This is appealing to anyone who wants to target a specific group of delegates. Knowledge is invaluable. Sometimes these conferences will be in glamorous foreign locations or on cruise ships and you should get costs covered plus a fee.

Public appearances: When a blog is established in its niche and read by everyone in the industry then that blogger becomes a celebrity figure within their chosen field. For example, if you have a successful motoring blog then you may be asked to open a motoring show. If you have a successful fashion blog then you may be asked to compère a catwalk show or even model in one! Many celebrity and music bloggers make a great sideline by DJing. Event organisers love it when bloggers are involved in their projects because it often inspires the bloggers' followers to attend the event, and the blogger normally writes about it afterwards, generating extra publicity. The fee can be similar to that of a speaking engagement. If you're giving up your time to attend an event and help the organisers create a memorable occasion, it's only right that you get rewarded.

Freelance contracts Many businesses are launching a blog element to their websites and need some help with the editorial side of things. For example, the fashion retailers Topshop, Very.co.uk and Missguided all have blogs and someone has to write them. Occasionally, the company bosses may spot your fashion blog and ask you to help develop theirs, write it and suggest opportunities. These businesses may be hoping that your blog readers will see you are writing extra content in a different area and follow you to the brand's website to pull in more traffic for them, but you don't have to promise this: you're being paid to write. Freelance blogging is a good opportunity to raise the profile of your own blog and be seen as an expert in the field, while earning money at the same time. Admittedly, you have to have a very successful blog to be spotted but some bloggers are proactive and contact businesses to offer up their services and end up getting paid well as a result of this.

You might have realised by now that there are more ways to make money blogging than you first thought! Chapters 8 and 9 of this book will go into more detail about direct revenue, and Chapter 10 is all about indirect money-making methods. But for now, let's get back to the overall plan.

WHEN CAN YOU EXPECT TO MAKE MONEY FROM BLOGGING?

For any business, the amount of revenue generated and the speed at which it's generated are closely related to the number of customers willing to buy the business's services. So the question of when a business can make money depends on how quickly it can grow its customer database. Applying this to blogging, you can expect to make money when you've grown your traffic to a decent level.

How quick is that? There is no one-size-fits-all answer to this, I'm afraid – it all depends on how much time you can commit. A shop that is only open three days a week will take longer to earn money than one that is open five days a week. If your other commitments prevent you from spending time working on your blog, you may find it takes you longer to make money from it. However, if you put a bit of time and effort into it then you should be pleasantly surprised by the speed at which you grow traffic and make money. I've been going three years and I now have a six-figure income.

So, how did I do it? By following the steps that I'm about to outline in Chapters 2 to 7. I approached blogging like a business, set myself small targets and checked things off on my to-do list. If you've got five days a week to blog, then you'll get through my checklists very quickly and be up and running in no time. But if you can only spend an hour a week, don't worry about it. It's better than nothing and you'll get there in the end.

WHO HAS MADE MONEY BLOGGING?

Whenever you start something new in life, you're bound to have doubts. Starting a blog is a scary prospect and you may be wondering if you have what it takes to work your way through the rest of this book. Stick with it! Otherwise you could be missing out on a chance to earn $30 million.

Seriously, that's what Tech blogger Michael Arrington earned when he sold his blog *Techcrunch* (techcrunch.com) to AOL in 2005. But it's not just the Americans who are working the blogging world – the best British example is Pete Cashmore who founded *Mashable*. He was 19 when he set it up from his bedroom in a small village near Aberdeen in Scotland. *Mashable* now gets approximately 50 million page views a year and has 2.7 million Twitter followers. As a result, Pete now earns upwards of £150,000 each month and has about 50 employees in offices in New York and San Francisco. It's estimated that Brit Nick Denton, of the Gawker media empire, makes £4,000 a day from adverts on *Life Hacker* (lifehacker.com) and he owns another blog called *Kotaku* (kotaku.com) that earns £1,000 a day. If you want this level of money then you have to be in it to win it.

WHAT ELSE YOU'LL GET OUT OF BLOGGING

You may have bought this book because you want to get financially rich, but I have some other happy news to spur you on in your blogging journey. Blogging enriches your life in more ways than one.

While researching this book, I spoke to some of the world's leading bloggers and found out what they loved most about their blogging businesses. Bear these happy thoughts in mind if you start to get disheartened. Blogging is enjoyable and rewarding – and it can also make you money!

Why did I start my blog? To have fun!

Perez Hilton, PerezHilton.com

I have turned *AMR* into a diary for my children to look back on when they are older so they can see what was important to us as a family, what we did and to record our experiences. I'm very aware that I only remember a small part of my childhood and I don't want my children to forget some of the fun we have had.

Pippa Wright, A Mother's Ramblings

As my eBay business petered out from the recession I needed a way to make a living without leaving the house. I knew how to build sites that would get attention so I figured blogging would be a good solution. It's a great way to earn money and be a mom.

Jessica Gottlieb, A Los Angeles Mom

I was working as an online marketing manager for a fashion group looking after brands such as Racing Green, Baracuta and Suit Direct and would often read blogs on my lunch break for inspiration. I found that there weren't many menswear blogs compared to womenswear so decided to set one up. There's a lot of satisfaction providing something new.

Craig Landale, Menswear Style

CHAPTER 2

FINDING YOUR SPOT IN THE MARKETPLACE – WHAT TO BLOG ABOUT?

Let the plan commence! If you want to be able to sell adverts on your blog and earn money through affiliate revenue, then you need some traffic. And how can you get that? By being businesslike, following a plan and doing it step by step.

When company directors are starting up a new business and think about attracting customers, the first thing they do is always the same. They think about who their customers might be. They ask themselves – is there a market of people keen to buy products and services from us? If so, who are these target customers? What are they like? When heads of business can identify their customers, they will be able to identify their customers' needs and satisfy them, and this keeps people loyal. Company directors always carry out this research before launching any business. Imagine if a shop picked a product to sell, started trying to sell it and then asked the customers if they wanted it! A start-up business always begins by figuring out what customers want and need.

Applying this to blogging, you need to ask yourself if anyone really wants to know or cares about what you're going to be writing about. If you can find a subject that people care about, then your traffic will grow... and you'll be on your way to getting rich.

CHOOSING A SUBJECT

When I started blogging, I was given some fantastic advice from a leading figure in social media and marketing. Let me share it with you:

> If you think blogs are boring, then the problem is you're reading the wrong blogs. Look for a blog that interests you and start reading that.
>
> Conversely, if you're not getting many followers then have a look at what you're writing about. Are you sure you're being interesting?
>
> *Stewart Rogers, founder of usfitties.com and Director*
> *of Communications for Crawford Technologies*

Here's what not to do:

- Rant about public transport. We know it's bad – what are you adding that's new?
- A funny thing that your child said. It may be funny to you, but will the rest of us care?
- Something personal to your local area. If you want your blog to be read around the country and across the globe, then

there's not much point in writing about the man who works at your corner shop.

- What you ate for lunch. Unless you're giving us a recipe or a preview of a new food, we don't care that you ate a supermarket sandwich and it was stale, because we could easily do the same thing ourselves.
- What your pet dog/cat/hamster thinks about a subject. It may be cute to you but we have our own pets – why should we care about yours?

It's vital to find a subject that makes people want to take time out of their busy lives to read up on. If any of my friends or family members started a blog, then I'd read it once out of loyalty but I wouldn't revisit if it didn't interest me. It takes time to go to a laptop, open up the Internet and read a blog, and that's time I could have spent doing something more useful – walking the dog, tidying my flat, calling my mum.

So how do we know if we're being interesting? If you're anything like me, you may be feeling a bit of pressure right now. When a singer goes on stage before a concert there's always a bit of fear as they never quite know whether the audience is lively or what songs are going to get them to their feet. What happens if they start to sing and nobody cheers? It's the same with blogging. There is a risk that nobody will read or engage with your posts. You need to pick your subject matter carefully.

One mistake that a few new bloggers make is to base their decision of subject matter on what other, more established, blogs are doing. It can be tempting to look at a list of Top 10 Money-Making Blogs In The World, see Tech blogs such as *Mashable*,

Techcrunch and *Engadget* are at the top and decide that's the path for you. But do you actually care about the subject? If not, this will show in your writing. It's clear to see when an author loves what they are writing about as their posts are more energetic, more enthusiastic and a lot more fun to read. If you're writing out of a sense of duty or obligation, it's always obvious.

When choosing a subject matter, the trick is to work out what interests you more than anything else in the world. Have you ever played the name game when meeting strangers for the first time? The rules are to say your name and tell everyone one thing you love to do. For example, I may say I am Zoe and I love reading magazines, newspapers and other blogs to get gossip. What would you say? Maybe you love scuba diving. Perhaps you're fired up by horse riding. Or do you love testing the latest beauty products? You need to blog about whatever you enjoy the most in life. If you write about how you took your dog to the vet when you really care about lipstick or mascara than that blog post about your dog is distracting you from your true vocation– beauty! Life is too short to waste blogging about a subject that you only have an average amount of interest in.

It's vital to pick a subject that you're passionate about is because you will need to blog regularly when you're starting to build up a following. If you're not interested in the subject then it will feel like a chore and you'll have a very miserable life. That's not the point of blogging!

If you want to be certain of picking a suitable subject matter, you need to do some soul-searching.

EXERCISE 1

What do I find interesting?

Take a pen and a piece of paper and complete the following question: 'If I won the lottery, a perfect day would involve…'

By listing the things you enjoy, from spending more time with your family to driving round in a super car, to flying to a luxury holiday destination, let your imagination run wild. Now put that piece of paper to one side for at least an hour. When you come back to it, look carefully at the things on your list. Could you base your blog around one of these subjects?

EXERCISE 2

Take a trip to a store that sells magazines and newspapers. Look at all the different section areas – celebrity, women's lifestyle, men's lifestyle, gadgets, home, fashion, music, film, sport and fitness. Imagine the newsagent was burning down and you only had time to visit one section. What would it be?

Go over to that area and look through the titles. Which magazines grab your attention the most and what kind of articles do they feature?

Working out what you like to read about is a good indication of what you'll enjoy writing about.

Need a bit more inspiration? Here's a list of what other bloggers have done. Would you enjoy blogging about any of the following?

YOUR HOBBY OR INTEREST

If you play netball or hockey, then you're probably part of a team and it's likely your team-mates would be interested in a blog about their favourite sport. Now imagine how many similar teams exist around the world, as most countries have hockey and netball teams on a national level and thousands more amateur sides. Most people who play sport want to learn more about it so your potential readership is huge.

Further reading: *Kickette* (kickette.com), *Rugby Unplugged* (rugbyunplugged.com)

POLITICS

Everyone in a democratic state will – or should – vote at some point in their lives. If your blog has information about all the political parties and up-to-the-minute commentary on the latest party news, people have a reason to visit your blog to educate themselves before they vote.

Further reading: *Guido Fawkes* (order-order.com), *Left Foot Forward* (leftfootforward.org)

PARENTING

It goes without saying that there are a lot of parents in the world. Otherwise the population would die out. Ask anyone and they will say they want to be a better parent, so there's an opportunity to share what's worked for you. Consider doing product reviews, offering family-friendly recipes or simply sharing practical parenting tips such as discipline and sex education. Be warned – this will encourage a variety of debate and discussions.

Further reading: *A Mother's Ramblings* (amothersramblings.com), *Mumsnet* (mumsnet.com)

FOOD

Every human being needs to eat and so blogs about food have a massive potential audience. Most of us are always searching for a new taste experience, a way to eat more healthily, or a recipe that's quick and cost-effective. Add photos of dishes you cook and people will stop, salivate, take part and let you know if your advice worked.

Further reading: *Love Food Love Drink* (lovefoodlovedrink.com), *Maison Cupcake* (blog.maisoncupcake.com)

EXTRAORDINARY NEWS

People like to be entertained, but we don't always have time to search the Web to find something that makes us chuckle. There's a market for being the destination surfers check out first when they need a laugh. Some popular blogs offer a round-up of everything weird and wonderful on the Web. They might suggest the top five quirky YouTube videos to watch that day or even post a daily selection of cute animal photos.

Further reading: *Fail Blog* (failblog.org), *Cute Overload* (cuteoverload.com)

SPECIALIST NEWS

If you turn to the gossip section of a newspaper first, then you're not alone – why do you think it's always spread over the same pages of a newspaper or magazine? Depending on the publication, this may be towards the front if it's a specialised gossip title or towards the middle when the title covers more general news. You may turn to the sports' section first and know it's normally going to be at the back of a newspaper or in a pull-out supplement. Editors know that some people are interested in certain subjects more than others and cater for this by making it easy for them to find their favourite topic. If you have a specialised blog, you can focus solely on one subject area and busy people will come to your blog because they know they'll get the best information in one place without having to spend time browsing sections they don't care about.

Further reading: Gossip news at *TMZ* (TMZ.com), sports news at *Us Fitties* (usfitties.com)

TECHNOLOGY

Do you know exactly how to get the best from every item of kit you own? Most people only use gadgets like their phone, their TVs and their computers half as well as they could, so there's an opportunity to educate them about the gadgets they own. You might tell them how to resolve common problems or whet their appetites for new technology – who doesn't want to make life simpler by using a new gadget?

Further reading: *Techcrunch* (techcrunch.com), *Life Hacker* (lifehacker.com)

THREE ESSENTIAL QUESTIONS

If you've found something that interests you, congratulations, you're getting there! When you're interested in a subject, you can make it interesting to other people and they will come and visit your blog. You've got a potential readership. Hurrah!

But before popping the champagne corks, you need to analyse the market. A business must always consider if a market has the right conditions to encourage long-term growth. For example, people may be interested in your subject matter now, but will that always be the case? Also, are you trying to enter a saturated market? If you can't be any more interesting than anyone else, then I'm afraid there's no reason for people to visit your blog. You must ask yourself three questions before making your final decision on what to blog about.

Question 1 Can I contribute anything unique?
It's vital to remember that people have busy lives. If you are pointing out something obvious, which the reader could have worked out for themselves, or if you're reiterating an old point, then you're wasting everyone's time.

I'm speaking from experience. I find stories about celebrities really interesting and at the start of my blogging career I thought all I had to do was put them on my site, sit back and wait for the traffic. A lot of the time I would read all the newspapers, magazines and other entertainment blogs for celebrity stories and just rewrite the articles slightly before posting them on my own blog. What was I thinking?! The information I was putting on my blog was in no way unique to me so there was no compelling reason for a reader to come to me. Wouldn't anyone prefer to go to the source of a story rather than read a copycat?

When I realised I was making a mistake, everything fell into place. I would love to say that I had some divine intervention but actually it was a lucky accident. One afternoon, I was shopping in a Waterstones' bookstore in London, and I found out *X Factor* winner Leona Lewis was signing copies of her book in-store. I love interacting with celebrities, so I decided to queue up for a signed copy. After an hour of waiting in line, I was almost at the front of the queue and I got out my camera ready for my big moment with the superstar. There were five people between Leona and me when something very strange happened – a man jumped out of line, ran over to the singer and slapped her round the face. He was a tall, quiet man and for the whole hour we'd waited in that queue, he seemed on edge. I'd asked him a question and he grunted in response, signalling he didn't want to talk. However, as he ran towards the star while she was signing her books I sensed that something was not quite right so I turned on my camera, switching it from stills mode to video mode to capture the drama as it unfolded.

The following day I posted the footage on my blog. It was exclusive to me because nobody else had reacted quickly enough to record any evidence. And traffic went through the roof! The post was spotted by ITV and BBC and made it onto the national news programmes, with the URL of my blog appearing as a caption while the video was being played. After this it was picked up by international news channels in the US and Germany, where Leona has had hits, and they also mentioned my blog URL. I was contacted by magazines and newspapers from around the world and asked how much I would charge for the photo. Finally, I thought I had achieved success. Millions of people were visiting my blog... for that week.

I learned the hard way that the 'uniqueness' factor was the

reason for the traffic spike. After the Waterstones' incident I went back to posting old, generic celebrity news and my traffic dropped and dropped. There were no TV crews asking for my content and the magazines that had been so eager to have the Leona Lewis photo were strangely quiet. Clearly the millions of people who had found out about my blog because of the Leona scoop didn't see a reason to return afterwards. This served as a big wake-up call. People had enjoyed my unique content about Leona Lewis but stopped visiting when I posted a random story about a celebrity event that I may not even have attended. I realised I needed to get more new content, more exclusives and more first-hand reports if I wanted to keep my readers interested and also have a chance of being picked up by magazines and TV programmes to attract additional readers.

So I started to attend more functions and events and posted bird's-eye views of what I was doing. I wrote about what I was wearing as I walked the red carpet. I'd interview celebs myself and ask them fresh questions, and I stopped reworking older articles that I'd spotted in magazines. My readers now know that if they visit my site, they'll find stuff they can't get elsewhere. My traffic's growing all the time and I'm enjoying life a lot more. Creating new content is fun!

One of my most successful pieces of unique content was when I saw Beatles' legend Paul McCartney at a party. For a while they'd been rumours he was planning a duet with Bob Dylan, so I swallowed my nerves and decided to approach him and ask about it. Getting to Paul was hard as he has a lot of staff around him but I was driven. I knew that my traffic would increase if I got a quote so I'd need to be brave if I wanted to raise the profile of my blog. I made my way over to his group, waited for a gap in conversation, introduced myself in a direct way and asked the question. The end result was a video on YouTube that was seen by 16,000 followers, which was an impressive number of hits for a blog that had only been running for a few months at that stage.

I always make an effort to go to the Brit Awards and the BAFTA Awards to get unique content, no matter how difficult it is to get into the actual event or one of the after-parties. I must admit that when I first started the blog it was hard to get any invites, which .was a shock coming from the *Sunday Mirror*, where I could attend whatever I wanted. However, I knew that if I wanted to get fresh content from lots of celebrities in one place then it was important for me to be at or around those events. I researched the events in some detail and found out that it's possible to buy tickets to be an audience member at the Brits. I figured this would enable me to be in the vague proximity of the celebs and I could see what I could get from there. The ticket would entitle me to access to the stadium so the organisers of the event could not throw me out of the arena if I decided to hang out around the VIP entrance that led the stars to their dressing rooms. The worst they could do was move me on, which they eventually did, but not before I had my photo taken with Mark Ronson and chatted to Adele, which resulted in hundreds of thousands of hits. With the BAFTAS you can register to be in the fan crowds by the red carpet outside the Royal Opera House and most celebrities spend as much time chatting to the fans there as they do with the press. It was an effort to wake up early and queue for a coveted fan pass, but it was worth it as the post that I did about the BAFTAs was read by thousands of people. A video that I recorded of Jonathan Ross's screenwriter wife Jane Goldman had 45,000 views on YouTube. Both of these events helped to increase my traffic so the following year I was invited by the organisers, who wanted me at the event knowing that my blog post would go out to a growing community of readers, which was just as large as the readership of some national magazines.

Whether you have a mum's lifestyle blog, a gadget blog or a fashion blog, you always need to keep it unique if you want to grow your traffic.

66

The Clothes Whisperer is different because it focuses on written editorial that is up to print standards but expressed from a subjective and more informal perspective. I have a Masters from Oxford in Classical Literature; I know a thing or two about sentence structure and like to think my site also has a sense of humour that many others lack.

Kirstin Know, The Clothes Whisperer

99

If you look at some of the world's leading blogs you will see there's always one thing they do better than everyone else. It may be because they get better photos or perhaps use the photos in different ways (one of the reasons why superstar blogger Perez Hilton is huge is because he was brave enough to doodle on celebrity faces). Some bloggers have a reputation for breaking stories before anyone else, while others are better at building a rapport with key figures and carrying out exclusive interviews.

> ### EXERCISE
>
> Make a list of other blogs already existing in your chosen subject area. You can find these by entering the words related to your niche into the dedicated blog search engine *Technorati* (technorati.com) or *Google Blogs* search (blogsearch.google.com).
>
> Ask yourself: what do they do well? What can you add that hasn't already been done? Is the content presented in the most eye-catching way? Are there enough photos and videos to engage the reader?
>
> If you cannot think of one thing you'd do differently from the blogs already existing in your field, it's going to be impossible to make your blog unique. If it's not unique then it's not interesting enough. Time to go back to the drawing board?

Question 2 Will anyone care in twelve months?

If a blog is based on an event that takes place at a specific date and time, it has a limited shelf life. It will be popular in the run-up to the event, and climax during it, but what happens after that? For example, I noticed a few blogs centred around the London 2012 Olympics. Before the event they posted team news, interviews, outfit details, information about ticket sales – it was all great content. During July and August 2012, these blogs were a brilliant source of information about medal wins and injury news. However, where are they now? I don't know about you but I don't have time to read a blog about an event that happened in the past.

Equally, you have to be careful if you're basing a blog around a specific band or TV show. The artist/TV series that you choose to write about may not be so popular in a year's time. A musician could hastily rush out a song that fails to chart, a band might split up and go their separate ways and ratings' figures for TV shows can drop if production staff or writers change.

TIP

Before setting your heart on a specific blogging subject, look carefully at what you are planning to do. Could anything change in the next year to make your subject matter less appealing?

Question 3 Can I start conversations about my blog?

Part of what makes your blog unique is you. If a reader feels they have the opportunity to interact with you and influence what you do, it's a lot more interesting to them than a site they visit to get a five-minute update of the news before getting on with the rest of their lives.

For example, think back to when you've ever commented on a blog post or on a friend's Facebook wall. Whenever I do this, I always return to my comment to see if anyone's responded to it. If you start a blog and don't, or can't, give people the opportunity to comment on your blog posts, then you are missing out on this repeat traffic.

Get this right at the start and you'll grow a lot quicker than I did. For some reason, I didn't think to ask questions of my readers when I first started out. I wrote my news post, hit publish and walked away. That was it as far as I was concerned. 'I've said my bit – I'll come back and say some more tomorrow,' I thought. See ya later!

I realised the error of my ways after reading other blogs and websites in the celebrity news arena. *LaineyGossip*, *PopSugar*, *Gawker* and *PerezHilton* all have the opportunity for people to comment underneath posts, or they refer readers to a Facebook page where they can comment. Was I missing a trick? The answer turned out to be a huge 'yes', because as soon as I started asking questions and talking to my readers, my blogging career became a lot more interesting.

Through engaging with my readers, I had a lot more fun. And as my readers gained more enjoyment from the site, they were more likely to recommend it to their friends. I started to talk to my readers directly on Twitter and Facebook, and saw numbers grow from a few hundred to several thousand within months. Sometime long threads would start from some of the posts I'd written and if I didn't respond immediately, one of my readers would look after another person on my behalf. Occasionally, if a regular participant hadn't visited the site for a while, other regulars would notice and try to find out if the missing person was OK. I wish I'd known the importance of conversing instead of showing off when I started, because if you are able to start conversations you'll inspire people to come back to the blog.

When you're thinking of a subject for your blog, you need to consider if it's possible to formulate interesting questions that will provoke comments. I don't just mean writing 'What do you think?' at the end of every blog post. If you have 'What do you think?' at the bottom of every single article then it becomes standard and people stop seeing it as a question and start thinking it's part of your writing style. You need to ask questions that are imaginative enough to grab your reader's attention. For example, a celebrity blogger may ask questions that require their audience to imagine an entertainment scenario. A good question that I've asked has been 'What would you do differently if you were a TV producer on *The X Factor*?' A music blogger may ask if they think the act they've blogged about is similar to any other artists. If you've got a motoring blog you could ask your readers to tell you if the car you've reviewed would be on their shopping list if they won the lottery and their reasons for this. If your subject area is too narrow then it becomes very hard to think of questions that will inspire debate. Even if you can think of some interesting questions now, is there enough material to encourage debate and conversation long-term?

66

Know these answers: What is your voice? Who are you talking to and why do they benefit from your perspective? Create a strategy first, then develop your execution plan. When you are very clear on your purpose and your why, the rest falls into place. Be patient! It takes time.

Michelle Rice, Breakthrough Biz Strategies

I think your tone of voice has to come through in what you're saying. A blog is about you as a person as much as the topics you're covering, and that's what my readers like about mine. I'm chatty, and I'm honest with what I say too (sometimes a little too honest) and people respect that.

Hayley Carr, London Beauty Queen.

99

CHECKLIST

Have you:

☐ Made a list of what interests you by checking through some magazines to see what subject areas you feel passionately about?

☐ Taken the subject matter that interests you and asked yourself if you have any new or fresh information?

☐ Asked yourself if there could be something that might harm the longevity of your blog. Is there anything that could possibly date it?

☐ Thought of a few ways to start a debate and discussion around your subject matter?

CHAPTER 3

LOOKING GOOD – THE IMPORTANCE OF AN ATTRACTIVE DESIGN

If a business is trying to attract customers, it needs to get its premises in order. The offices must be clean and the shop has to be tidy. In the same way, if you want to attract traffic and you would like advertisers and sponsors to buy into your blog, then you need to think carefully about the design. The better it looks, the more money you stand to make out of it – so this is an important chapter.

Image is key in any field where money and investment are concerned. Imagine you are a fly on the wall in the boardroom of a large corporation and all the directors are sitting around a large mahogany table, wearing designer suits and expensive watches. If someone enters the room dressed in a T-shirt, shorts and flip-flops, they would never be taken seriously. The casually dressed delegate might be a genius and score the top marks in his year from his country's leading university, but if he hasn't made the effort to fit in, his lack of finesse will distract the board of directors from what he's saying. Conversely, if a delegate goes to the trouble of dressing better than the other people in the boardroom with a bespoke suit, a bigger watch, thicker hair and shinier shoes, then you can imagine the directors sitting up straight and paying attention.

If you want people to give your blog a chance, you need to make it attractive and, ideally, better than anything else operating in the same subject arena. When it comes to my own blog, *Live Like A VIP*, I am constantly looking over my shoulder at other entertainment blogs to see if they're implementing new features. If Perez Hilton updates the photo at the top of his header, is it time to change mine too? If the *I'm Not Obsessed* blog trials video advertising and I only offer banner advertising, maybe I need to follow suit? If I go to an event where I know there will be cameras, I make an effort to look my best. Remember that while it may be tempting to airbrush a photo of yourself and stick it at the top of your blog, people will notice if that image is not consistent with other pictures of you.

When designing a blog, the key thing to remember is clarity. Make sure people can navigate the site and find the information they want quickly. Blog readers don't have time to search around and if they can't access the information from you fast they'll visit another blog that presents the information more clearly. Clarity is the key goal to have in mind when working through this chapter.

Anyone can do it! I know this from experience. As long as you read the following steps carefully, you will end up with a great-looking blog, whatever your level of creative skill. Before I started blogging, I was a writer. I was confident using Microsoft Word but I could not draw or paint, and if you'd presented me with a piece of paper and asked me to 'design a blog' I would have panicked. But by looking at what my competitors were doing and having one key goal to make it clear to read, I found the task was less daunting than I first imagined. After I'd made a list of elements the other bloggers had, I could logically work out how to spread them around my blog in a clear way. Once I had achieved clarity, I could add the bells and whistles and make it more fun to read. Instead of having plain titles in the top bar of *Live Like A VIP* I enveloped the words in stars. Further down the page, I used polaroid frames to display photos, making it a bit more exciting than standard square-shaped pictures. At the bottom of the page, I made it look as if I was sitting on a table, ready to share the latest news with the readers to encourage them to sign up for my newsletter. I found it easier to be creative once I had the basic elements in place rather than being faced with a blank page and told to fill it. Like most things in life, anything is achievable if you take it step by step.

DESIGN CONSIDERATIONS – FROM THE START

Designing a blog is a two-part process but before you draw up an outline of what you'd like your blog to look like and let the creative side of your mind run riot, you need to think about how you're going to host your blog online. It's all very well mocking up your ideal design on a piece of paper, but how are you going to get it onto a server? Just like any other type of website, a blog must be stored on a server connected to the Internet so web users can access it whenever they want.

Some bloggers add their blog to an already existing website and use the same hosting server as that website, which is called self-hosting. Others may take advantage of dedicated blog hosting services such as WordPress or Blogger which take care of all the technical details of running a blog. If you have an account with Blogger or WordPress you need never worry about where your blog is stored as you simply log onto your online account, create your content, hit publish and your blog will be stored on your host's server.

It's vital to weigh up the advantages and disadvantages of each option as your choice of host affects how much freedom you have when designing your blog. Using a hosted blogging service can be the equivalent of living in a rented house: while it's very convenient that someone else has the responsibility of owning a house (and you can get some stunning rented houses), you are never free to knock down walls and truly customise. On the other hand, you can do whatever your heart desires to a house that you own – and you have the same freedom if you decide to self-host your blog.

PROS AND CONS OF HOSTED BLOGGING SERVICES

THE ADVANTAGES OF A HOSTED BLOGGING SERVICE

- You can be up and running in as much time as it takes to crack open a bottle of champagne (i.e. not much time at all). All you do is visit the website of the blogging service, sign up for an account and you're ready to start creating content. Check out WordPress (wordpress.com) or Blogger (blogger.com) or OverBlog (en.over-blog.com) and you'll see just how easy it is. Out of the three, I would recommend WordPress, as it's the most flexible in terms of design customisation, but you may find a template that you like straightaway at Blogger and therefore not require any customisation. Go and investigate!

- You don't need to have any technical knowledge about building websites or any knowledge of programming code or HTML (hyper text mark-up language). All the tools you need to create, manage and publish your blog are online-based so you just log in to your account, hit publish and it appears online without you having to worry about how it got there.

- It's completely free of charge. If you own a website on a separate server you'll pay a rental fee, but there are no start-up or ongoing hosting fees to operate a blog on WordPress, Blogger or OverBlog.

- Your data is stored on the blogging service's domain and normally backed up automatically, so you don't have to worry about doing this yourself.

- It's less likely that you'll experience technical issues such as servers going down as these organisations have a massive team to ensure all goes smoothly.

- If it goes wrong then you can email the support desk and they'll fix it for you.

- Most of these programs have close links with Google to get your blog spotted in search results. If you open up a WordPress account you have the option of downloading a plug-in called WordPress SEO (search engine optimisation), which automatically elevates your blog in search engines. This means you won't need to spend time learning about search engine optimisation, nor will you have to pay someone to do it for you.

THE DISADVANTAGES OF USING A HOSTED BLOGGING SERVICE

- Design customisation is limited to the templates provided by the hosts. While they may be easy to navigate and follow a traditional blog design format, you may feel that you want more 'special touches'.
- You don't fully control your own blog so there is a risk you may not be able to use it if the host company carries out maintenance on its servers, or even worse, goes out of business.
- If you don't control your own data and the company goes bust, you may not be able to get it back. Data is vital for any business, especially if you have pre-sold advertising on a newsletter and need the data in order to send it out.
- The URL of your blog will contain some reference to your blog host with the format being yourname.wordpress.com or yourname.blogspot.com This indicates to future advertisers that you don't have 100 per cent control over your blog and you'll find it more difficult to monetise the blog.

PROS AND CONS OF SELF-HOSTED BLOGS

THE ADVANTAGES OF SELF-HOSTED BLOGS

- You are able to customise your design as much as you want. You're free to choose exactly where to put your logo and key images, and you can make your blog look gorgeous.
- You'll be taken more seriously by the blogging community as it's easy to tell the difference between a self-hosted blog and a hosted one. If you self-host then it shows that you're making a long-term commitment and you'll be sticking

around for a while – otherwise you would have gone with a free service.

- You are free to choose your own URL, which is easier to remember than one with WordPress or Blogger in the title, and this makes it more brandable. It's hard to fit a long WordPress URL on a pen, for example.

- Having your own URL shows to advertisers you have ultimate control over your blog. This makes you look more professional. Also, when you purchase web hosting you automatically get an email address, which will be the same name as your blog. This is a million times better than having a free account from a blogging service and contacting advertisers from your hotmail email address.

However, self-hosted blogs do require a lot more technical knowledge.

THE DISADVANTAGES OF SELF-HOSTING

- You're only as free as your knowledge. If you don't know HTML coding and graphic design, then you won't be able to take full advantage of the ability to customise your blog. It's one thing having the freedom of the software, quite another being able to use it.

- It's more expensive. If you don't know the technical jargon, you'll need a designer. On top of this, you cannot avoid spending money as you must think about domain name registering and web-hosting subscriptions. Registering a domain name has a one-off registration fee plus a yearly fee, while hosting fees are normally paid quarterly or yearly.

- Backing up. If you install your own software, you are responsible for backing it up regularly in case anything breaks.

THE KEY FACTOR IN THE HOSTED VS SELF-HOSTED DEBATE

Advertisers won't take you seriously if you're using a free blogging service. If you've got your heart set on making some money from your blog, then you should host it yourself. However, this does require an initial spend so it's worth considering if you're really sure you want to be a blogger before you shell out. I've seen a lot of people start up blogs only to ditch them a few weeks later. What a waste of money!

TIP

I interviewed a lot of successful bloggers and most told me they started with a hosted blog so they could focus on creating great content instead of worrying about anything behind the scenes. As soon as they were confident in their ability to blog and saw themselves continuing it long term, they switched to a self-hosted blog. If in doubt, sign up to a blogging service to test the waters and switch servers at a later date.

WEB HOSTS

If you self-host, then you need to get your hosting from some-where. Let me explain. Whenever you write anything on your blog it has to be stored somewhere online. Web hosting provides the server where all your writing, images and graphics are kept. You pay a monthly fee to a web host for space on their server just as you pay Council tax when your house occupies a place on a street.

LOOKING GOOD – THE IMPORTANCE OF AN ATTRACTIVE DESIGN

Like any business outlay – from stationery to telephone systems – it's important to shop around to get the best deal when it comes to web hosts. Just as two telecommunications companies may charge different prices for phone and broadband services or two utility companies can offer slightly different rates for electricity and fuel, the same is true for web-hosting companies. If you're buying domain registration and server space from a company, then you could potentially save a bit of money by getting the right deal.

The two most important things to look out for when choosing a web host are disk space and bandwidth. The amount of disk space depends on how much content you will be uploading to your blog. If you are uploading large image files and video, you'll need more than if you simply write blog posts. Blogs with photos can use from to 5 to 10GB a month, video files considerably more. Bandwidth relates to how many visitors you expect your blog to have. Just as you can't fit lots of people in all at once if you have a small flat, if you buy a small bandwidth then you won't be able to welcome lots of visitors to your blog at the same time. If you develop a popular blog and receive lots of traffic, you will need to invest in bandwidth or face the prospect of your server crashing as it is unable to cope (the virtual equivalent of your windows falling in).

Other considerations are email addresses and technical support. If other people contribute to your blog, then you may want to give them an email address associated to the URL. If the server crashes, can you reach someone 24/7 or will your blog go down – thus costing you money in terms of lost advertising opportunity – until the following day? Shop around.

SETTING UP SELF-HOSTING

If you're keen to self-host after weighing up all the advantages and disadvantages, then be prepared for a tricky start. You need to find some blogging software, work out a way to load the blogging software files onto your computer, run the script, modify the code for your server and generally fiddle about in the inner files of the software until it looks the way you want on your domain.

For software, WordPress provides an option for bloggers wishing to self-host in addition to its free service. You can download all the files you need from WordPress.org. However, to upload it to your server, I recommend asking an expert for advice. As you're just starting out in business you may want to keep costs down, so consider IT students at universities and colleges. If they too are just starting out, they will need work for their CV and may charge you less. Of course your best way to find what you want is to use the Internet. Once you've identified a college, contact them and ask if they'll notify the IT class of your request. This may sound bold, but if you don't ask then you don't get. And if you're too timid to approach a school, how will you ever approach a potential advertiser?

TIP

If you decide you like blogging, then consider taking a basic programming course to understand the basics of self-hosted blog installation and design. If you decide to change your blog design in the future, you'll save yourself a lot of money. Also, if something goes wrong within your design template, you'll be able to fix it yourself without going back to your original designer.

There are courses that will give you an overview in less than twenty-four hours. Search Google for lessons near you.

A FINAL DESIGN LIST

Whether you choose a self-hosted blog and play around with your own design, or have a hosted blog and pick a template, it's important to make sure your design is the best it can possibly be. Have you looked at other blogs in your subject area to see how they're designed?

If you want a sleek, well-designed blog, you need to remember the phrase 'ARE CAPTAINS'. Each letter stands for a design element that you must have on your blog. Get your blog design right and you can sail off and captain your blog to find the treasure waiting in the blogosphere. And by treasure, I mean money, which you will earn if you get the design right.

ARE CAPTAINS

A – Attractive 'wow' elements For example, I use stars in the *Live Like A VIP* header instead of block page dividers. Since the design is different from anything seen before, it stands out.

R – Readable It's vital to make sure people can go to your site, get the information they want and leave quickly. Check there are no fancy design elements getting in the way of how easy it is to read and navigate the site. It's all very well having a pretty pastel font, but if it's illegible, it will be a hindrance to traffic and not a help.

E – Easy to brand You need to keep getting your logo in people's faces so they start to remember you. If you brand T-shirts and posters to drive traffic, then you must have the same image online to make sure that people realise they are in the right place. Moreover, the more someone sees an image, the more it will stick in their head.

C – Comments space If you want to build a community, then it's a good idea to install some comment facility when you design your blog.

A – Advert space If there is no space for adverts in the sidebar, you will never be able to make money from your blog. It sounds obvious, but so many bloggers overlook this when trying to fill up their blog with special features.

P – Picture sizes If you're going to have pictures in the main section of your blog, then how big should they be? This depends on what size you've designed the main section. The size of your sidebar is also important if you plan on having some banner ads. Most ads can be up to 300 pixels wide, so make sure you have sufficient room.

T – Tone The tone of the colour used in the design will influence how people react when they see your site. Pinks get us all in the mood for a girly gossip while a black-and-white site is best suited to a businesslike news blog.

A – 'About us' section If you want potential advertisers to contact you about possible deals, it's vital you have a space to explain how fabulous you are, as well as how they can contact you. Where will this sit?

I – Information search box As blogs display the most recent information at the top, it can be hard to find articles that were written a few weeks ago. Most bloggers like to make life easier for their readers by installing a search box so they can easily locate an article on a specific subject (I have one at *Live Like A VIP* in the top right). Leave room for this search box somewhere in the design of your site.

N – Names of other bloggers you rate in a list – a blogroll This is brilliant for search engine optimisation, which I'll explain more in Chapter 6, so you need to design your blog with this in mind.

S – Statistics monitoring tool Make sure you sign up for an account with Google Analytics (google.com/analytics) and install its code so you can monitor your blog's traffic. This will be vital when you're ready to talk to advertisers and monetise the blog.

CHOOSING A NAME

With the business looking clean and tidy, it's time to put a name above the door. Choosing a name for a blog is like choosing a name for your child – getting it right is a huge responsibility. Pick the right name for your child and they're off to a great start in life as people they meet think their name is cool. Pick the right name for your blog – describing what you do in a catchy way – and you'll gain added respect.

Now I'm not suggesting you take it to the extreme, like a hairdresser called To Dye Or Not To Dye or a flower shop known as Flower To The People, but you can't help but laugh when you read these on a street sign. Things that make us react with an emotion such as laughter or horror automatically stick in our heads; we need to be creative with our own virtual street signs.

The top tip I can give anyone trying to think of a name is to remind yourself of the unique selling point of your blog and have a thorough brainstorm to find a name that reflects this. To maximise your chances of coming up with a brilliant name, ask yourself:

What is the topic of the blog? There can be a benefit to using the topic of the blog in the name as this will help generate a lot of search engine traffic. If you have a blog about cars and someone types 'cars' in Google, there is a higher chance of your blog coming up than if you called it after the name of your car, e.g. Betty the Beetle.

How confident are you in the direction of your blog? You may be interested in cars now, but in the future what happens if you want to write about cars and motorbikes? You can still use the word 'car' in the title, just make sure it gives you room to expand should you wish to develop your blog. Carsandthings.com might be a potential way of getting round it.

What tone will it be written in? If it's penned in a newsy, serious tone then the title of the blog needs to reflect this to gain credibility. However, you can have more of a play on words or use a pun if you're writing in a more light-hearted style.

Who are you trying to appeal to? Consider your target market and what types of things they find interesting, funny and attention grabbing.

What are your long-term plans? If you want to sell your blog then it's unwise to have any reference to your own name in it, unless you want to take on a consultancy role afterwards. Arianna Huffington from *The Huffington Post* is still linked to her blog, even though it's now owned by AOL.

Is there anything that could date your blog name? It goes without saying that if you have reference to a date in the domain name then it's going to limit the viability of your blog. For example, if you call your blog *Olympics 2016* then you're going to have to search for a new domain name in 2017. Similarly, if your blog title references one specific TV show and that TV show is discontinued, then you'll have to scramble for a new title and start a new brand all over again.

How long is the name? Ideally the name should be as short as possible so it sticks in people's minds. Also, the longer it is the more chance it might be misspelled, and then people won't be able to find your blog.

.com vs co.uk? A 'dot com' has global appeal so unless you are targeting a specific country (because your products are only sold in a certain country), then you should always try to buy a .com. It is also advisable to buy a .co.uk (if you are based in the UK), or a .fr if you're based in France, .jp for Japan or .ru for Russia. When buying a domain name from a domain registrar, you'll be automatically presented with a list of domain endings relevant to different countries and you can simply select the ones most relevant to where your business operates. The more endings you have, the more you pay but it's worth doing as some people may mistakenly type in the wrong domain ending when looking for your blog. If another company has bought that ending instead of you then they will benefit from your traffic. Some bloggers also have the domain ending .org (short for organisation) to further protect their names. If your blog becomes successful, then other people will want a piece of the action. Saving money by not buying the .org in the first instance is a false economy as it leaves it open for another company to buy it. When you're successful, you don't want another company buying your name with the .org ending and automatically benefit from being associated with you. Mark your territory now!

Can your name be translated? Be aware that different names mean different things in different countries. What might seem an amusing name in one country could be a swear word or an insult in another territory!

TIP

If you're stuck choosing a name then there are some genius online name-generating programs available. *Bust A Name* (www.bustaname.com) enables you to enter words related to your blog and it will randomly generate different combinations of those words.

66

It was supposed to be a little joke suggesting that the blog was gourmet and chic, but spelling 'chic' as 'chick'. Tenuous, I know.

Gourmet Chick

This is very silly but I was listening to 'Girls on film' by Duran Duran and talking to my fiancée about the blog idea. Somehow swapping 'Girls' for 'Clothes' happened and the more we repeated it the more it stuck. I like the title because it does not alienate readers the way that 'costume' might. To many, costume still means period garb or what Superman wears to save the world. I wanted to feature contemporary clothes from contemporary films.

Clothes On Film

I decided I would be talking about menswear and men's style so *Menswear Style* seemed like a nice fit.

Menswear Style

I played around with the word beautiful and thought about how make-up made me feel.

Beauty Fool

CHECKLIST

Have you:

- ☐ Looked at the advantages and disadvantages of hosted blog platforms?
- ☐ Investigated popular hosted platforms such as WordPress and Blogger, just to see what they're about? Visit wordpress.com and blogger.com for an idea of what templates you can use.
- ☐ Looked at the advantages and disadvantages of self-hosting?
- ☐ Worked out what it truly means to self-host? Have you lined up a web host? Who will install it for you?
- ☐ Used the phrase ARE CAPTAINS to check your blog design is professional and readable?
- ☐ Thought up a name for your blog? Play around with words that describe your subject matter to make sure the name sums up the blog.

CHAPTER 4

PREPARE FOR BUSINESS – WRITING WITH YOUR READERS IN MIND

It's almost money-making time! You've worked out a few ways in which businesses lay foundations before launching so they can ensure customer growth and customer satisfaction. In Chapter 2 you analysed the market to check there would be a group of people wanting to read your blog. Then in Chapter 3 you worked on the design to make it welcoming and easy to use. Now it's time to install the furniture before you invite customers, or readers, through the doors.

If you want to make money from your blog, keep treating it like a business. Would you welcome customers to a store with no products for sale? Would you entertain clients in an office with no desks? Before you launch a blog, or any kind of business, you must have some content. When the blog is in operation, you need to keep it in good shape. Would you spend money in a shop that had mashed-up hangers and clothes jumbled up all over the floor? Of course not.

I know how tempting it is to want to rush into things. For most of us, money is the issue. I'd quit my job to start my blog and I had no other revenue stream, so I made the mistake of putting it online before it was ready. With hindsight, making money from a blog is not related to it just being online, otherwise every blog out there would generate an income. When businesses make money, they do so because they have products people want to buy and when blogs make money it's because they have content that people want to read.

When I launched my blog, I had only written one or two posts, which looked unprofessional and made readers question if something was missing. I've always felt uncomfortable if a shop only has one or two items for sale because this gives the impression that it isn't doing well because it can't afford to stock products or perhaps it doesn't care because it hasn't done a good job of stock-taking. It's equally off-putting if a blog has only a few posts. Most people visit blogs looking for information and if yours is lacking in content they'll visit a rival blog, just as any unsatisfied shop customer will visit the shop next door. Waiting until you have a decent amount of content before launching your blog benefits you in the long run as it will mean that your first visitors are not frightened away.

FLAGSHIP FURNITURE

If you want to get your blog off to a good start, make sure your best stock is up at the beginning. In the blogging world, this is what's known as flagship content. Flagship content is what draws a reader into the site.

Business and entrepreneurship blogger Chris Garrett

(*chrisg.com*) likens the idea of flagship content to stores in a mall. Wander into any indoor shopping mall and you'll find the shops at the entrances and in the corners are usually large big-name stores. Shoppers make their decision to visit a mall based on what the big stores are. In between the big stores are smaller retail units where people will still spend their money, but if it wasn't for the flagship content, they wouldn't have visited the mall in the first place.

It's time to think about what your flagship content will be. You need to have a few posts that attract readers to the blog so they look at other posts while they are there. It's unrealistic to think that every post you write will make people stop and stare and tell all their friends about something fantastic they've learned but if you can aim for one or two awesome posts a week, it's enough to make people visit your blog as opposed to another one operating in the same subject field.

Your flagship content needs to be on your blog before you launch so that people see how fabulous you are right from the start. It must be unique so people come to you because it's the only place they can get it. What do you do better than any other blogger out there? And what can you tell readers that nobody else is telling them?

If you can't immediately work out what your flagship content will be, then you need to do a bit of thinking.

EXERCISE

Ask yourself, when you were choosing a blogging topic, why did you choose it? In most cases, you will have chosen to blog about a subject you know a bit about.

Also, this will help you identify content that others are likely to find interesting.

Now take that subject and go online, grab some books, attend a few lectures and research it in more detail. What issues and debates come up time and again? What advice and explanation could people benefit from that no one has shared with them properly up until now?

If this doesn't come easily to you, cast your mind back to when you first became interested in your subject area. What do you wish someone had told you about that subject?

With an interesting idea in mind, your flagship content could take the form of:
- A 'How to' guide.
- A series of FAQs.
- Weekly jargon-buster updates.
- A series of case studies/interviews.
- Reviews of products used in your niche.

Almost ready to start creating your content? Before you get going, ask yourself two questions. Firstly, is there enough opportunity to create ongoing content? If not, it's like a shop opening with fabulous artisan products on day one, selling out of the stock and replacing it with something they found at the local cash and carry.

Secondly, it's a good idea to do some market research to ensure there's a need for that content. Going back to the shop analogy, it's highly unlikely that a shop will open without surveying shoppers in the vicinity and looking at what the locals need. In a residential area inhabited by the over-sixties you won't find many shops selling baby products because there's no demand for it. Equally, you may think you are doing people a huge favour by explaining the point-by-point workings of a topic, but if no one cares it's the equivalent of helping a little old lady across the road only to find out that she didn't want to cross!

It may take a while to think of your flagship content, but if you pick the right subject it will guarantee tons of traffic to your blog. As I keep on saying, readers mean revenue. Also, imagine if you started working hard to create flagship content, posted it on your blog and nothing happened. It's much better to spend a bit more time planning than to ultimately waste time failing because you acted too quickly.

The only way to check you will genuinely be helping people with your flagship content is to ask. If you interact with communities on Twitter, Facebook and Google+ you'll see what subjects come up time and again. Join in the debate, suggest you may be able to help and see if people get back to you. Perhaps you know of some forums or message boards that people visit to ask questions about your subject area. Start contributing to these and test the waters. Trust me, you'll soon find out what they care about based on the responses you get.

POLISHING THE FURNITURE

When a business has a good product they normally place it at the centre of their operation to draw attention to it. The flagship stores of shopping malls are by the entrances and exits; the most in-demand items in a store are at the front of a window display. In the same way, you want to make extra sure that you show off your flagship content so your hard work is spotted by more people.

Choosing appropriate headlines for each of your flagship articles is very important for two reasons. Firstly, if you use clever keywords in the headline then it will show up in search engine results and this means you're more likely to attract new visitors. Secondly, you can share headlines with your Facebook and Twitter followers, and an attention-grabbing headline is more likely to make followers click through to read that article on your blog.

If you've ever wondered how some headlines sound more exciting than others then I'm about to let you into a little secret. There are three weapons all bloggers can have at their disposal to make their headlines more snappy:

Meet a need Headlines containing 'How to' in the title have a high click-through rate as people believe they will learn something from your blog and will therefore take time to check it out. Just look at the success of beauty blogs with titles such as *How To Apply Pink Lipstick* or *How To Get Lady Gaga's Eyes*.

Call to action If you tell people to do something, there's a high chance they will do it. Headlines containing 'see' or 'watch' or 'discover' also show people they will get something from your post. They're far more effective than blandly stating what's in the post. A headline is a way to show readers what's in it for them. Too vague and there's no definite incentive for them to read on.

Use alliteration This is the icing on the cake. After you've included a call to action or a phrase indicating you're meeting a need, it's time to focus on the rest of the words in the headline. Alliteration instantly makes a group of words appear livelier. Also, consider mashing up two of your keywords to bring a smile to people's faces (or at least nod in recognition of your effort). To use a classic, 'eggs-cellent' is a great way to communicate a blog post about Easter or eggs and something that you've enjoyed.

Finally, remember to keep all headlines under 140 characters. Search engines are only designed to display results that are under 140 characters. You won't want to go to the effort of thinking of a great headline only to discover that it won't come up in search results because it's too long!

TIP

If you find it tough to think of headlines then carry a notebook and call it your headline book. Keep it with you whenever you read other blogs or newspaper articles. When you see something you like, jot it down in your headline book. The next time you're stuck for a headline, read through your book and see if someone has previously said it in a clever way.

POSITIONING THE FURNITURE

Make sure the link to your flagship content is visible at the top of your blog in the sidebar or below the header so that people can find it when your blog updates. Realistically you will only have time to add flagship content once or twice a week and it will get pushed down your blog as new posts go to the top. If you don't make the link easily visible, the effort you spent creating the content will all be for nothing.

❝

I always try to put myself in the shoes of the reader, or simply think about what content I wish was available on the Web that would tell me what I want to know. Then I simply go out and try to create that type of content based on the topics I'm more of an expert in. Everyone has hobbies or interests they know everything about, so it's just a case of sharing what you know to help out newcomers to these topics.

Chris Spooner, Spooner Graphics

I have three regular series to draw in new readers. I love writing *The Lazy Girls' Guide to Glamour* as people so often think it's so high maintenance to look nice, but it really doesn't have to be! I also write a series of red lipstick reviews and finally, I started a campaign for clearer clothes sizing, which was picked up in mainstream press.

Gemma Seager, Retro Chick

CHECKLIST

Have you:

☐ Prepared some flagship content? Will it take the form of FAQs, a how-to guide, interviews or product reviews?

☐ Thought of appropriate headlines for your flagship content? Now check the headlines appear to meet a need, drive a call to action and are less than 140 characters.

☐ Prepared a place to store your flagship content? Try to make the link at the top of the page so that it's clearly visible.

CHAPTER 5

SPRUCE THINGS UP – AND STAY TIDY

If you want people to keep coming back to your blog, then not only do you need to keep the business tidy, you must keep it fresh too. By definition, a blog is constantly updated with new posts at the top of the page, so a reader visiting your blog for the first time will see your most recent content at the top followed by the next most recent content. Do these look similar to each other? Are the images the same size? And are there any cool elements, like video?

A business that is trying to increase its number of customers tends to be equally focused on generating new customers while pleasing existing ones so they return. Without returning customers, profit would never rise as the business would each time be selling to fresh customers. It needs to have a regular database of clients and expands by adding to that database. If any customers are lost, then it must try and get them back! To keep existing customers interested, it's vital to keep the shop looking tidy. And to attract new customers there must be fresh reasons to draw them in.

Bloggers can draw in new readers through their use of images and videos. However, you need to take care. Posting poor-quality videos and images looks terrible and I cannot overemphasise how important it is to keep your blog in order so your readers enjoy hanging out there. If it's messy or they can't find the information they want, then they won't come back. If you put effort and time into designing a brilliant blog template and ruin it because you cannot maintain it then you're letting yourself down… and you're losing money. After all, a decline in readers means a decline in revenue.

Look at some of the most successful blogs and you'll see what I mean. How beautiful are the images at *The Clothes Whisperer* (clotheswhisperer.com) and *Style Bubble* (stylebubble.typepad.com)? Using gorgeous images and taking time over the presentation of their blogs helps the blog owners earn respect in the fashion industry. As a result, more fashion brands want to advertise on the blog and the bloggers get invited to collaborate on projects, advise clothing labels and even design their own products so their earnings go up and up and up. Susie Lau from *Style Bubble* gave up a successful job in one of London's best advertising agencies because her blog earnings were on a par with her office job, and if your site is a well-designed showcase of your best content, you could be looking at a salary way into six figures. But do you think anyone would have taken Susie seriously if her blog was difficult to navigate, or if it didn't look like any thought had gone into the design? No way.

Before I started *Live Like A VIP*, I was very much a writer and I had no idea what to do with images. At the beginning, I congratulated myself if I even managed to upload one (which you should do too, by the way – each baby step shows you're en route to something fabulous). However, I was never happy with the way my blog looked compared to others. Please learn from my mistakes:

- **DO NOT** upload a blurry image. It just makes it look as if you can't be bothered to find a high-quality image or you're too cash-strapped to buy a good camera or hire a professional photographer.

- **DO** work out what size images look best on your blog and keep to those sizes. Unless you're aiming to be hip and edgy with the way you display your images, if the images inside a post are all different sizes then it doesn't look uniform.

- **DO NOT** steal images. Ever. When your blog takes off it'll be seen by a lot of people and one of those viewers will work out that you don't own the image. Then you'll be forced to take it down amid huge embarrassment. You may even get sued. If you're impressed by someone else's image, then contact them and ask if you can use it in return for a credit on your blog – but never take without asking.

- **DO** make the most of free online editing tools to touch up your images and video before posting online. In less than two minutes you can alter the colour and exposure levels, and this has a significant effect on how bright your blog looks.

- **DO NOT** take too many photos and display them underneath each other. While readers love to see photos, if you pile them on top of each other it means that the blog post is going to be very long and earlier posts will be pushed further down in your blog and will not be visible to new readers. All the effort you put into creating yesterday's content will be for nothing if no one can see it because the following post is too long.

Display your images in a gallery instead (I'll explain how to do this properly later in the chapter, page 73).

WHERE TO FIND IMAGES

Copyright is a murky area for bloggers. In essence if you did not create an image then you do not own the copyright, so you cannot reproduce it on your blog without seeking permission or paying for it. Therefore the images on *Live Like A VIP* contain a lot of photos taken by me or a member of my editorial team so we are completely sure we own those images. When it's not physically possible to take your own photos, there are two options.

You can buy an image from a photo agency such as Getty Images (gettyimages.com) or Rex Features (rexfeatures.com), which typically costs around £60 per image for use online. You'll need to visit the agencies' websites, sign up for an account and receive a password before you can browse the full selection of images. However, be careful as the images often look so clear and lovely, you could easily end up spending a fortune.

The other option is to search online for free images, which you can find in directories like iStockphoto (istockphoto.com) or Image Collect (imagecollect.com). Enter the name of what you're looking for in the search box of these directories and you'll be presented with a decent selection of images that are generally free to use. If there are terms and conditions regarding their usage, these restrictions will be clearly displayed next to the photos in the search results to avoid confusion.

Do not be tempted to copy photos from Google Images (google.com/images). Even if there is no watermark on an image, it doesn't mean it's free to use. I learned this at my peril when I used Google Images to look for a photo of a singer at a gig I attended. After finding one that didn't have a watermark, I posted it on my blog, but the person who took the image spotted it. They were, quite rightly, rather annoyed and ordered me to pay them a ridiculously high usage fee or take it down. I ended up taking it down, which affected my blog's credibility. If a blogger posts something and then takes it down a couple of hours later, it looks weird.

BUYING IMAGES

If you're just starting out then you'll probably want to keep costs down. Some of the larger photographic agencies have special rates for bloggers. Since the photos are only published online rather than in newspapers or magazines, they can be of a lower resolution and therefore the price you pay is less than that quoted to printed media. Contact Getty Images (www.gettyimages.com), Rex Features (www.rexfeatures.com) or Wire Image (www.wireimage.com) for rates.

I've found Image Collect (imagecollect.com) to be a great low-cost option if you want celebrity photos. For a fee of $99 a month you can download 15 images from the site's collection of up-to-date photos taken at film premieres and showbiz events. When you consider that paying for a single agency photo from Getty or Wire Image might be £50, Image Collect is excellent value for money.

> **TIP**
>
> Have you heard of iStockphoto (istockphoto.com)? Bloggers use it in two ways – to search for low-cost, quality images and to sell copyright of images they've taken themselves. If you take a lot of images for your own blog then you may as well see if you can sell copies afterwards. After all, you own the copyright! It's really easy to upload your images to the site and you can earn between 15–40 per cent of the sale price. When you've sold your own images you'll have more money to pay for other people's. At iStockphoto you can buy six credits to use whenever you want for just £10.

SEARCHING FOR FREE IMAGES

Every blogger should bookmark Everystockphoto (everystockphoto.com) and Creative Commons (http://search.creativecommons.org). Here you can find free images to illustrate virtually any subject.

When you use these search engines, the information box by the side of the image will give you some terms and conditions of use. For example, sometimes you are required to credit the photographer underneath where you've posted their photo in your blog post. This is a small compromise to make in return for getting an image for free – think of the money you'll save in the long term.

EDITING TIPS

If you want to go that extra mile with your blog, take a bit of time to perfect your images before publishing them. For this you need an editing tool, some of which are more hi-tech than others. If you prefer to play around with colour balance and advanced editing tools then you will have to invest money, but if you just want to resize, crop, adjust red-eye and make collages, there are some fantastic free editing packages available. I recommend investigating the following:

Picasa The website picasa.google.com is a free image-editing software that you download from Google. It's not as powerful as some editing applications such as Photoshop, but it's a very good application for editing pictures due to a selection of easily visible buttons and sliders. Because of its speed and simplicity, many people prefer using Picasa for quick image editing. It also offers the benefit of saving the original image, which is useful if you want to change it back.

The benefit of Picasa over other free editing tools is that it's integrated with the social networking tool Google+. In Chapter 6, I will fully explain how to register for a Google+ profile and suggest how to use it alongside Facebook and Twitter to communicate with your blog readers and grow your brand. When you understand the basics of the Google+ circles, which I explain in that chapter, you'll appreciate the value of Picasa seamlessly interlinking with Google+ and enabling you to share images directly with your circle as soon as they've been edited. You do not need to use an editing tool to save the image to your desktop and upload it manually, you can just click on the relevant button in Picasa and it's with your Google+ following straight away, saving you time and effort. Who doesn't like to save time?

Once you've edited a photo in Picasa both images are

automatically stored in an album so that you can easily search for old photos in case you want to use them again.

Pic Monkey At Picasa you have to download software from Google, but Pic Monkey (picmonkey.com) lets you upload a photo to their website and edit online before saving it to your computer. This is useful if you're travelling and in an Internet café, or using a friend's computer and therefore unable to access the Picasa software.

iPhoto If you're a Mac person then the chances are you will have used iPhoto as it's built into all Apple devices. Already you have all the basic tools for cropping, straightening, resizing and adjusting colour and brightness.

It doesn't offer as many features as Picasa, but if you've used it before then you're likely to be more confident with it and to try new things rather than have to learn Picasa from scratch.

Adobe Photoshop Elements This package costs around £100 but has lots of advanced editing features. You can rotate images, stack them on top of each other in a collage and adjust the colour balance manually by lifting the hues of blue, white or red in the post.

Professional photographers use Adobe Photoshop, which costs around £600, but if you're only working with images for your blog then Elements will suffice. Yes, the added features on the full package should make your blog look absolutely superb, but if you're only using small photos on the blog you have to wonder if people will really notice the difference. And the price gap means you can save your business money for advertising, merchandise or even extra design help.

Instagram We all look great with a bit of soft focus and

Instagram (instagr.am) allows users to take a photo, apply a digital filter to it and then share it. Every blogger should use Instagram at least once a week for two reasons. Firstly because it shakes up the variety of images you are using on your blog – we can't always have a photo of you standing by the thing you're blogging about, no matter how pretty you are! The second reason is that millions of people are using Instagram and if you're on it too, you're more likely to attract new readers. In December 2010, Instagram had one million registered users. In June 2011 Instagram announced it had five million users and it passed 10 million in September of the same year. In April 2012, it was announced that over 30 million accounts were set up on Instagram. To be in with a chance of reaching out to this figure, you need to be in it to win it. Visit the Instagram website for more details. If you have an iPhone you can download it from the App store.

TIP

If you want to make your blog look visually exciting then you need a variety of image types – photos of you in front of an object are all well and good but you must have some of the actual object too. Change between close-ups and panaromics. If you really want to add interest then use your editing tool to merge some images together into a collage.

Study the fashion magazines and you'll see they keep their pages interesting by creating a mash-up of objects dotted around the page rather than in a straight line. You can do this too by investigating the collage templates available online. Try Pic Monkey (picmonkey.com) or

Polyvore (polyvore.com), which is simple to use to create beautiful collages and can then be shared with other Polyvore subscribers. Just sign up for an account and follow the instructions.

TOOLS FOR CREATING GALLERIES

There are several good reasons for bloggers to use photo galleries. Firstly it keeps your site in order and makes a blog post easier to navigate. I know if I'm reading a blog that has lots of images I prefer to see them in small thumbnails and I can click on the ones that interest me most. I don't want to have to scroll down through them all – I haven't got time.

Secondly, galleries help with the blogger's page view figures. When you're ready to talk to advertisers about your site, which I talk about specifically in Chapter 9, they'll ask for your page views and the good news is that photo galleries always help to boost page views. This is because each photo is automatically uploaded to its own page. Displaying the images thumbnail size and indicating where people have to click through to the gallery to see the full size alerts their curiosity and they'll end up browsing. Also, the longer they browse, the longer they spend on your site, which is another piece of information advertisers may request. Therefore it is a good idea to get used to galleries at the start of your blogging journey so you understand the process and get quicker at doing it. The quicker you are, the more galleries you can have and therefore more page views.

If you want to have a gallery that brings people to your site then it has to be with a blog plug-in. Photo sharing services like Flickr (flickr.com) offer galleries, but these work by uploading your photos to Flickr, creating a gallery inside Flickr and then generating a code to put into your blog post. They may look lovely and increase the time people spend on your site, but they won't actually improve your page views as the images don't live inside your site.

Blogger, OverBlog and WordPress all have gallery options which you will see if you type the word 'gallery' into the help box of your service provider. I use WordPress with the Next Gen gallery plug-in. It's easy to use, the results look fabulous and it helps my SEO (search engine optimisation). Triple result!

WORKING WITH VIDEO

One of the easiest ways to mess up a blog is to attempt to cash in on the popularity of YouTube without fully understanding what you're doing. Every video you release is a reflection on you and your brand. Do you really want the blog you've spent so long designing to be associated with a quickly released, badly shot, pointless video? Would a business approve a release of a product before it was tried and tested? No!

Whether you are looking to have video as your flagship content or as an added extra to give more weight to your writing, the key thing to remember is there should always be a reason for it. What are you trying to communicate? Humour? Shock? Instructions on how to do something? Remember if you want it as your flagship content, the more you can provoke a reaction such as 'laugh out loud funny' or 'gasp in horror shock', the more likely it is to be shared.

Ideally you want to make the video quality the best it can be so that other bloggers will spot it and talk about it, and ideally take the link and embed it on their own blogs. Would you put someone else's long and badly lit video on your blog? Nobody would, so you need to become accustomed to some basic shooting and editing tools if you want your video to be picked up and spread in a viral way. Just look at how many videos there are on YouTube right now. You can see how many times a video has been viewed by looking at the number in the bottom right of the player. Some have 10 million hits and some struggle to get 100. Normally, you'll find the least popular videos are the ones that have been shot in a rush, whereas the more popular ones contain something that grabs your attention.

SHOOTING VIDEO

No matter how good your editing skills are, if you shoot good-quality video in the first place you'll make life lots easier for yourself. While you can touch up sound and colour levels in the editing suite, if the sound is barely audible when it's shot there's not a massive amount you can do. Similarly, if you jerk the camera up and down, the most sophisticated image stabiliser software in the edit suite won't be able to fix it.

The first step is to get an appropriate video camera. If you only want a quick point-and-shoot camera to do interviews or to take on roving reporting missions, there are some great portable HD cameras. I have a Flip Camera, but a Sony Blogger is equally good. These are designed with bloggers in mind as they have an inbuilt USB key meaning they can be read straightaway by a PC or a Mac. Simply push a button, out pops the key and you can transfer the data to any PC with a USB socket. If you want a higher quality, news-bulletin-style feature then you'll need a better camera.

Ideally, you want a camera with the socket to plug in an external microphone – one with a lot of inbuilt memory and high-definition HD quality is important. These can be found on most mid-range cameras costing in the low to mid hundreds. Some bloggers spend a lot of money on professional cameras worth thousands but I think it's a waste of money. I have a Panasonic video camera that cost £500 and I've never had any complaints. Your readers are not expecting videos of that standard – they'll watch TV if they want that. However, it's not just about getting a camera, it's about using it too. I have a checklist of five questions I ask myself every time I leave the house with a video camera:

- **Is my battery fully charged, and do I have a spare?** There is nothing worse than having a battery run out mid-flow, especially if you're recording killer content! Batteries are inexpensive so it's a good idea to buy a spare one to give you peace of mind.

- **How much space is on my memory card, and do I have a spare?** If you run out of memory you'll have to delete something so you can't record the entirety of what you set out to do.

- **Have I checked sound levels?** Before going into the full video shoot, I always record a minute's talking, asking someone what they had for breakfast to check I will be able to hear them when recording has finished. If you check before you start then there's no chance you'll be faced with the embarrassing task of having to repeat it because you can't hear anything.

- **What is the person standing in front of?** If there's something distracting in the background or your subject is standing in front of a tree and looks as if they have a bird on their head, then it's distracting for the viewer – they'll be drawn to the background and not the main body of your video. And yes, I have filmed in front of a tree before. Never again!

• **If I'm doing an interview, shall I bring a tripod?** If I'm likely to be standing in one place then a tripod is genius as it means your camera won't shake and you won't get arm ache either.

If in doubt, ask someone to film for you. Spending some money on hiring a professional will end up making your blog look more professional so it's a worthwhile investment.

EDITING VIDEO

It's not as hard as you think to edit video. Nowadays there are some fantastic tools available. The price of these tools depends on what you want to do with your video. If you require lots of advanced editing functions and graphics, then consider investing in a video editing package like Adobe Premiere Pro or Mac's Final Cut Pro (both available on Amazon.com) or one of their more basic (and cheaper) packages such as Adobe Premiere Elements or Final Cut Express. Personally I recommend the cheaper packages as once again professional video quality is wasted on a web audience.

If you're just starting out I recommend using the free software available on your PC – Windows Movie Maker – or on your Mac – iMovie. This is because it has all the basic tools you need. It may not have as many options in terms of transitions, screen backgrounds or credits, but you can still improve your video enormously by using it. Therefore it's a good idea to see how you get on with the free software, and if you find out you have a natural talent for it and you want to keep on doing it, then it's time to upgrade.

The best way of using video software is simply to get stuck in. Actually using it is a lot less frightening than reading about how to do it. Sometimes the possibilities of what you can theoretically do can be overwhelming and you find it a lot simpler once you're using it. Very soon it will become instinctive and you won't even have to think about it. You need an editing program that will allow you to:

- **Trim the clip** Whenever I get my video camera out, some of what I film is fantastic, other parts are boring, and the parts are not always linked. There may be something fabulous followed by something dull and then topped up with something super amazing.
- **Apply transitions** so the video doesn't appear to jump between sections. Even a simple fade to black after each clip is smoother than stopping one part and starting on the next straightaway. Other basic video transitions – available even on the free packages – are spin in and spin out, or swap screens.
- **Zoom in and cut out** some of a clip. This is a good way of eliminating annoying distractions.
- **Insert still photos** to remind people of a similar event or to break up a long interview.
- **Add titles and credits** to a clip. If the sound quality is bad or you're not sure your viewers will recognise who is talking, you'll want to be able to use titles and subtitles at the bottom of the screen, or before a specific section, to explain things. This is also useful if your sound hasn't turned out as expected.

- **Add a soundtrack** over a sequence of images if you wish. However, be careful where you get the soundtrack from as it's very easy to infringe copyright laws. The free soundtracks in iMovie or Windows Movie Maker are not licensed for commercial use and you must also steer clear of any song recorded by a professional musician. You only own copyright if you've produced and recorded the track yourself, or if you have a written agreement from the original artist to use it for a specific purpose.
- **Add a watermark** over the video. If you're going to share it on websites such as YouTube, you want people to know where it came from and to visit your blog as a result.

SHARING VIDEO

Once you have carefully made your video, the next steps are to publish it on your blog and to alert people that it's ready to watch. Most bloggers upload their video to a third party website like YouTube (youtube.com) or Vimeo (vimeo.com) and create a blog post containing a link to where it's hosted on the third party site, as opposed to manually uploading video to their own server. The reason for this is partly because most blog services can only handle small files and video files tend to be beyond their capabilities. However, another reason is because YouTube and Vimeo are used by millions of people around the world, who may not have known about your blog before. In fact, it is estimated that YouTube has around 500 million registered users. All these visitors need something to entertain them so they'll go to YouTube, search for what interests them and be presented with a list of matching video. You need to upload your video to the site so it will come up in search results and advertise your blog to a whole new market. Although Vimeo has less users than YouTube, the more places your video is, the more chances you have of people spotting it and visiting your blog. The US White House has its own vimeo account at vimeo.com/whitehouse so if it's good enough for the American President, it's good enough for the rest of us!

To upload a video to these video-sharing services, simply visit the Vimeo or YouTube website, sign up for an account and locate where the video is saved on your computer. Click the button that says Upload. You are then given the option of adding tags. Pick wisely as this will make your video more likely to be seen in search engines. YouTube is owned by Google so it takes notice of the words you tag your video with. It's a good idea to make the tags the keywords that you want your blog to be known for (in my case 'celebrity' and 'gossip' as well as the names of those starring in the video and any topics that you have noticed trending at the time).

Once your video has been uploaded, it gives you the option of sharing. Click this button and then the embed button. Choose the size of the player, copy the code and enter it in the dashboard of your blog when it's in HTML mode (as opposed to publish). You now have video on your site!

TIP

YouTube and Vimeo allow you to subscribe to other people's feeds and comment on their videos. Search for others who are uploading similar videos to yours and comment on them. The more you engage people, the more likely they are to check out your video in return, and this means your videos get more views.

Most bloggers have an account with both Vimeo and YouTube, even if they just use one or the other to embed the video to their blog. This is because each video-sharing service has a different community and the more communities you engage, the more traffic to your blog. Also consider putting the video on Yahoo Video (http://video.yahoo.com), Metacafe (www.metacafe.com) and Blip.TV (www.blip.tv). The more people you reach, the better!

CREATING A PODCAST

I had no idea what the word podcast meant when I first started blogging. To put it simply, a podcast refers to the action of posting some audio or video content online and making it available for a viewer to download and play back at their convenience. It's a great way of reaching the driver commuting on a long journey or the mother with her hands tied in trying to entertain her kids. However, podcasts were more important to bloggers a few years ago before the invention of mobile devices with Internet capacity. These days, most smartphones have access to the Internet, which means busy people can just as easily watch content on their phones tuned into YouTube. Now they don't need to download anything – they can put their phone next to them, use its 3G to start up YouTube and listen to music or even catch up on a TV show. Therefore, you need to consider if making a podcast is really worth your time. Like anything in business, you must have a good, well-thought-out and cleanly edited podcast if you expect downloads, and that requires planning in advance. Where are you going to find the time to do that if you're already trying to improve your images and get great video?

Sometimes it's OK to focus on quality rather than quantity and admit you don't have time to do something. Podcasts are brilliant ways of engaging with people, but concentrate on videos and photos first, make some money, employ some staff and start podcasts at a later date.

> Some new bloggers tend to go overboard with colours, fonts and masses of 'arty' pictures. In terms of great blog design, less is definitely more. Make sure things are tidy but don't worry about touching things up to perfection. It's better to update often than spend hours on one post.
>
> *Elinor Shields, Mumsnet*

> Self-timer is a wonderful invention. If you want to make sure you own the copyright then take the images yourself!
>
> *Sara Louise Wilson, Sara Luxe*

> I take photos myself. I don't like to use images from Google unless it's necessary (i.e. if I don't have the product myself). I've taken up a keen interest in photography to get the most out of my work.
>
> *LaaLaa Monroe, Dolce Vanity*

CHECKLIST

Have you:

☐ Contacted photo agencies to find out how much they charge for images? Visit Getty Images (gettyimages.com), Rex Features (rexfeatures.com) and WireImage (wireimage.com).

☐ Browsed the directories Image Collect (imagecollect.com) and iStockphoto (istockphoto.com) to use as a source of stock photos?

☐ Bookmarked Creative Commons (search.creativecommons.org) and Everystockphoto (everystockphoto.com) as a source of free images?

☐ Investigated image-editing software? Play around with Picasa (picasa.com), Pic Monkey (picmonkey.com), Instagram (instagr.am), iPhoto and Adobe Photoshop Elements.

☐ Found a gallery plug-in that's compatible with your blogging software?

☐ Bought an appropriate video camera and tested how to use it?

☐ Investigated the video-editing tools Windows Movie Maker and iMovie? You need to be able to trim clips, apply transitions, add titles and credits plus a soundtrack and a watermark.

☐ Started an account with YouTube (youtube.com) and Vimeo (vimeo.com)?

CHAPTER 6

DEFINE YOUR IDENTITY – BUILDING A BRAND

Once your blog is up and running, you need to keep treating it like a business and use basic business strategies to encourage customer, or traffic, growth. Without traffic your blog will never make you rich, just as a business would never turn over profit without customers. How, then, do businesses acquire these customers?

Looking at the corporate world in detail, it's clear the most successful global corporations don't just sell things to customers. They *are* things to their customers: they are brands. You may have a blog, but if you want to be successful you need to turn your blog into a brand that's instantly recognisable to potential customers. Think of the differences between Louis Vuitton and a fashion stall at the local market. After all, both sell clothes. The difference is that Louis Vuitton has a unique LV logo and it has an identity. Customers expect to gain similar advantages from the Louis Vuitton experience wherever they are in the world. They expect the stores to be clean and staffed by smartly dressed and helpful assistants, showing them high-quality, luxurious products. In contrast, you're never quite sure whether the market stall owner will turn up or if he will be able to offer anything that's high quality. Does your blog have an identity? If not, you must create one if you're to stick in people's minds.

Once you have an identity it's easier to promote your brand as you can be more focused on spreading the word in places your reader is likely to hang out. You know who you are, you know who your readers are, and now you can go out and gather them up in the most effective manner possible. As the clothing retailer H&M aims to appeal to a young fashion forward market, it might advertise at a festival. Apple might promote heavily at tech conferences, and you often see Nike posters in gyms. When a promotional campaign is focused more people react as a direct result of experiencing the promotion, and the amount of money the brand has spent on the outreach campaign is justified. That's why being focused and having an identity is particularly important for bloggers who do not have a lot of capital at the start of their blogging career. You don't have time to spend on an advertising campaign which doesn't bring readers into the blog because you failed to identify your target market.

All of the best known TV channels, magazines and newspapers have identities. My previous employer, the *Sunday Mirror*, was a tabloid newspaper. You know that if you pick up a tabloid newspaper, you'll get gossip, scandal and shocking stories. In contrast, a broadsheet newspaper such as the *Daily Telegraph* or the *International Herald Tribune* has more political features and in-depth analysis of current affairs. The BBC has a very different identity to MTV. If you're looking to watch a music video, MTV will be the first channel most people turn on. It's time to work out what you want to become known for and how you can make your blog the first destination people check out.

BLOG IDENTITY – HEADER LOGO

The first step in creating an identity is to think visual. If I mention the word Nike then most people immediately think of the company's signature tick logo and its slogan 'Just Do It'. When talking of Apple iPods and MacBooks a lot of us visualise the iconic image of an apple with a bite taken out of it. Mention Rolls-Royce and there's the infamous flying lady on the bonnet of all its vehicles, the epitome of luxury. What defines your blog? Is there anything to get you noticed?

If you want to start thinking of yourself as a brand, then you need a header. You want people to see your logo on a physical product or a blog post, and for this to make them think of the blog. Therefore it's worth spending some time designing a logo. Make sure the design sums up what your blog is about. *Live Like A VIP* has lots of stars in the design because 'star' is another term for 'VIP' in the celebrity world. Here's a look at what some of the superstar bloggers have done:

Mumsnet The UK's leading mummy blog website has a simple yet effective icon of women multi-tasking, from playing a trumpet to juggling the baby. This sums up the type of women they aim to appeal to, but the angular, geometric design means it is easy to reproduce.

Techcrunch A simple T and C are easy to recreate, but the

pixelated nature of the letters indicates that it's a blog about the computer industry.

The Clothes Whisperer A beautiful illustration shows this blog is about the sophisticated and classy side of the fashion industry. Luxurious and aspirational.

Lainey Gossip A silhouette of a woman sipping a martini is easy to sketch out and therefore to transfer. It's very effective in summing up the way Lainey writes her blog, as if she was in a bar having a gossip with friends.

Autoblog A simple semi-circle and line made out to look like a speedometer shows that *Autoblog* is about all things fast and fabulous. It's easy to use on posters, pens and other promotional material.

BLOG IDENTITY – BRAND PRINCIPLES

The second step towards creating an identity is to lay down some ground rules. Looking again at well-known brands such as Nike, Apple and Rolls-Royce, another characteristic emerges. They all have a strong sense of business identity and brand values. Each produces a specific type of product and attempts to be the best at it. Originally, Nike was a running shoe specialist. The company used scientific analysis to work out what materials best supported feet and made cutting-edge trainers based on those principles. Nike doesn't make stilettos and they don't produce loafers. When they release shoe after shoe after shoe, it's always a sports shoe.

Applying this to blogging, you need to define what you're blogging about. If a reader knows what to expect from your blog and you keep on giving them what they want, then they'll keep coming back. What would happen if you put up a real-life feature about how to apply fake eyelashes on a blog that's normally about PCs and gadgets? It may cause a drop-off in traffic as readers desperate for a gadget fix would look at what a competitor was offering on that subject. Don't lose your readership by veering off course.

At the same time, don't lose them by failing to decide on a theme. When readers don't know what your blog is about, there's an element of risk involved and also an element of doubt. If they don't know what they'll get when they turn on the Internet and visit your blog they're more likely to visit another site where they do know what's on offer. People have busy lives; they don't want to waste time visiting a blog that might not give them what they're looking for. To return to the market stall analogy, a blog without an identity is just like a market stall that may or may not decide to open. People don't trust it! Your blog becomes a collection of posts with nothing to define it, just as a market stall is simply a collection of clothes. If you want to be like an international clothing chain as opposed to a small town market stall, it's vital to work out who you are and what you blog about and get that across to your readers as clearly as possible.

TIP

To stay on track when I first started blogging, I made a short mission statement. I asked myself how I could sum up what made my blog interesting in one sentence. Why would a reader visit my blog? In my case, readers would visit *Live Like A VIP* to find out how they can live like celebrities.

I wrote down my mission statement on a Post-it note

(pink, of course) and stuck it to the side of my laptop. Each time I thought about writing a blog post, I asked myself whether it contributed to my blog's overall selling point of explaining to readers how they could live like VIPs. In this way, I made sure I kept my editorial standards high and my subject matter consistent. My readers want to know what they can buy to make them look and feel fantastic, not how they can save money on their local grocery shop or find the best weedkiller for garden patios.

PROMOTING THE BRAND

Once you've worked out the concept of what your blog stands for you have something consistent to promote. Congratulations! Now it's time to get proactive and tell people you exist and what you're about. When enough people know about your blog they'll spread it among their friends and traffic grows via word of mouth. However, most bloggers feel they need to do something to get readers involved in the first place. Here are some cost-effective suggestions:

MERCHANDISE

If you really want to stick in people's minds you need to be in front of them 24 /7, so that means transferring your online identity onto something physical. Most people have a pen near them at all times – in a handbag, in a pocket, in an office drawer or pen pot. If your logo is on that pen, then they'll be looking at your logo all day long. They may not actually read the words every single day, but it acts as a subconscious reminder that your blog covers a specific subject and reminds them of the URL. Pens start at just 10p per item, which is a pretty good deal for something likely to be in front of a person for long periods at a time. Especially compared to an advert in a magazine which people scan for one second, turn over and eventually throw away.

Moo (moo.com), Vistaprint (vistaprint.com) and Zazzle (zazzle.com) all offer competitive rates on a number of different products, from T-shirts to stickers to handbags. Take care to check you're happy with the proof of the design before going to press as it can be very easy to misspell the name of a URL. If that happens you will have wasted your money and you'll also be stuck with stock that won't direct anyone to your blog.

Consider carefully the places where you think you'll meet the types of people who are likely to be interested in your blog. There's no point in handing out pens at a Women's Institute meeting when you blog about heavy metal music. Remember that product has cost you money to produce. Do the people you're giving it to deserve it?

If you blog about music, take your merchandise to a gig or a bar near to the gig venue. Blogging about cars? Then go out to a car show. Think about where your average reader hangs out and go there, because that's where you're most likely to meet like-minded people.

SENDING OUT A WEEKLY NEWSLETTER

It's important to remind your readers that you exist. If they've been on holiday or been extremely busy with work then they may have got out of the habit of reading your blog. Sending out a weekly reminder with the best bits you've published in the last seven days is an ideal way to win them back.

The three most popular e-newsletter service providers are *Mail Chimp* (mailchimp.com), *Constant Contact* (constantcontact.com) and *Vertical Response* (verticalresponse.com). Simply register your details online, pick your favourite template and upload it with your content. Tease people by giving them a sentence of the story and tell them to visit your blog for more.

The success of a newsletter depends on how many email addresses you have in your database. Even the best written newsletter in the world is useless if nobody reads it. Make sure there is a newsletter sign-up feature on the homepage of your blog and on your Facebook page and point it out occasionally in your blog posts so that people spot it. All of the e-newsletter providers have newsletter sign up form templates that you can embed in the sidebar of your blog. In the 'help' section of their websites you'll find instructions about how to add the functionality to your Facebook page.

HOSTING A PROFILE-RAISING EVENT

An event is a great way of getting your brand in front of people. You can brand a room with posters and then you can talk about how fabulous it is to people when you're at the event. If you're the host, people have to listen to you!

Personally, I've found putting on events to be one of the best ways of raising awareness of *Live Like A VIP*. A summer get-together to thank PRs, celebrities and my staff for working with me earned coverage in national magazines and photos were published on the *Mail Online*, which gets eight million users a day. What a great way to generate publicity! I invited a radio crew to interview people at a Christmas party and they broadcast their report to their thousands of listeners the next day, crediting my blog. If I was to buy advertising on the radio channel or in the magazines, it would have cost me a five figure sum, but I got it for free and I enjoyed a fabulous evening with a friendly crowd. However, good planning is essential. You need to be careful because if you host an event and something goes wrong, it could leave a lasting bad impression in people's minds and drag your brand down rather than elevate it up.

Firstly, take care with the guest list. If there is only a limited amount of space available then make sure everyone deserves their place. Target the editors of print publications, ask important PR companies and key industry figures. Parties can be expensive so it's important to make sure you invite people who have something to offer you. Make them sing for their champagne!

Secondly, you want to keep costs as low as possible, especially when you're first starting out. This is difficult but I am living proof that it is possible to pull off a five-star party for next to nothing with a bit of bartering and a refusal to take no for an answer. One of the most spectacular parties I hosted was at the five-star hotel, The Arch, opposite Madonna's house in Mayfair. There was lavish catering, there was champagne, there were vodka cocktails and it was attended by celebrities who normally charge a fee for their time, including up-and-coming girl band Stooshe, supermodel Sophie Anderton, *X Factor* band The Risk, the Streets performer Leo The Lion and reality TV star Calum Best. I even secured a magician and an in-house photographer to entertain the guests. How did I do this? Firstly, I admitted I may not have money to get what I wanted but perhaps I could offer everyone involved something that money couldn't buy. When it came to the venue, I asked myself how it positioned itself in its marketplace and what it would need to be successful. I worked out that the key thing a hotel needs is VIP customers who will have money to spend on rooms and so I pitched the idea of having a room for a couple of hours in exchange for bringing in a lot of new potential clients to the hotel. This worked well for me as a celebrity blogger, but if you have a fashion blog, you could hold an event in a shop. If you have a tech blog, what's stopping you from hosting an event after-hours in a gadget store?

To get the VIPs and the press to the event is a game of cat and mouse. Important people like to be written about if they have something to promote and journalists always need content. Tell the celebs that the media are going, and tell the media that the event will be attended by key industry figures and it will all fit into place. Once you start receiving RSVPs from journalists, you'll find it easier to get a drinks sponsor. Drinks brands have a large budget for advertising but it's a lot cheaper for them to provide a few bottles of stock for an event and get photos in magazines of famous faces drinking their product than it is to take out an advert in those publications. If you contact ten drinks brands and pitch them this idea, you should get at least one to provide you with heavily discounted refreshments.

When you're at the event, it's vital to stay focused. I always avoid all alcohol and work my way through the following checklist:

- Do I have people's email addresses so they can stay in touch with my news and updates?
- Have I talked to enough people? If I've made people feel

personally welcomed, they're more likely to visit my blog because they feel a connection to me.

- Have enough photos been taken? I always like to have photos of an event on my website afterwards as it serves as a sign that my blog is interesting and that I go out and interact with readers. The people who attended the party also enjoy seeing whether or not their photo has made it onto my blog.

- Can I get everyone out on time and make them leave on a good note? While it's tempting to party all night, I like people to leave wanting more. I want them to come back to my next party and not overwhelm them all at once. I like them to take away a good lasting impression of my blog so I always give them a goodie bag. Everyone appreciates a free gift and it doesn't have to cost you anything. Ask the drinks sponsor if they have any miniature bottles and ask the venue if they have any branded items. If you've invited some key industry figures to the party, ask them if they want to promote their product to the guests by slipping something into the goodie bags. For example, I often have beauty PRs at my parties, so I'll ask for nail varnish samples or mini eyeshadow compacts. PRs know that everyone who is attending the party is either a journalist or a celebrity or a highly respected industry figure and in a position to spread awareness of that brand by word of mouth or through the publication they work for. If only one journalist writes about the product they picked up in the goody bag it saves the beauty brand advertising in that title. It's not hard to do the maths, most businesses would rather spend £200 on supplying product for goodie bags compared to more than £2000 advertising in a newspaper or magazine.

Finally, after the event you need to capitalise on the buzz. I always email everyone with a simple 'Thanks for coming and visit my blog to see the evidence'. That day I will make sure there is something super fabulous up at *Live Like A VIP* for them all to see. There is no point directing people to your blog without bothering to freshen it up for the new traffic and you need something amazing that will encourage them to revisit the next day to continue the story.

Try sending photos and a press release to relevant media outlets in the industry and in the local area. The fact that you're getting out and doing something is news. If you can get your blog mentioned in an industry or national title then it will bring in tons of traffic, so do everything that it takes. Follow up on your press release with a phone call to the news editor explaining exactly how fabulous it was. When you're on the phone, remember that enthusiasm is infectious.

SEARCH ENGINES

Having an identity helps you define your keywords and this is vital for search engine optimisation, or SEO as it's more commonly known. This may be a scary sounding phrase but it's also an efficient way of promoting your blog without you having to host a party or pound the streets distributing merchandise. All you need to do is to use a few SEO tricks when writing your blog posts and search engines such as Google and Yahoo will promote your blog for you. You'll stand out as an expert in your niche, and anytime anyone is looking for news about that niche the search engine will push you forward, thus exposing you to readers who exactly fit your demographic.

Entire books have been written about how to boost SEO, and some businesses make a huge income from charging companies to boost their SEO and promising to get them on the first page of Google. If you have money to spend then it's worth investigating, as getting on the front page will bring you tons of traffic but I believe a lot of these companies are charging you for something that you yourself could do. Why not start by doing the basics yourself and get a professional opinion later down the line.

To start, bear in mind when it comes to SEO, Google and other search engines trawl the Web to find new content to offer their users. In calculating how to order the search they consider two things: what keywords you use most often on your blog, and how many links you have to other sites and other sites have to you. Change both of these yourself and you'll get further forward in Google search engines without having to pay for it.

Links are important because the search engine software detects how many times other people link to your site. If lots of people link to your site, you're perceived as a trustworthy source of information. Increase the number of links and you'll be further forward in the search engine's rankings, and it's not so hard to do. For this, I suggest creating what's known as a blogroll, which is a list of other blogs you like. You'll find lots of bloggers have these in the sidebar of their homepage. Tell the bloggers in your blogroll that they've made your list and hopefully they'll link to you in return. Secondly, if your blog is established you can flatter other bloggers and ask them to consider doing a guest blog for you. When they post on your site they will almost certainly mention to their readers that they've done it and link to your site so their readers can view the piece. That means it's another link for you! Text based links inside blog posts rank higher than blog roll links at the side of your blog, so don't skip this step.

With keywords, you need to pick ones truly relevant to what your blog is about. Search engines take note of the number of times you use a keyword as a measure of how relevant that keyword is to your particular page, so to get further forward in Google you should try to get your keywords into every single blog post. The more often you repeat them the better, which is why you should always pick those that sum up your blog. If you kept mentioning tenuous phrases all the time you may get good Google rankings, but you also alienate your readers who will then wonder why your writing standards are declining. Keep it relevant and keep it balanced.

TIP

Make sure your blog is actually registered with the major search engines or they'll be less likely to find you. As soon as you've published your first blog post you need to notify the main search engines in which you exist. It's a straightforward process and simply requires entering your blog's URL. The three most important links you need are: Google (google.com/addurl), Yahoo! (siteexplorer.search.yahoo.com/submit) and MSN Live Search (search.msn.com/docs/submit.aspx).

ADVERTS RELATED TO KEYWORDS

Choosing great keywords will also help you to formulate an efficient strategy for paid-for adverts. I'm always wary about spending money on advertising before you have much income coming in but Google AdWords, based on your blog's keywords, is a cost-effective way of advertising. It's guaranteed to bring readers to your blog as you only pay if someone clicks through the advert and visits your blog.

The adverts are content specific so you can also rest assured they'll be seen by people interested in your subject field. You can see how it works in practice by going to Google and searching for a particular term such as 'vanilla cupcakes'. Notice how there are some small text-based ads in the sidebar. Now change search terms and enter 'pink shoes'. You should see a completely different set of ads in the sidebar. Other benefits of AdWords are:

- There is no minimum spend. If you took out a banner advert then you may be asked to commit to a minimum budget, but you can start a Google AdWords campaign for less than £50. Once you've set your budget you pay for the actual clicks to your site, not the impressions, so you get value by knowing your traffic is increased as a result of your investment.
- You can expand or cancel depending on your company's growth. If your blog grows quickly and you start to have more of an advertising budget then increase your daily spend. Conversely, if you decide to stop, then you can do so at any time.
- You can start straightaway. As soon as you decide you want to advertise, visit Google AdWords, create an account and your adverts will be live the same day. There's no need to design hi-tech banners either!
- Google provides you with a raking tool so you can monitor how successful your campaign is. If you see your ads are not being clicked that much, maybe it's time to change the keywords?

Setting up Google AdWords is so simple. Here's a step-by-step guide to getting the best from it:

Step 1 Visit the Google AdWords homepage (google.com/adwords). Enter your personal details and pay an initial deposit via PayPal or credit card so that you have a budget to start with. You need to have credit in your AdWords account before you can buy ads.

Step 2 Walk away from your computer, go somewhere comfortable and make a list of keywords related to your blog and your subject area.

Step 3 Create a text-based ad containing those keywords. Each ad has a headline, a few words and a URL linking to your blog.

Step 4 Set your budget and work out how much you want to spend per day on your campaign. This requires deciding how much you are willing to pay for each person that clicks through to view your site. Google uses a complex formula to calculate where to place your ads, depending on how much you're willing to pay per click. The more you are willing to pay, the better your ad placement will be, and the more frequently it will be viewed by web surfers putting those key terms into a search engine.

Step 5 Monitor how well your ad is performing. Google has a service that lets you track this. What's important to look for is Cost Per Click CPC and Click Through Rate CTR (I explain these in more detail in Chapter 8). If you can find a low CPC and a high CTR rate then the ad is financially effective. Most bloggers experiment with different combinations of keywords until they find an ad with a low CPC and a high CTR.

> **TIP**
> For a quick overview of search engine marketing tips and tricks, visit Search Engine Watch (searchenginewatch.com).

ENGAGING MAINSTREAM MEDIA

Ask any brand what happens when their product is featured in a national newspaper, a magazine or trade title and the result is always the same: sales increase dramatically. Magazines, newspapers, radio stations and TV shows reach hundreds of thousands if not millions of people, and if they mention you for any reason it means the name of your blog is being exposed to that number of people too.

I experienced this first-hand with the coverage I received after I blogged about Leona Lewis being attacked in Waterstones. Since I was at the event, I had unique footage and magazines, newspapers and TV programmes all picked up the content and credited my blog. Traffic literally went from hundreds to millions overnight. I knew that if I wanted my blog to take off, I had to get more media coverage. I do this by sending out email alerts to newspapers and magazines when I have content they may be interested in, and it works. I once attended the Cannes Film Festival, where I got exclusive photos of Brad Pitt and Angelina Jolie and interviewed Kirsten Dunst. It was published by leading UK gossip magazine *Now* after I told them about it. I emailed people after the Brit Awards and the BAFTA Awards with interviews I'd had with Adele, Lily Allen, Jessie J and Mark Ronson, and I managed to secure coverage in magazines such as *More*, *Heat*, *The Daily Star* and *The Mail On Sunday*.

DEFINE YOUR IDENTITY – BUILDING A BRAND

You can always tell the effect a published article has had on your web traffic by studying your Google Analytics report. Back in Chapter 3, I explained you needed to include Google Analytics when you designed your blog, saying you should register for an account to generate code to install on your blog. As long as this code is correctly installed, you can keep a close eye on your statistics wherever you are in the world by signing into your account at google.com/analytics. Simply enter your user name and password and you'll see Google has monitored the traffic associated to the code and presented you with a selection of reports, including visitor numbers, traffic sources and search terms. The day a published article is out, there will be a huge spike in the number of visitors to your blog. If the blog is also published online, you may be able to see that magazine's website has been a source for traffic to your blog.

The skill of getting a media publication to write about a brand is known as PR. PRs act as the middle ground between journalists and brands and work to make the brands sound exciting enough for journalists to write about. PR account executives get to know journalists to find out what they are interested in, and then report back to the brand. Once they know what a journalist is likely to write about, they can tailor a press release to make a brand fit that theme and the brand may get coverage in the press. For example, say a PR had a fashion client and knew a fashion magazine journalist was working on a festival fashion spread. The PR would go back to the brand, find out what clothes the brand had that fitted a festival theme, and would then target the journalist with the desired information. Through good PR and knowing what

101

journalists want, the brand is more likely to gain coverage than by sending out a generic press release.

Therefore if you want your blog to be mentioned in the press you need to hire a publicist or learn more about the practice of PR. Some bloggers do hire PR companies as it can be a time-consuming process to build a relationship with journalists and keep on checking what they're up to. However, this is best done when it's time to go from relative success (and some level of income) to massive success. It's a pretty expensive process and if you're not earning anything at all from your blog, it's best to focus on that and then expand. When it's time, shop around for the best price. All PR companies specialise by sector, so to find one relevant to your niche, do a Google search with the subject field you write about and the term PR agency. Call up for a quote and ask what coverage you will get for that price.

Before hiring professionals though, you can learn what to do yourself to maximise exposure. There are two major elements to PR: targeting relevant journalists with a suitable story, and communicating your information in a professional way with a press release.

First, you need to compile a list of specific reporters, writers and editors and the subjects they typically write about. If a publication carried a similar story to what you suggest in the past they're more likely to take your content. Do this in a methodical manner by writing down a list of magazines, newspapers and broadcast media outlets that you want to be featured in. Next, contact each outlet and ask for the name, title, direct phone number and email address of the appropriate reporter. Sometimes the receptionist may not give out this information, especially if it's a popular magazine, because they're trying to protect their staff from being bombarded by cold callers. Imagine how many PRs are trying to get something in the same magazine and if everyone was allowed through, the journalist would never get anything done. However, do not give up. If you can get the relevant direct contact details it shows you have done some research and immediately puts you head and shoulders above everyone else who is trying to contact the title. You didn't give up at the first hurdle when it came to blogging, so don't give up now. Go out and buy a copy of the magazine, as sometimes the reporters' contact details are listed. Alternatively, search for the information through Google or another search engine. Or, if you're going to be promoting your blog a lot through the media, you can buy access to a database containing journalists' contact details through a specialised service called Gorkana (gorkanapr.com). This is expensive so consider how much use you'll get out of it before visiting the website to take out a subscription.

With your target list in mind it's time to tailor-make a perfect press release. A press release is the easiest way of communicating with journalists as it lays down all the facts and figures and shows you're an expert on a particular subject in a gentle way. You're not physically calling up a reporter, screaming 'pick me, pick me!' without giving them any reason why they should. As the former editor of a newspaper column, I have had people do that in the past. Needless to say, I didn't include their stories!

A typical press release should be around 500 words. It should be a concise summary of all the facts reporters and editors need to know, with facts rather than opinions or descriptions. Answer the questions who, what, when, where, why and how and then include your contact details. Some brands include quotes from relevant people in their organisation but I don't think this is vital. If a journalist is interested, they will contact you for quotes.

When thinking of what to cover in a press release, you need to look over the most interesting thing you've covered on your blog recently and lead in with that. Your job is to convince a journalist to publish something, and for that you have to tickle their imagination and make them appreciate the relevance of the story. If in doubt think themes – Christmas, Valentine's Day, Summer Getaway or Autumn Break. Remember, magazines work ahead so you need to think about what's coming up rather than what's happening now. Some publications start planning their Christmas features in August.

TIP

If you want an example of a good press release, there are several forums on the Web designed to help. Visit:
- Publicity Insider (publicityinsider.com/relese.asp)
- Wiki How (wikihow.com/write-a-press release)
- Press Release Writing
  (pressreleasewriting.com/10_essential_tips.htm)

If you send a well-written press release to the appropriate journalists then you're in with a good chance of getting picked up. However, do follow up with a phone call if no one replies to you. This is your chance to ask the journalist what sort of things they cover so you can make your next press release more relevant. If you keep on doing it, you'll build up a relationship with that journalist, and as any PR will tell you, relationships are key. If a journalist likes the person who's promoting a product then they're more likely to choose that brand over similar products.

TIP

If you have a really fantastic story and you think it may appeal to a wider market than the publications you normally deal with, you need a quick service to reach as many journalists as possible. PR Newswire (prnewswire.com) is a fantastic press release distribution service, which will distribute your release through email and fax to all journalists signed up to the service (all around the world). Gorkana (Gorkanapr.co.uk) offers a similar service in the UK. Within hours, thousands of reporters, editors and journalists will get your press release in their inbox without much effort at all. And the catch? You do have to pay Gorkana and PRNewswire for the service. Look online for rates.

PROMOTING YOUR BRAND ON SOCIAL MEDIA

Ever heard of the term 'viral'? It's when an article or a video spreads out over the Internet like a virus, resulting in millions of people seeing it. One person picks it up and shares it with their friends. If all their friends like it, then they share it with all their friends and those friends share it again, and so on and so on. If that content is associated with a business or a blog, then everyone who is opening the content is seeing the blog's logo – it's essentially free advertising.

The ultimate goal of any social media platform – whether it's Facebook, Twitter, Google+ or the photo sharing service Pinterest – is to create content worth sharing to get your brand name out there. I explain how to use all four of these platforms in more detail at the end of the chapter to give you the knowledge needed to grow your online community but remember, we all have to start somewhere. Your first posts are unlikely to go viral and may just be shared by one or two people but you need to keep it up. Every time one person shares some of your content, you're reaching a whole new audience so celebrate that, keep posting more, keep updating your followers with your latest news and eventually more and more people will subscribe to you. Hopefully these new subscribers will also share your news with their friends, who may in turn subscribe to you so your number of followers is continually growing and growing. Some advertisers now take into consideration social media presence as well as unique users when discussing ad terms, so read my full guide at the end of this chapter carefully.

Each of the four leading social media platforms listed above should be approached as a different entity. If you're starting out and unsure as to how they work, see page 120 of this chapter, where I explain how to set up accounts with each of these social beasts. If you already have accounts and want to know how to use them better, read on below.

HOW TO INCREASE YOUR FACEBOOK 'LIKES'

With over a billion of the world's population having membership to Facebook, it is vital to play the Facebook game correctly. Get it right and you can find out what people like and potentially appeal to a lot of new people. If you were to add up the amount of time people spend on Facebook around the world, it could be as much as 700 billion hours a month – what great exposure! Moreover, by putting your time and energy into Facebook you are reaching a market of people who actively use the Internet. As they're online already, it won't be difficult for them to click through to your blog. The best form of marketing and brand exposure reaches people where they are.

To use Facebook effectively, you have to remember you are only as powerful as the number of people who 'like' you. Only the people who 'like' you receive your news and updates. Therefore the goal of any blogger is to increase their number of Facebook fan page 'likes'. To do this you should:

- **Name your page something interesting** Often, the name of the page will determine whether users click on it. If the name is boring, it is unlikely that users will bother reading that page. Once you reach 100 friends or 'likes', you cannot change the title of your page so you need to get it right in the first place. The easiest thing to do is pick a name related to your blog so that people can easily find the page. My page is called LiveLikeaVIPdotcom.

- **Run competitions** By creating a contest that must involve Facebook interaction you will increase 'likes' in a short space of time. Clearly state in the rules that people have to 'like' the page in order to enter the competition. If the prize is good, people will tell their friends about the competition and their friends will enter it too, further increasing your fanbase.

- **Have a Facebook link on your brand's website** If it is there in front of their eyes when visiting your main site, then it is easier for them to click. It is vital to remember that consumers can be lazy. It's your job to make the navigation process to the Facebook page as easy as it can possibly be.

- **Update Facebook regularly** Although this seems obvious, many brands fall at this hurdle. You need to look at Facebook as an extension of your blog and you update your blog regularly, don't you? Give people a reason to keep checking in with you.

- **Pay Facebook to advertise your page** This is possibly one of the quickest ways to gain followers. Visit Facebook.com/advertising to create your campaign. You will have to surrender sensitive information about you and your brand, but this means your ads will only appear on people's Facebook accounts who fit your targeted demographic. You can set the ad budget but remember, you get results based on how much you spend.

- **Join pages which relate to yours** This might sound obvious, but it really does work. If you 'like' pages similar to yours and start up conversations and debate on them, you will instantly get noticed. You could even post content from your site to these pages if it is relevant to the conversation within the community. This will not only gain you more 'likes', but will put your content out there. It is possible the owner of the page may take the content down, but if you create enough buzz around it then it is more difficult for it to be removed. It may be an advantage to you if the post is removed as fans of that page will be interested in the rest of the debate/story – which could give you automatic Facebook 'likes'.

- **Link to other social networking sites** Curiosity will naturally send your Twitter and Pinterest followers onto your Facebook page. Whenever you add information about yourself to a user or contributor page, make sure you include your Facebook link too.

- **Promote your page everywhere** Never miss an opportunity to promote your page. Whenever you write anything online, always insert a link to your Facebook page. Don't overkill it, but at least one link per article is acceptable, if not two. If you are guest blogging, ask the host if you can put your link in. Bloggers like to help each other out, so this should not be a problem. Tell anyone you meet about it, and if you have business cards, have the Facebook link printed on them. Adding a link to your email signature line is also just as effective.

TIPS FOR GROWING TWITTER FOLLOWERS

Twitter is not used by as many people as Facebook but it's a more powerful tool for bloggers due to the intelligence of information you can gain from the Twitter software. You can use a program like Tweet Reach (tweetreach.com) to learn how many people you've reached from just one tweet. This could prove very useful to potential advertisers at a later date. Through Tweet Reach you can also keep track of what subjects your followers find interesting. If they keep choosing to retweet your messages about a particular musician, then you know that musician is popular and you should be covering them more on your blog.

People have written entire books about how to use Twitter for personal use, books on how to use it as a business and even novels about how Twitter has changed their lives. I do recommend purchasing at least one of these to get more information, but I have summed up the basics below.

Again, the key to Twitter is to build up your followers. It's only when people choose to follow you that they see your status updates. If nobody's following you, then what you post isn't being seen by anyone so there's really no point in sharing your news on it. If you want more people to follow you then:

- **Tweet at peak times** Monitor when people are tweeting the most and start doing the same. Although there is always a steady influx of tweets, studies have shown that top Twitter activity usually takes place between 10am and 4pm, with most responses being tweeted between 1pm and 2pm. There is little or no point tweeting during the middle of the night, unless you are aiming your tweets at people in different time zones.

- **Interact** You will never get your followers up if you don't interact. Twitter is an online community and with that you have to be social. Although it is important to tweet, if you do it too often, you are likely to lose followers. Stick to one topic at a time and follow it through. Wait a fair amount of time before changing topic or retweeting someone else's message to avoid overkill. And if anyone does engage and ask you questions, make sure you answer him or her.

- **Target popular and influential Twitter users** to get interaction going. Following, tweeting and retweeting people who are well respected in your industry creates a buzz around your account. You may not get them following you, but others will pick up on you and will follow. This has worked for me when I have sent Twitter messages to celebrities and the celebrity has replied to me. I have 10,000 Twitter followers but some celebrities have millions, so if a celebrity namechecks you there is a good chance that all their followers will go to your Twitter account to see who you are. Whatever industry you're in, there are popular people so in fashion you may target a designer, in beauty you could target a make-up artist and in tech you might target another high-profile blogger. Just look out for who talks about a similar subject to you and who has more followers than you then ask them something interesting to grab their attention.

It's important to plan what you're going to write as you want your tweet to stand out from the hundreds of others they receive daily. Motivational quotes, funny scenarios or thought-provoking questions are the best. If at first you don't succeed, try, try again. By monitoring what they have been saying to other people and trying to generate a debate, it looks as though you have a genuine interest in what they have to say. They'll notice you in the end!

- **Make people aware of your Twitter page** Be sure there is a link from your blog to your Twitter profile and connect your Twitter to your Facebook and Pinterest profiles.
- **Utilise Twitter hash-tags** You may have heard people talking about hash-tagging and not really known what it is. This little Twitter tool is vital in getting your tweets out there. Some people search Twitter through categories, so if you hash-tag the category you are talking about, it will make it a lot easier for people to see your tweets. For example, if you were tweeting about the football World Cup, you would use the hash-tag like this: #worldcup2012. If other Twitter users are interested in the content you are posting and hash-tagging, then they will see your content in the search results when they use Twitter's search facility. Once they see you share an interest in the same topic, they may start to follow you for more updates. If I was writing an article about Beyoncé, I would search Twitter and I would see all the recent tweets from anyone who had used #Beyonce. If someone had posted a lot

of Tweets and used the hash-tag Beyoncé each time then I'd deduce they were a Beyoncé expert and start to follow them.

- **Tweet photos and videos** People love looking at what someone is doing as well as reading a status update. Get a reputation for giving your followers a little bit more than they'd get in an average Twitter message and they're guaranteed to tell their friends about you. This works especially well if you give them access to somewhere they could never normally hope to be, such as backstage at a gig or a fashion show, or at the press preview of a new gadget.

- **Stay current** Twitter moves very fast, so be careful not to get left behind. Keeping up with newsworthy events is important as people are keen to talk about the here and now, not what happened two weeks ago. They want to know what is going on at that particular moment. Being a few hours late to a conversation can be detrimental, as it limits your exposure to a new audience. However, if you do join in late then make sure you can link the debate smartly into your tweets and blog.

- **Start a contest** Similar to Facebook, Twitter competitions will increase your followers fast. Get people to answer questions or retweet the competition tweet and you'll come up in their status update, which will be seen by all their followers. Some of those followers may decide to follow you. Make sure you hash-tag the competition when you announce it, as this will enable more users to see it in search results. The more people who see it, the more will spread the word.

HOW TO INCREASE YOUR GOOGLE+ FOLLOWERS
Google+ is the fastest-growing new social media platform.

Facebook took four years to get 60 million users and Google+ has managed to achieve this within a year of launching. Industry analysts forecast it will reach 400 million by the end of 2012 and be on track for 1 billion by the end of 2013. It's time to get cracking! If you build up your followers now, then you'll be up and ready for when everyone else starts to really join the party. Here's how:

- **Invite people to your circle** Circles enable you to fine-tune who you are following and who you want to keep in touch with, making it easy to keep your colleagues, business and friends separate from each other. You can choose which posts go to which circles. For example, your business acquaintances may not want to know which Madonna track you love the most – this could be kept to your friends and family circles.

  However, the reason you need to start by inviting people to your circles is because circles are completely private. If nobody knows you have an account because your profile is not visible, then they can't add you so make sure you invite them to a circle and you'll have more people to interact with.

- **Follow people** Again, this seems absurd to say, but the followers will not come to you. You have to seek people out. Divide them into different circles depending on the areas you are interested in. It's best to have lots of smaller circles than one big overcrowded circle. This is one advantage of Google+ over Twitter as it means you don't miss anything if you're following too many people. To keep track of each group of people, log into the relevant Google circle, see the news and log into the next.

- **Create a cool Google+ profile** If your profile looks interesting then it is more likely to be followed. You need to make it easy for people to find you via the Google search profile. The best way to do this is to turn off the privacy settings for the parts you want to be made public and upload a decent picture of yourself or your brand. Then think of your ideal audience, or blog reader demographic, and tailor this to your description.

- **Post regularly** It's the same for Google+ as for other networking sites. Be thoughtful and have a point of view so users can comment and form an opinion on what you are talking about. You don't have to create controversial topics, but you should ask questions, which encourage comments. If you see another post similar to yours, why not share it with your followers? This will create a new thread and keep discussion flowing.

- **Be visual** Similar to Facebook, Google+ lends itself well to visual stimulants. It is important for users to see what you are talking about, as well as reading about it. Try to post images to accompany your text to break it up. Make sure the photo strip across the top of the page is populated with interesting images to catch the attention of new visitors – it will keep your existing followers interested too.

- **Shamelessly promote yourself everywhere** First of all, you need to alert your blog readers that you are on Google+ so they can find you. One way is to display your Google+ profile on the top bar or the side bar of your blog using a widget. Don't be scared by the term 'widget', it's actually one of the most useful things a start-up blogger will encounter. The term is given to a stand-alone program like a clock, a timer or a map that can enhance your blog without you having to know any technical detail about how it was made. To install it on your blog, all you need to do is copy the code from the program's maker and paste it into a sidebar page or the top bar page, which should be visible to you when you log into your blog service provider. Instead of creating a post, you go to the area pages are stored and slot in the code where you want the widget to appear just like you would do if you were embedding a YouTube video into a blog post. If you have a WordPress account, it's worth searching the widgets database because you'll be amazed at how many ways you could potentially improve your blog. In the home dashboard of your WordPress account, you'll see a sidebar on the left and one of the headings in the side bar is appearances. Click on that and you'll see a sub-heading for widgets. Once in the widget area, either search for Google+ or widget wander to your heart's content.

If you don't want to install Google+ on your sidebar and spoil your blog's design then another option is to repeatedly mention that you have a Google+ account when writing your blog posts. For example, you could tell readers that if they want to leave a comment then you are temporarily only accepting comments on your Google+ page and not on the blog. Keep referring people to Google+ and eventually they'll start using it on their own accord.

You could also use the link of your Google account alongside your email signatures or add them to your business cards too – and any other sites you contribute to.

- **Comment on other media platforms** The more you comment on other blogs and websites with links to your Google+ account the better. Only do this on sites relevant to yours, as the readers of the site you are commenting on are likely to be interested in yours too. However, you may find it's best not to comment on the same site too much as the founder/author of the site may block you, or report your comments to the system provider.

HOW TO INCREASE YOUR PINTEREST FOLLOWERS

Pinterest is a fantastic tool for growing traffic. If your readers like your content then they will 'pin' what you say on their virtual pinboards and all their followers see it. How fabulous is that in terms of brand exposure?

You can install Pinterest 'share this' buttons onto your blog so that your readers can take content directly and start 'pinning'. However, if you already have a Pinterest account and have a lot of followers, it's an additional way to ensure people see your content. To attract followers:

- **Optimise your boards and images** In the same way you use SEO (search engine optimisation) for your blog or website, you need to use keywords to describe your images. The idea is to use a few keywords and not to overload your description as it won't make any sense. Think about everyday words that shoppers use, and if you get stuck why not try Google AdWords (google.co.uk/adwords) to help. You'll need to sign up for an AdWords account and then use the Tools and Analysis button in the top bar, which is between Opportunities and Billing. If you enter a search word that you think is related to your blog's subject area, the AdWords tool will suggest a list of similar words and phrases that you may not have considered. If you place these keywords in your key line and image description, it's more likely to be found by Pinterest users searching for images on that subject. If you want to increase your followers then you need to be found so picking the right tags is vital.
- **Make your board visually attractive** You would be amazed at how many people don't think to do this. If something looks

boring, people will not follow it. Make sure your main image is attractive and has useful or humorous quotes, and relevant pins. It's important to give your followers something they can visualise in their minds.

- **Remember not to over-self-promote** Your fans will see through this and it's an easy way to lose followers. Stumble Upon (stumbleupon.com) is a great site to get some free wallpapers and images to make your site look more attractive. If you post images from Stumble Upon as well as your blog it shows you care about a subject, and readers like it when others care.

- **Link to existing social networks** One of the fastest and easiest ways to gain more Pinterest followers is to link your existing social networking accounts to your account. By doing this you will notify your Twitter and Facebook followers that you have pinned something new, thus creating an interest in your account. Since you have already established connections with these social networks, you will grow your Pinterest followers more organically.

- **Make sure your pin content is useful** Remember the phrase 'less is more'. Although it is important to upload lots of content, potential followers only want useful and decent content. Make sure your pins are relevant to you and your users. That's not to say that you can't throw in the odd random pin you find interesting, but if you want to create a large amount of useful followers then just think: would I want to follow this person?

- **Update pins regularly** Just as you would update Facebook and Twitter, Pinterest needs to be refreshed just as often.

Consistency is important. Aim to update several times in the morning and again in the afternoon.

- **Communicate with other users** If someone 'likes' your pins, 'like' some of theirs back. This will gain you long-term followers and builds up rapport with people in your niche. The more you give, the more you get.

- **Be a pioneer pinner** Don't just re-pin what others have already pinned. Although this is great to do, just as it is useful to retweet on Twitter, don't do it all the time. Always be on the lookout for new pins that no one else has found. You will gain much more respect from fellow pinners as they will think you know what you are talking about, and you are much more likely to have a lasting following.

- **Pin video** Not many people do this, but it's just as effective as images. Perhaps create an introduction video, explaining your account and blog and where you can find your work – this not only interacts people with you, but will promote your blog too. Perhaps you should pin one video out of three to keep your account interesting.

EXPERT ADVICE

I asked some of the most successful bloggers how they increased their number of followers on Facebook, Twitter and Google+. Here's some insider information:

66

Twitter and Facebook can act as a kind of extension of your blog, a place to continue the conversation. The more you converse on these channels, the more visually present you are in people's timelines and they'll head to your blog to check out more. You'll find there are a bunch of interesting conversations going on at any one time, about current affairs, things that affect us all – involve yourself in them. Often, those conversations can generate ideas for posts, so a discussion on Twitter or Facebook may lead to you writing a blog post on that topic, where you can lead people to continue the conversation. Be involved, reply to people, engage and be engaging.

Muireann Carey-Campbell, Bangs And A Bun

Blogs, like bands, need to use social media, but they need to use it carefully and cleverly. If all you do is post links to your blog on Twitter, I'm not going to want to follow you – there needs to be something more to what you do.

Peter Robinson, Popjustice

Twitter is brilliant for getting a following but again, it's best used as a conversation and not solely to promote yourself. Followers [on Twitter and Blogger] want to see a person's personality. Some people try to be PC but the best tweeters give an honest and funny opinion on anything from fashion and beauty to reality TV and politics. It's also a great exchange of information. If a media-related person comes to know you as you engage well in conversation (just as in real life), they remember you and also sometimes seek out your blog.

Karen Hendry, Katie Chutzpa

A NOTE ON SETTING UP
SOCIAL MEDIA ACCOUNTS

FACEBOOK

When you're using Facebook to promote your blog you need a Facebook fan page. Never use your personal account as it looks unprofessional. Most of us have occasionally been tagged in horrendous photos or posted politically incorrect status updates on our personal Facebook profiles. You don't want your blog readers or potential advertisers seeing these. This is how to create a Facebook fan page:

Step 1 Go to Facebook.com/pages and click 'create page' in the upper right-hand corner.

Step 2 Pick a page category. Facebook selects six categories: local business or place, company organisation or institution, brand or product, public figure, entertainment and cause or community. A lot of people are tempted to tick the box brand or product and then tick the box website, but this may not be the best category. If you have a website category then people will only find your page if they want to see you. However, if you tick the box related to the industry you blog about and people look for that subject when they search Facebook, then your page will come up in the search results. Say you have a blog about fashion. Lots of people search for fashion because they want to find out more about it. If you choose a website category, you would not get that traffic as your blog would not be indexed in relation to fashion.

To pick the best category, first you need to read through all the page types before you decide. Clicking on each category box will bring a scroll-down menu. Look through everything before making your final decision as you may find a suggestion that you didn't imagine but fits perfectly. As a general rule, local business or place is most appropriate if your blog relates to a physical place that you want people to visit, as it gives the option of listing opening hours. Company organisation or intuition is most relevant if your blog is about an industry, so if you blog about the motoring industry or the computer industry then pick this. Brand is relevant if your blog is sufficiently popular that people are likely to go to Facebook to try and find you. Artist or public figure can be useful for two reasons. If you want to become famous out of your blog, you could list yourself as a public figure. However, the problem with this is you may be missing out on traffic as, realistically, people won't search for you initially.

For start-up blogs, the best way to use the entertainment category is if you have a fan blog about a film or music star. The entertainment category is great if your blog is centred round a particular genre like a sports team or a TV show. Got a blog about Chelsea Football Club or a fan blog for *Glee*? Entertainment is the category for you! Finally, there is cause or community. This is the least useful of all categories as there is no drop-down menu to choose from. Therefore, if you have a blog about a non-profit charitable organisation, you're better off going to company or institution and scrolling down the menus to non-profit. The more boxes you can tick, the more ways you will come up in people's searches.

Step 3 Once you select the category for your business, you can fill in the name, address and phone number. Check the box next to 'I agree to Facebook pages' terms' and click 'get started'.

Step 4 Upload a picture for your page. It can be a logo, a photo of a store or a photo of a person – whatever makes the most sense for building your brand. The file needs to be smaller than 4MB, and it can be square or a vertical rectangle. However, note that the avatar that shows up next to status updates and wall posts is square, so if you don't want anything chopped off, square might be the way to go.

Step 5 Get your page started off with some 'likes' by recruiting your own friends. Start typing in names and when you drag the cursor over someone's name, it will highlight in blue. Click once to check the person and add them to your invite. Click 'selected' to see who's on your invite list. When you're ready to invite, click 'send recommendations'.

Step 6 Click on 'import contacts' to reach out to your email contacts about your new page. You can upload a file (Outlook, Constant Contact, .csv) or you can enter your email login information so Facebook can access people in your email contact list. Again, you can check the box next to the names you'd like to invite, and you can preview the invitation to see what it'll look like. People already on Facebook will get a 'recommended pages' widget on their Facebook, while everyone else receives an email.

A NOTE ON SETTING UP SOCIAL MEDIA ACCOUNTS

Once you have a photo uploaded and a few fans on board, you can start engaging.

TWITTER

Step 1 Register your interest. Enter your full name, email address, and desired account password. Make the password secure and not easy to guess.

Step 2 Confirm username and password. On the next screen Twitter will let you know if your username is available or not, judge the strength of your password and suggest alternative usernames you may want to consider.

Step 3 Celebrity followers. In the next step Twitter suggests some well-known celebrity figures you may want to follow.

Step 4 Personal followers. Now you can search Gmail, Yahoo, Hotmail and AOL email accounts to find which of your contacts already have Twitter accounts. Simply enter your email account details and Twitter will scan your contacts book to find registered users. Once the search has been completed you can then choose who to follow. Alternatively skip this step if you want to be picky about who you follow. You may like to communicate with someone over email for work reasons, but following them on Twitter and learning more about their personal life is a different level of intimacy.

Step 5 Confirm you're human. Check your inbox for a confirmation email from Twitter, as there are strict measures in place to prevent fraudsters from opening accounts. Once you get the email, just click on the activation link to fully activate your account.

Step 6 Start following in your niche. If you know some Twitter names you would like to follow, enter them in the following section. You can also search for any term related to the business sector/niche you're in or personal interests, and can invite your friends via email in this section.

Step 7 Polish your profile. Go into your settings, click on your Twitter name along the top and choose 'settings' from the drop-down list. Once in your settings, click on the 'profile' tab and choose a profile image. If you're using Twitter for blogging purposes I would suggest using your company logo; for personal use I would always suggest a photo of yourself. Once you've uploaded your photo, complete your bio. A bio in Twitter, just like tweets, is restricted to 160 characters, so be creative.

Step 8 Start tweeting! Tell your followers what you're up to and make it as interesting as possible. Put as much care into your Twitter as you would do your blog.

GOOGLE+

Step 1 To begin, launch a web browser and go to the Google+ homepage. To use Google+ it's necessary to have an account with Google. Those with Google accounts already – through Gmail or YouTube, for example – can skip ahead to Step 3; otherwise click the 'create an account' link to visit Google's sign-up page.

Step 2 Fill in the required information to create a Google account, providing an existing email address and choosing a password that's hard to guess. Under the 'get started with Google+' heading, fill in a location and date of birth before typing in the verification-word characters. Finally, click the 'I accept. Create my account' button to accept the terms of service and create an account. Google will send an account-verification email. Click the link contained within this email to open an account-verification web page. From this web page, click the 'click here to continue' link to return to the Google+ homepage.

Step 3 If the Google+ homepage displays a red 'sign-in' button, click it to go to the sign-in page, provide the correct email and password and click the blue 'sign-in' button. Once signed in, the Google+ homepage displays a box for creating a public profile. Add your name and gender, but don't worry about adding a photo at this stage. You may wish to click to remove the tick from the 'Google may use my information to personalise content and ads on non-Google websites' box before clicking the 'join' button.

Step 4 The next screen is used to add more information to your public profile. This is strictly optional, but I recommend providing a photo and at least selecting a country – this will make it easier for friends to locate and identify you. Click the 'change profile photo' link to open the 'select profile' photo window. To upload one from your computer, click the 'select a photo from your computer' button, find a good photo and double-click it to begin the upload.

Step 5 Once the photo has uploaded, crop it by dragging the corners of the selection or rotate using the links on the right. It's possible to make edits by clicking the 'creative kit' link, which opens a more advanced set of tools. Once you're happy with the photo, click the 'set as profile photo' button to accept it and return to the public profile page, then click the 'continue' button.

Step 6 The next screen provides an opportunity to find contacts from Yahoo or Hotmail who are already using Google+. If you're a user of either site, click the 'find people' button to open a login window for the relevant service. In this window, clicking 'what will I share?' explains what information will be exchanged. Click 'connect' to go ahead, or back out by clicking 'no thanks'.

Step 7 Google+ will now suggest various famous or supposedly interesting people that it thinks you may wish to follow. Click the 'add to circles' link next to any suggestion that seems interesting to see that person's public updates in Google+. I'll explain more about the concept of circles in Steps 11 and 12, but recommend adding any complete strangers to the 'following' circle rather than a circle you've created for a specific group of people, e.g fashion PR or London nightclubs. If you want to be selective at the start, there's no obligation to follow any celebrities or strangers, or indeed anyone at all; click 'finish' to start using Google+.

Step 8 After finishing these initial steps, Google+ will display the homepage, at the centre of which is a stream of posts from people who have been added to circles. Near the top of the website, to the right of the Google+ logo, are several icons for navigating: hover the cursor over them to see an explanation of each. Click the 'profile' icon to view your profile page, complete with the information and photo you added during the sign-up process.

Step 9 Adding more information to the profile will further help friends and colleagues to find and recognise you, and may help you make new contacts with similar interests. However, it's up to you how much information you fill in and how much of it is shared. Click the 'edit profile' button to add more details, then click any field to update its contents. Click 'save' after editing a field to close it and return to the profile-editing view.

Step 10 Google+ can detect profiles you may have on other social networks, such as Facebook. Click the 'other profiles' link on the right of the screen to review these and, if there are none, add them by clicking 'manage connected accounts'. In the new browser tab that this opens, click the 'connect an account' button, select the service from the list and add your account name or the web link to your profile. Click 'add' to save the change, close the web page to return to the Google+ profile, and click 'save' to close the 'other profiles' box.

Step 11 Once the profile is complete, scroll back to the top of the page and click the 'finished editing' button. The next step is to add more people into circles. Click the 'circles' icon to view the default Google+ circles and any people they already contain. Click 'find people' to display suggestions based on your existing contacts on Google services. Alternatively, look for specific people by typing their name into the 'type a name' search box. Drag people into a circle to add them – it's possible to add the same person to multiple circles, if necessary.

Step 12 To create a new circle, drag one or more people to the grey ring on the left and click 'create circle' to name it. Add more people if required, then click the 'create circle with' button to save the results. Google+ informs users when they've been added to someone else's circles, but they are never told which one. They may choose to reciprocate, but don't be offended if they decide not to. When finished, click the 'home' icon to return to the homepage.

Step 13 With more people added to several circles, your Google+ homepage should now contain many more posts than before. If there are too many, click the circles in the list on the left to see only the posts from members of that circle. The notification icon in the top right will turn red to indicate events, such as somebody adding you to their circles. Click it to view the details.

Step 14 To post an update, click once in the 'share what's new...' box under the 'stream' heading. If necessary, use the icons to the right to add a photo, video, web link or location. Before posting, think about who needs to see the update and whether there are people who shouldn't. When the post is finished and the permissions are set, click the 'share' button.

JARGON BUSTER: WHAT ARE CIRCLES?

Circles essentially allow you to customise and categorise your friends list. In the real world we don't share everything with all our friends in the same way. For instance, you probably share different things with your parents, college friends and your boss. Hence, you can simply create a circle with a particular designation and drag and drop your connections into them. Circles basically work like groups, so you can share different things with different groups.

PINTEREST

Step 1 Register your interest. For now at least, Pinterest is an 'invite only' application. You can request an invitation by clicking the red 'request an invite' button at the top of the Pinterest website, where you'll be asked to enter an email address for the invitation to be sent. Alternatively, you can ask any of your friends who already have a Pinterest account to email you an invitation.

Step 2 Enter your details. Once you receive your invitation, click on the link you've been sent and you'll be asked to sign in with either Twitter or Facebook. This makes it easier for Pinterest to find and suggest friends for you to follow. You will still be asked to create a Pinterest account name, password and associated email. A Pinterest account image will be created from the profile image of either Twitter or Facebook, depending on which network you chose to log in with.

Step 3 Choose your topic of interest. Once you've signed in using Twitter or Facebook, you'll be presented with a visual grid of 28 topics. You'll be asked to choose your topics of interest so that Pinterest can make better suggestions as to who you should follow. Pick some topics, then click the blue 'follow people' button at the bottom of the page. You'll see some static, non-clickable images of people (and their boards) that you are following, based on the selection of topics you just made.

Step 4 Experiment with some boards. Pinterest will give you a default selection of pinboards (or boards) to choose from, such as 'products I love', 'for the home', and many more. You can also click the 'add' button at the bottom of the screen to add your own board with a custom-made name of your choosing. These boards represent topics that you can pin pictures to. Create as few or as many boards as you like. You can also edit the titles of boards you've created or delete them altogether.

Step 5 Play with friends. If appropriate you can allow other people to contribute to your boards by clicking the 'edit' button at the bottom of your board. Next, find the option 'who can pin?' and change the setting from 'just me' to 'me + contributors'. Note that if you want someone as a contributor, you have to follow at least one of their boards first. Also, note that I pointed out allowing people to comment *if appropriate*. You don't want one of your embarrassing friends changing something that is business sensitive.

Step 6 Keep it switched on. You never know when you will find something that you want to pin, so make life easier for yourself with the 'pin it' button. Once you've created some boards, you'll be directed to a page where you can install a bookmarker called 'pin it' in your browser. The 'pin it' button gets installed on your browser's bookmarks bar so that when you find images on a website that you'd like to pin to one of your boards, you simply click the button. The Pinterest application will open, showing you a grid of thumbnails of all the images available on the website.

When you scroll your cursor over any image, click the 'pin this' button to pin the image to your board. A pop-up window will open and you can choose the board you'd like to pin the image to from a drop-down menu of the boards you've created in Pinterest. Select the appropriate board, give the image a description (this is mandatory) and click the red 'pin it' button. Another pop-up window will open, confirming your successful pin and providing you with the options to 'see your pin', 'tweet your pin', or 'share on Facebook'.

Pinterest takes care of attributing the sources of the images, and every pinned image contains an embedded, clickable link back to the original website from which it came.

Step 7 Manage who you follow. The next screen you'll see during the sign-up process is one full of images that are from the Pinterest users you are following. These were generated by your initial selections when you first signed up. In Pinterest, you can follow a user, or you can follow a specific board. Removing users or boards is easy, and the person is not notified.

To unfollow a person, click on the user name in one of the pinned items on your feed. You'll be taken to their profile page. Beneath their photo is a grey button that says 'unfollow all'. In selecting this, you'll unfollow the person completely. You can also use the same method to unfollow specific boards in that user's profile.

A NOTE ON SETTING UP SOCIAL MEDIA ACCOUNTS

This is a good way to keep your Pinterest feed manageable and useful. For a business, especially, you want Pinterest to do the work for you by keeping the users and boards that you're following to be on topic or part of your social media plan. Less is more; twenty good pinboards or five users are better than 1,000 random ones to sift through.

Step 8 You'll want to flesh out your account with links to your website and adjust settings to match Pinterest to your Facebook profile. For example, if you linked to your Facebook profile when signing up, Pinterest automatically adds your Facebook friends who use Pinterest to your Pinterest feed, and provides a link to your Facebook profile.

You will definitely want a link to your website and to add a useful description about you or your business.

CHAPTER 7

ENCOURAGE BRAND LOYALTY – AND KEEP READERS RETURNING

You're doing a great job so far by offering your readers what they want and keeping your blog looking tidy… but you could still do more. There is one final way successful businesses are able to keep their customers coming back and therefore widen their customer base: they have loyalty schemes and incentives.

Now I'm not about to suggest you start up your own alternatives to Air Miles and make your readers collect points for visiting your blog, which they can then exchange for rewards. However, you have to admit Air Miles is pretty addictive as customers feel valued and therefore use the service more and more to build up points. There must be some benefit in it as lots of businesses have loyalty cards. Go to Starbucks and if you drink ten coffees you get one free. If you stay in Hilton Hotels, you earn points at every stay. At my local hairdressers, you get a free blow dry after every eight visits. This is what keeps me coming back.

ENCOURAGE BRAND LOYALTY – AND KEEP READERS RETURNING

When you know there's another blog in your subject area covering similar things to you it's important to go that extra mile to encourage loyalty and give your customers satisfaction. If you look at any industry, you'll see that if you get customer service – with *service* being the operative word – right then it will guarantee good business. With the opening up of new airlines operating low-cost routes in the UK, for example, many people still prefer to fly British Airways, who make it their mission 'To Fly, To Serve'. When you decide where to go out for dinner, how important is food and how important is service? I get so angry when I go into a restaurant and have to wait ages to get noticed. How hard is it to say please and thank you and make me feel welcome as I walk through the door?

Sometimes it's the little things that make a difference and show your readers that you've made an effort. When I first started blogging, I knew that I couldn't compete with my former publication, the *Sunday Mirror*, which could feature promotions like 2 for 1 entry to a theme park or £5 off a £25 supermarket shop. Therefore I started writing a weekly post called Deals of The Week, where I trawled through online discounts and newspaper promotions to find the ones I thought my readers would be most interested in. Although I hadn't negotiated the discounts myself, I had taken the time to write a blog post tailored to my readers and it showed I was going the extra mile. When my blog became more established and traffic started to grow, I was approached by PR companies and asked if I wanted to run competitions to give away a product the PR was promoting. In effect, this was free advertising as I was linking to the product but it gave me a way of offering something free to my readers. Every time I posted a competition, I looked at my Google Analytics account to see how it affects my traffic and it always increased. Therefore one Christmas I decided to do an advent calendar competition, where I gave away a different prize each day of December. Sometimes the prizes were big, such as a stay in a hotel or a camera, and sometimes they were small, like a DVD box set or a cheap necklace, but it led to three times as much traffic in December compared to November. That taught me the power of competitions and of giving something extra to your readers. Obviously I now do an advent calendar competition every December.

There are a few other ways you can show readers that you're grateful to them for taking the time to read your blog so they keep returning. In this chapter, I'll explain how a blogger can make a reader feel valued so they stay loyal.

MAKING A READER FEEL VALUED – CREATING A COMMUNITY

Why? Look at any successful blog and you will see it's been designed so readers can comment underneath posts, or these posts point people to Facebook where they can give feedback. Starting up a blog without a comment option is the equivalent of opening up a shop or a bar and ignoring your customers when they come in. Give them time to browse, fair enough, but make it easy for them to contact you when they decide to reach out. Sometimes, people want to ask advice from a business owner. Let your readers do the blog equivalent of asking if their bum looks big in what they're wearing! Even better, be honest with your response and you'll stand out for your integrity as well as how you write.

When you start up a comments system you may find it slightly slow to start with, so it's important to work extra hard at making people feel welcome. If you can't provide interaction your customers will go off and visit another blog which is livelier and more fun. Readers choose their favourite blogs based on where they feel at home, and it's up to you to create this atmosphere so your blog is the first destination when they switch on their Internet. Instead of wallowing in self-pity if nobody has commented, it's your responsibility to go out and get the party started! Give people a reason to comment and they'll start to do it for themselves. Very soon you won't have to do anything and people will do it automatically; your blog will become a place for them to visit to interact with their friends. With regular interaction they feel valued. Not only do they get news from your blog, they also receive an additional reward – friends! It's your job to be the host with the most.

How? Encouraging comments is a two-step process. It's very tempting to throw a quick-fix at the problem and offer a prize for the best person who comments on a particular post. This will encourage comments on that post but it's not realistic to offer a prize with every post you put up – you may as well be a competition blog if that's the case! Speaking from experience, you need to look at your writing first, as you're often to blame if people aren't commenting. Only when you're sure you have created the ideal atmosphere to encourage feedback should you kick-start the promotional push.

Every time you write a blog post, think about if you're asking any questions in it. If not, there is no reason for people to comment. If you are asking for comments then what type of questions are you asking? It's always best to ask specific questions with an urgent call to action. If you always ask 'What do you think?' then people will come to accept it as part of your writing style rather than seeing it as a valid question meriting a reply. Furthermore, if someone asks me what I think, then my automatic response is 'What do I think about *what*?' In a blog post, the chances are you've probably made about three or four points to back up your opinion or to communicate a message. Which part are you asking for feedback on? If a reader has to think too hard about what he or she is meant to comment on then they won't do it. They worry that if they answer the wrong thing they'll look stupid.

You need to read back over your post and think about how strongly you've asked the question. Research has shown that if a reader is going to comment it's a gut instinct and they leave a comment immediately, which is why you need to write the question in such a way that it looks like your life is not complete if you don't get an answer. For example, let's say we wanted to start a debate about Kylie Minogue's outfit. We might start with a specific question such as 'Do you like Kylie Minogue's outfit?' But it's more likely to get people interacting if you ask something like, 'Should I get an outfit like Kylie's? Tell us whether you like it or not below and if there are more likes than dislikes, I'll get the outfit and show you a photo.' The more people see their reply makes a difference, the more likely they are to reply. Or consider a question relevant for mum's lifestyle bloggers: 'What do you think about the use of swearwords on TV before the watershed?' This may encourage a reply, but you'd probably learn how strongly people felt on the issue if you made it more personal by saying something along the lines of 'We're thinking of making a petition to the government saying there are too many swearwords before the watershed – will you join us? Register your interest by commenting below this blog post.'

To further encourage urgency, ask yourself if you can write a post in such a way that a comment would enable the reader to show off. When a blogger suggests they don't know all the answers to a subject and asks readers for their help to fill in the gaps it strikes an emotional chord. In real life, if a friend says he or she is stuck on a problem and really needs your help to clarify the issue then you don't hesitate to help. You don't sit back and see if someone else will respond. It's part of human nature to try and help, no matter how much we might pretend otherwise. People feel satisfied if they help someone else; it adds purpose to their life. Capitalise on this sentiment by writing with humility. Make some valid points throughout the blog post with facts to back them up. Later on in the post, raise another question and suggest you don't know enough to be able to have an opinion. Play it right and you should get your readers offering up their expertise.

For example, if you had a parenting blog and were writing a blog post about a behavioural tip to get a child potty-trained you could admit you were having difficulties and ask your readers for advice as to what they would do in the same situation. Or if you're looking for a new buggy, you might ask your readers to suggest shops they like.

Fashion bloggers writing about a specific shop can ask people to say whether they know of a better one. Tech bloggers can ask whether their readers know of any additional functions for a certain device, or if they know of a cheaper place to buy the gadget. Whatever type of blog you have, you will always find a way to get your readers involved and give them a chance to show off their knowledge.

EXERCISE

Is there anything else we can change with our writing to encourage comments? It's time for a bit more market research, looking at other blogs in your subject areas. Have you noticed some get a lot of comments while others receive hardly any? What are the talked-about blogs doing that the others aren't? How can you apply this to your own blog?

Finally, to get comments going in the first place, you could have some incentives. I found getting comments difficult at the start of my blogging journey until one day I linked a competition post in with a blog post. I wrote a normal blog post, probably on the subject of some showbiz party I attended, and asked readers to comment on what they would have done differently to me if they'd been at the event, saying I would give the best answer a meal for two at a top restaurant. Until this point, I'd always had blog posts asking for comments and competition posts asking for readers to email me with their responses to a set question. However, I was surprised to find that this new approach of having a comment-based competition question attracted more than 50 responses. Although it was not that many compared to the entries had I asked for emails, none of my blog posts had ever attracted that level of feedback before.

ENCOURAGE BRAND LOYALTY – AND KEEP READERS RETURNING

To capitalise on the initial buzz from the competition, you need to act quickly, preferably with another competition, to keep comments flowing. After my initial success, I wrote another blog post naming those who had left useful comments and saying what I thought was good about their answers. I also made it crystal clear how grateful I was for their feedback by securing a bottle of expensive wine and offering it as a runner-up prize. As readers were not expecting two prizes, it showed I had carefully read and reviewed all comments before picking the best. Finally, I announced another comment-based competition the same day, setting an equally good prize for readers who left feedback on a post about a different subject.

As the second competition was running, I made it more of a priority to go to the comments and join in the debate. For example, after every ten reader entries I would leave a comment, whipping up the debate. I might even refer readers to a similar blog post I had written, where I raised a similar subject to show off to other readers that I wrote lots about what they were interested in. At the same time, I would join in with the comments under other posts, maybe thanking people for their feedback and suggesting if they had more points to add they could be rewarded by entering the competition that was currently running.

I made the most of every opportunity to promote the competition to my existing readers by mentioning it in any relevant blog post and linking to the competition post in that site (as entries required people to comment under that specific post). I also mentioned the opportunity in my weekly newsletter to ensure people saw I encouraged and rewarded feedback on my blog posts. An added bonus was that I found competitions encouraged a new base of reader to my site. For some people, entering competitions is a daily habit and there are websites advertising new competitions. The best of these websites receive massive levels of traffic, the top two being Loquax (loquax.com) and Martin's Money Saving Expert (moneysavingexpert.com). When you have a competition on your blog you can notify these places; if they pick it up and mention it on their site, you'll see that you get a lot of extra entrants and many more comments. Even better is that most of these readers would never have visited your site before you began encouraging comments, so they're starting off their interaction with you with comments coming naturally. This is what we want – for people to start leaving comments of their own accord, because they automatically see your blog as a welcoming place without you having to consciously and continuously do things to prove you're welcoming.

TIP

To submit a competition to Loquax, the first step is to visit the website (Loquax.com) and sign up for a new account.

To submit a competition to Martin's Money Saving Expert, the first step is to register with the site (moneysavingexpert.com). Then search the forums to see where the competitions are being talked about on the site.

It's a slow process; it took about six months of continued competition and comment-based activity to get comments on my blog up to a decent level but the more time and effort you put into it, the more likely you are to see it take off. You need to reward comments with feedback from yourself. Part of the reason we read blogs is because we like the personality of the blogger. I love the way Perez Hilton is not afraid to be cheeky with celebrities, and how *The Clothes Whisperer* talks about fashion with intelligence. If I left a message on their blogs and one of my comments provoked a reply from either one of them I would keep commenting in the hope that they would interact with another comment. It goes back to what I said earlier in this chapter: if you make people see that their comment genuinely makes a difference to the blog then they're more likely to do it. And one way to show comments are being taken on board and used is to join in the debate, supporting those whose points you agree with and challenging those you don't.

Hopefully you'll start to enjoy it at the same time. Some comments may make you laugh, others could bring a tear to your eye. When you interact with the people who comment, be honest about how you are feeling and they will warm to you. If you look like you're just engaging in the activity to get numbers up then people will quickly see through this. No one wants to feel just like a number in a crowd – your job is to make people feel special. And let's face it, you really should be grateful it's not just your mum who cares what you think anymore!

TIP

At the start, if you're still finding it difficult to get comments on your blog, ask your friends and family to help out.

Where? Are you sure it's easy for people to comment? If they can't find the box where they can leave their reply straightaway then they won't do it. When you write a question, point out exactly where they can write their opinion. Is it below your post? Do they have to log in first?

What? Sometimes it's a good idea to make readers log in before they post a comment to protect against spam. You have a choice between doing this in-house or using a specialised third-party software that is specifically designed for handling comments and provides extra tools and functions. If you only want the basics – the important thing is the ability to remove comments from the thread that do not seem to come from a legitimate place – then most blogging platforms (WordPress, Blogger, and so on) have their own in-house comments systems. The advantage of these is that they are styled after your blog's design. This keeps the look and feel clean as well as uniform, and gives your readers a smooth transition from post to comments. You have more control as it's hosted on your server so you're not screwed if their server goes down; and your formatting isn't messed up because you decide to switch off and go back to your own system. However, I prefer the third-party-comment services because of the range of options they offer. Comments are vital to bloggers and I would rather have the option of being able to do as much as possible with them, rather than just moderation.

If you're getting a lot of spam, you could investigate getting some additional elements around your comment system to deter attacks. Remember, every hurdle you put up to deter spammers also makes it more difficult for genuine readers to leave a comment, so I suggest only using these strategies if you have a genuine problem with spam.

Firstly you can use CAPTCHA – a challenge response test – to check if the person leaving the comment is human. These work by selecting a randomly generated series of numbers and letters and asking the user to duplicate the series before entering a comment. Normally, spammers target blogs and are not smart enough to be able to read and recreate the randomly generated series of letters and numbers. However, spammers are getting more inventive so some CAPTCHA systems are being based on a simple mathematical question like what is 2+2, or a logic question such as 'What colour is a pink elephant?' Most blog softwares and third-party-comment software have built-in CAPTCHAs.

Another way to fight spam is to install a registration option where people have to submit a valid email address before they can comment on a blog post. Spam scripts are normally indiscriminately sent out, without being attached to an email address, so asking users for an email address means genuine subscribers will fill in their emails and spam messages, not associated with an email, will not show up. Not all of the inbuilt blog comment systems have registration options, so you may need to look for a third-party-comment service if you prefer user registration to CAPTCHAs.

Finally, I recommend all WordPress bloggers use a third-party software to filter out keywords usually associated with spam. Even if you are going with your inbuilt comment service, a keyword filter won't affect the design of your blog and there is no issue with control. If it breaks, it won't leave you any worse off, but when it works it is genius. The way it works is that it associates keywords with spam and filters out comments containing those words. We all know that words like 'Viagra' are hardly ever used in genuine comments so the keyword filter stops posts containing the word from appearing on your site. You can add words to filter out, depending on what type of spam links you have the most problem with. Just like an email address, you'd check your spam folder once every week to make sure you're not missing any genuine comments.

The most popular anti-spam system for WordPress these days is Akismet, although Security Ninja is also good. To install, simply search the widgets, download the plug-in on your blog and generate an APIkey – a string of numbers and letters. Then visit the Aksimet website (http://akismet.com) to register your blog and submit that API key number.

TIP

Did you know that if you're on WordPress you can get software that sends an email to people thanking them for their comment? If it's the first time they've left a comment, the 'comment relish' plug-in sends an automatic thank you that can be personalised to your needs. This should encourage people to keep on leaving comments and read more regularly. To install, look for the plug-in option in the sidebar of your WordPress dashboard, search for 'comment relish', download and activate it on your blog. Simple, yet effective!

MAKING A READER FEEL VALUED – DISCOUNT INCENTIVES

Why? Everyone likes to get something for free, and everyone likes a bargain! Look in any newspaper and there is always an advert for at least one supermarket, shouting about what's on special offer that week. The special offers are what draw people into the stores. Buy One, Get One Free, Two for £5, Three for the Price of Two – there's always a saving to be had. Sometimes they're enough to make people go out of the way to find their nearest store. When the supermarket Lidl sold lobster at the bargain price of £5, my parents got in their car and drove to the next town so they could shop at Lidl instead of their local Tesco. Make your blog something people want to run to their computers to check. Even when they're on holiday they should want to go to the Internet café to find out what your latest deal is.

How? I looked at how businesses organise special offers and I noticed two things: the offers need to run for a limited amount of time only, and they must be chosen with the target customer in mind.

Targeting and focusing the offer is the most vital part of the equation. It's better to have a £5 saving on something your readers want than a £50 saving on something they don't need in their lives. No matter how big the saving, the discount won't draw them to your blog if they don't care about the product. I wouldn't put a discount for a car tyre or a stair lift or a zimmer frame on *Live Like A VIP* because I don't think my readers would care. Notice that when supermarkets and grocery stores pick their discounts, they always have them on household essentials like milk and bread, cleaning products or healthcare brands. You don't often see supermarkets advertising that they sell pickled onions cheaper than a rival store. This is because they know all their customers use healthcare brands and everyone needs bread and milk. Not everyone likes pickled onions.

When picking your discounts it's important to profile your reader. What are their likes and dislikes? What are their hobbies and interests? What might their bathroom cabinet look like? Once you know what your readers need you can fulfil that need and people will visit you over a blog that doesn't serve them in the same way.

Secondly, a special offer should only ever run for a limited period of time. It needs to drive people to action so there must be a sense of miss it, miss out. If a supermarket always had something cheap then we wouldn't rush down to the shop because we'd know it would be in-store the following week. In the same way, keeping the same discount up on your blog for too long won't drive anyone to check your site on a certain date as they won't expect a fresh offer. Played correctly, discounts on products and services can ensure repeat traffic on a certain day each week. If it changes on a specific day then people may mark that day in their diaries and check what the deal is!

An additional benefit of running deals for a limited period of time is that you always have something new to incentivise readers to visit the blog. You have something new to talk to them about on Facebook, Twitter and Google+, asking them if they've seen the new deal yet. If not, they need to get it now. You couldn't do this if the offer was up all the time – you'd just be repeating yourself.

What? It's natural to feel more than a little intimidated right now – how are you going to get something fabulous for all your readers? The answer is, you're not. You're going to think about what they might want and then get someone else to do all the hard work for you.

Your chosen brand is the 'someone else'. They will be the ones in charge of explaining how to redeem an offer or shipping product to customers. All you have to do is show the reader it's out there and tell them it's out there because of you; only if they enter a certain code related to you will they get this saving. You put the offer on your site, give a code to quote at the venue for a free drink or a code to enter into the checkout in an online store, and it's up to the merchant to fulfil the order. Once you've got the deal and put it up on your blog, that's all that's needed – and you can then work out what you want to put up the following week.

OK, how do I get the offer in the first place, you may ask. In answer to this question, have a look at your Google Analytics statistics right now and check how many readers you currently get. All brands are constantly looking for ways to increase their exposure and reach new customers. The brand you're targeting may have recently spent a lot of money on paid advertising. If so, it can afford to give you some products at 20 per cent off. If you're not charging for an ad and it's reaching all your readers this is a no-brainer. You'll be beating away the discounts in no time! When you have a lot of discount options you may want to charge for the opportunity, but it's a good idea to keep it free at the start to make sure you actually get some offers.

Take it from me: putting discounts on your blog is all about momentum. Once you've put the first few deals online, other companies will contact you to ask if you'll put their deals up and then you won't have to do any work at all. I advise starting local. If you know a particular brand well through an event collaboration or you know someone involved with the company, pitch them first. If you have any personal contacts at a company they're more likely to listen to you than if you contacted them with a cold call. The discount does not have to be with a global brand. Even it's for a new shop or a start-up business, if you feel it would benefit your readers then get it up. What happens if you're not that well connected? No worries, simply go for budget. Look through all the magazines on your subject matter to see who is advertising right now. Which of the brands on that list have you spotted advertising a deal elsewhere? They're the ones to approach first.

It shouldn't take much time at all. All you need to do is compose a short email mentioning your readership statistics, where you plan to promote them on the homepage or sidebar, and stressing it's all free of charge. I'd be very surprised if you contacted ten brands and didn't get at least one or two deals out of it. Just keep them relevant! If the company says they're not interested and recommends something else that doesn't fit with your blog then you are allowed to say no. In fact, they'll probably respect you more for it, making you a serious contender for future business.

MAKING A READER FEEL VALUED – GOING BACK TO THE SHOP FLOOR

Why? No matter how large a business gets, people will desert it if the boss of the company doesn't appear to care. It's great to interact with your readers through comments and social media, but imagine how much more fabulous it would be if they got to meet you. When Richard Branson travels on a Virgin plane, the atmosphere is incredible. Here's the owner of a brand showing he's done all he can to raise the standards of the brand, and he loves it so much he's not ashamed to meet other customers to see what they think about it. Are you proud of your blog? Get out there and find out what your readers have to say. If you think you could improve, go out and ask your readers what they'd like to see you do more of. Just a thirty-minute interaction every week will be enough to show that you care about your readers and make them loyal to you in return.

How? It's not hard to install a chat box on your blog to converse with your readers in real time. Simply set a regular time slot aside each week, and tell your readers that if they visit the blog at a certain time you will be there to chat with them. The social networking site Myspace occasionally has live web chats with music artists, and so does MSN UK. These are advertised on the homepage a week in advance and interested fans can simply visit the site at a certain time to take part. However, if you had a specific day and time in mind when you were always free, even better – people would mark it in their diaries as a regular slot.

Alternatively, you could make use of the new technology available and do a video chat. Google+ has a fantastic 'hangout' application, which enables groups of web users to converse in real time and see what everyone looks like. Just make sure you do your hair and have a clean and tidy background – your image is your brand, remember!

What? For a good-quality chat box, I recommend Box, which is a third-party chat box application. Simply register with the Cbox website, customise your box and you're given an HTML code to insert wherever you want the chat box to appear on your blog. Don't be scared about HTML – it's as easy to embed as it is to embed a YouTube video. Here's a step-by-step guide:

Step 1 Visit the Cbox website (cbox.ws) and enter your registration details.

Step 2 Start configuring your chat box. Under the 'Cbox options' tab, configure the display, date and post options. Note that under post options there is an 'anti-spam' feature. Tick that.

Click 'colors & fonts' and select the colours that will blend well with your blog.

Step 3 When your box looks pretty, click the 'quick setup' tab to get your HTML code.

Step 4 Log in to the dashboard of your blog software. You can create a new blog post for the chat if it's just something you do once a week. Just before you want the chat to go live, open up a new post, make sure the writing area is in HTML (not visuals) mode and paste in your code. Hit publish and you will see the box on your blog. You can now start using it. Enjoy!

Step 5 Moderate the debate when you get started by blocking nasty people. If you should receive any spam post, go to messages, ban the user and delete the message. Under 'blocked users' you can change the duration of the ban.

For video, hosting a Google+ hangout is a great way to make ten of your readers feel special. Google+ has a limit of eleven people conversing through video at once because if you tried to see more than ten readers you'd never fit them all on your computer screen, but this is a good thing as it makes it more in demand. Maybe your winners could win a web chat with you – then you get publicity from the competition as well as interaction through the actual chat. And if you wanted to reach out to more than ten people, set aside an hour for the chat and chat to twelve groups for five minutes at a time. This will mean that 120 of your readers (ten in each group and repeated twelve times) have got to meet you.

To set up a Google+ hangout, here's what you do:

Step 1 Tell everyone who wants to be in the chat to create an account with Google (google.com/accounts). They'll do this if they want to chat with you that much.

Step 2 Add everyone to your circle in Google+. If they're not in your circle then you can't chat with them. (For a reminder of what a Google+ circle is, see the social media notes of Chapter 6, page 128.)

Step 3 In your Google+ dashboard, click on any of your circles on the left.

Step 4 When you're viewing a circle, click on 'start a hangout' on the right-hand side of your stream screen.

Step 5 To add or remove people, click the 'x' button in the upper right corner of any circle to remove the circle. Click 'add more people' to open the hangout to more people.

Step 6 Once all guests have been invited, click 'hangout' to get started! You'll immediately see a screen with anyone else in the hangout, along with your own video so you can see how you look.

Step 7 If you're in the middle of a hangout and want to invite more people, just click on 'invite'. You'll then be taken to the invite screen where you can invite more people.

Step 8 Hangouts makes it very easy to share videos if you're in the middle of a chat and decide you want to watch a music video or a film trailer. Simply click YouTube and everyone will get a player window pop up in their homescreen.

Step 9 When it's time to finish, log out by clicking 'end hangout'.

> Word of mouth should never be underestimated, so it is imperative to make visitors (and especially those kind enough to comment) feel welcome in the hope that they will spread the word. The key to building a successful blog (regardless of its size) is developing a reputation, and the best way to do this is through your regular readership.
>
> *Gary Collinson, Flickering Myth*

CHECKLIST

Have you:

☐ Made sure that it's easy for people to leave comments under your blog posts? Do they know where to leave them?

☐ Realised the importance of asking questions as a drive to starting comments?

☐ Worked out how to moderate comments and prevent spam attacks? Will you be using a pre-installed moderation system or a third-party system? Will you have CAPTCHAs?

☐ Negotiated some carefully selected discounts for your readers with relevant brands?

☐ Tried and tested a web chat and a Google+hangout?

CHAPTER 8

START MAKING MONEY – DIRECT ADVERTISING FROM DAY ONE

This is where the fun part begins. Keep working on what you've learned in the previous chapters, as you want to keep traffic growing all the time. More readers means more revenue.

At the start, growth can take a while, so you'll be pleased to know that it's possible to earn some pounds and pennies from day one without much effort at all. Hurrah! Every pound counts towards that first million. When a shop opens for the first time, it won't get millions of customers walking through the doors to spend money but it will have a cash register, just in case. Make sure your blog has the basic money-making tools from the start. You don't want to open the shop for business and then discover you don't actually know how to use the cash register!

Prepare yourself for the Triple As: three simple ways bloggers can monetise their blogs from the beginning:

Banner/text/link-based ad sales Most bloggers design their sites with some space for adverts. As you start blogging, you may not have time to sell the ad space yourself but you can sign up to an agency or get a Google AdSense account. Both match advertisers to bloggers and take a commission. They may take 50 per cent of what the ad is worth, but remember: 50 per cent of whatever they sell is better than 100 per cent of nothing.

Affiliate revenue Bloggers can earn money from giving product recommendations in their blog posts. If you sign up as an affiliate of an online retailer – for example, Amazon, ASOS or Net A Porter – and drive traffic to their website through links in your posts, then you will be entitled to a percentage of the sales generated by that traffic. You can do this from your very first post.

Advertorials It's possible to sign up to an agency that matches advertisers with bloggers who are willing to be paid for writing a post about a certain product. You'll be given a brief but the post can be written in your words so that it fits the style of your blog. The agency will typically pay a blogger between £50 and £100 for this endorsement. It's a nice little earner at the start of your blogging journey, and you can always re-evaluate the fee at a later date.

But did you hear me say prepare? Before you can do any deals, you need to focus. It's one skill to sign up to a money-making model and quite another to ensure you're making as much money as possible from it. To keep it simple, this chapter will be divided into two sections. First, I'll talk you through how to get started with each of the Triple As, and then I'll explain how to maximise your earnings on each platform.

SECTION ONE: GETTING STARTED WITH THE TRIPLE AS
A IS FOR... AD AGENCIES

If you have space for adverts on your site but feel sick with fear at the thought of calling up a business and selling it, then you need to find someone else to sell that space on your behalf. Most bloggers use a program called Google AdSense from day one, and some bloggers also sign up to a digital ad agency.

Where to start with Google AdSense:

• Visit the Google AdSense homepage (www.google.com/adsense) and click on the 'sign up' button in the upper right-hand corner of the screen.

• Fill in the online application form, which will ask for the URL of your blog, its primary language and confirmation that you agree to the terms and rules of the Google AdSense program. It will also ask you for your bank details so you can receive payment for the money you generate from your blog.

• Have a detailed look at what type of advertising is available to you. You have the option of image-based ads and text-based ads, and you can pick the size of your adverts.

• When you see a type of advert that you'd like to use, it's not that much more complicated than embedding a YouTube video into your blog. Remember I explained how to do that in Chapter 5? In that case you copied and pasted the video embed code given to you by YouTube into a blog post while your blog was in HTML mode (as opposed to visuals mode). With Google Ads, you'll see HTML code next to the ad you like, and you copy and paste the code into a blog post.

- If you want the advert in the sidebar, you just need to enter the HTML code into a different section of your blog design template, using what is known in the blogging world as a 'widget'. 'What's a widget?' you may cry out in panic, but don't be scared. If you have a WordPress account, when you log into it you will see what's known as a dashboard. Look in the left sidebar and you'll see a section named 'appearances'. Click on 'appearances' and you'll see a further section called 'widgets'. Now click on the 'widgets' option.

- Once in the 'widgets' menu, you will notice a large table containing rectangular boxes. Can you see a rectangular box that is labelled 'text'? On the right of the menu there is a list of boxes labelled with different areas of your blog, such as header, right sidebar, left sidebar and so on. If you want the advert in your left sidebar, click on that rectangular box and it will expand.

- With the rectangular left sidebar box expanded, go back to the main table. Now click and hold down your mouse on the text box to drag it into the left sidebar box. Once you let go of the mouse, the text box will stay in the left sidebar area.

- Click on the text box itself and it will expand.

- Paste the HTML code into the text box and hit save. Hello adverts, hello money!

TIP

To see a step-by-step video demonstration of how to install Google AdSense on your blog, go to Google and search for 'AdSense Installation Video'. A video tutorial shows you exactly what to do and where to click, and you can pause it as you work through the installation process.

Once you have got to grips with Google AdSense you will need to get started with a digital ad agency. As blogging has become increasingly popular, businesses and brands are allocating more of their advertising budgets to online activity. This means we're seeing a rise in the number of specialist online-based advertising agencies. The ad agency staff make deals with large companies and distribute the ads among the bloggers they already have on their books.

Given the choice, most bloggers would rather use an agency than Google AdSense as there's more human interaction and control. With Google AdSense there is always a risk of an unsuitable advert popping up on your blog as Google's content-matching algorithm can be temperamental at times. Also, ad agencies have more transparent pricing structures. Google never makes it clear what percentage of commission it takes for selling your ads, but agencies tend to split revenue 50:50 and give you a contract at the start, laying out terms and conditions. However, not all bloggers are able to sign up with an ad agency at the start of their blogging journeys as the agencies have specific criteria as to what they take on. Of course ad agencies are staffed by real people and these people must be paid. If an agency doesn't believe it can match your advertising space to any of its regular clients then it will refuse to take you on as you won't generate any revenue.

The only way you'll find out if you qualify is to ask. Investigate the websites of Handpicked (handpickedmedia.co.uk) or Glam (glammedia.co.uk), to see how to submit your blog. If they turn you down, then you've still got Google AdWords making you money.

If you want some insider information on what makes an agency more likely to take on one blogger over another, I got the low-down from a Glam Media account director.

INTERVIEW

Izan Nash, Glam Media Account Director

Q: What is Glam?

I: Glam has been going in the US since 2005 and 2008 in the UK. We have over 2,500 publishers worldwide and 300 in the UK. Our publishers want to be part of the Glam portfolio because generally they aren't big enough/powerful enough to sell their advertising space themselves and/or don't have the contacts to speak to big brands.

Pre-Google, advertisers knew they could go to the likes of MSN, Yahoo! and AOL to reach most of the online audience. Once Google came along, people found it easier to find the niche content that they wanted to read. It was women who led the way in this, and as they generate more online spend than men, they were a really valuable audience to reach. Glam saw value in harnessing these sites together and offering up the fantastic audiences that they provide to big brands.

So, in simple terms, we give the bloggers tags (which will create advertising spaces) to put in place on their site and we can serve advertising into them. There is no cost. We sell your space for you and whatever revenue we get, we split it with you 50:50.

Q: What benefits does Glam bring to a blogger's site?

I: Glam offers bloggers the opportunity to be part of a unique portfolio of sites which in turn creates more inbound and outbound links, helping to grow traffic. Our sales team then introduce your sites to premium brand advertisers – like Coty, L'Oréal or Net-A-Porter – that the blogger might not have relationships with already. Our editorial team on Glam.co.uk feature blogger content, link to their sites and extend invitations to brand press days and create opportunities for bloggers. With our sales opportunity, bloggers can also get involved with spokesblogging programs for extra monetisation, which means a company paying a blogger to write and manage their company blog. On top of *all* of this, Glam Media offers networking and educational events for blogs and sites on SEO, selling their sites and so on.

Q: How is a blogger approved to join Glam Media?

I: Glam Media chooses the best bloggers with niche content around style, family and parenting, entertainment, luxury, living and health. Our experts handpick bloggers and publishers with interesting and engaging content, and help to grow and monetise their businesses. We don't just go for the biggest blogs, we have a breadth of sites from *E! Online* to those starting out and needing guidance.

Q: What bloggers are currently with Glam?

I: Some of our publishers include *Face Hunter*, *Fleur De Force*, *Female First*, *Unreality TV*, *Rotten Tomatoes* and *E! Online*.

A IS FOR... AN AFFILIATE REVENUE SCHEME

With affiliate advertising you earn when you refer a customer to a product and it results in a sale. If you mention a specific product in your blog post and create a link from that post to an online shop selling that product then you are driving traffic to that retailer. It's only fair that you take some commission for this.

Bloggers can earn as much as 8–10 per cent of a sale through affiliate revenue. You don't need to negotiate payment terms or talk business with any ad managers, and you can always expect a cheque to arrive in the post each month.

When starting out, most bloggers prefer to join a network of affiliates rather than to start accounts with lots of individual retailers. You could deal directly with large retailers like Argos or Amazon, but you will receive your commission in fits and starts and you'll have to deal with correspondence from each individual affiliate. If you join a network that has several brands on its books you earn whenever you promote one of these brands, giving you more potential income – plus you will receive payment from one central source.

For example, when I started out I joined Link Share, which controls the affiliate programs of several major brands including Topman, Puma, Benefit Cosmetics, French Connection and Coast. If I wrote a post about where to buy a celebrity's outfit and I linked to a top from French Connection and a skirt from Coast and both resulted in a sale, then I would have made a nice income from one article. I would receive payment by cheque as soon as the earnings in my account reached £25.

Getting started is easy. Simply visit an affiliate network's website, sign up to create an account and you're away. Each time you log in to your account on that network, you'll see which brands you can link to and how much commission you make from each brand. Signing up for an account with one network does not preclude you from joining another, but do remember more schemes means more stress as you'll need to monitor your earnings from all the different places.

Some popular affiliate networks are Affiliate Window (uk.affiliatewindow.com), Buy.At (buy.at), Link Share (linkshare.co.uk), Affiliate Future (affiliatefuture.co.uk) and OMG (uk.omgpm.com/affiliate/). Take a look and see what suits you best!

TIP

Skimlinks (skimlinks.com) is swiftly becoming the UK's fastest-growing affiliate provider as it gives its members access to all of the affiliate networks. I swear by it!

Once you have an account with Skimlinks, you'll automatically be able to earn money from all the brands on the database. There is no need to sign up to each affiliate individually. It's also really easy to keep track of earnings as they create monthly reports so you can monitor the most clicked links on your blog, how many times they were clicked and how much you earn from those clicks.

A IS FOR... ADVERTORIALS

An advertorial is when an advert is designed to look like editorial content on your blog. This essentially means an advertiser will ask you to write a post about a certain subject and recommend a specific product and you'll be paid when you publish it.

Some bloggers view getting paid to post as a dirty business, but if you have tried out the product and believe it works, what have you got to lose by writing a blog post and earning money from it? If a PR sends me a sample of a new shampoo and I like it, then I'd probably review it. So why is it different when an advertiser sends me a sample of a product and tells me I'll earn money if I review it?

At the start of your blogging career, advertorials are a fantastic way to earn income, typically earning bloggers between £50 and £100 per post. In month one of your blog you won't be earning that much from Google AdSense or affiliate networks.

If you'd like to start getting advertorials, sign up to an agency like ebuzzing (ebuzzing.com) or PayPerPost (payperpost.com).

SECTION TWO: ACHIEVING AN AMAZING ADVERTISING INCOME

If you want to maximise your blog's money-making potential, then you need to understand what the advertisers and affiliate networks are paying you for.

ADVERTISING JARGON

Banner adverts The most popular form of online ads. These are normally rectangular or square and are displayed in the sidebar or below the header of a blog. When a reader clicks on the banner they are taken from your blog to the advertiser's website.

CPC (cost per click) This is typically the model used by Google AdSense. In a CPC ad model, you receive income according to how many people click on the ads, regardless of how many times the ads are actually shown.

CPM cost per 1,000 impressions (M is the Roman numeral for 1,000) This is the term favoured by digital advertising agencies. They quote their clients a figure based on how many times their adverts are being viewed by blog readers. If you set a £10 CPM, then every time the advert is shown on your blog 1,000 times to different readers, you've generated £10. If you want to make £100 then you need to make sure 10,000 readers view the ad, and if you want to make £1,000 then you must get the ad in front of 100,000 people.

CPA (cost per action) This is the information used by affiliate networks whereby a blogger only gets paid if the advert has resulted in a sale. A click is not enough – the person who has seen the advert must actively engage with what the advertiser has been promoting.

Cookies If you work with affiliate advertising, you always need to know whether it's monitored by cookies and how long the cookies last. Get a good cookie deal and the results should be delicious! A cookie is the technical term for a small text file placed on a computer's hard disk by a web server. If you're using it in relation to affiliate marketing, it means that each time someone clicks on the link you've made directing them to an external website, they get some cookie code with your affiliate number in it. Then when they visit this website, the website will pick up the cookie containing your user ID and credit you for the sale. The longer a cookie is active, the greater your chance of making money.

GROWING REVENUE WITH GOOGLE ADSENSE

If you want to get good money from Google AdSense, you need to keep monitoring how your readers are engaging with it. If you're not getting a lot of click-throughs you may want to change how the ads are being displayed on your blog. Google AdSense lets you customise the following factors:

• **Positioning** The number of times your ad is clicked on depends on the number of times it's noticed. If people don't realise it's an ad or can't see it because it's buried in your content, then they won't click on it. When a visitor first looks at your page, their eyes are normally drawn to the top left of your blog. This is where your blog logo and header typically is. If possible use an ad banner directly under this area. It is vital that your advert is as high up the page as possible as a lot of readers never stay on a blog for long. Some don't even bother to scroll down, so if your ad is at the bottom they may never see it.

Another tip is to make sure there is a space between the ad under your header and the ads in your sidebar. If you put one lot under the header and the other directly underneath, you'll cause what is known as 'banner blindness'. You're also at risk of banner blindness if you have a loyal following of visitors. The more people see your ads in a certain place, the more they see this as a design feature of your site and so they don't click on them. If your blog attracts regular readers it's a good idea to swap the position of ads round often.

A million-dollar question is whether or not to have ads within the content. Research has proven that people are more likely to click on ads in this way, but it can be annoying if they click on something they don't realise is a link. If they keep on doing it, they may desert your blog as it's too hard to read. Do it sparingly.

- **Size** Mix up the sizes of ads on your site to keep it visually interesting and ensure people don't fail to see them. Research has shown that wide skyscraper ads of 160 x 600 pixels perform the best in terms of click throughs, so you should aim to have at least one this size. Experiment with the others as you'll only work it out through trial and error. The size that works best for your friend's blog may not be the same as what works for you.

- **Colour** Most successful AdSense users seem to be taking the approach of blending their ads into the overall theme of their page. This often means making the ad's background the same colour as the background of the page and making the title and URL the same as links on the rest of the page. In this way the ad does not stand out as being 'ad-like'. Having said this, I know of a few bloggers who take the opposite approach and make their ads as bright and ugly as possible in the hope of attracting the attention of their readers. I prefer the blending method, as ugly ads make your blog look cheap.

GROWING YOUR AFFILIATE REVENUE

With affiliate networks, you earn when your readers buy a product through your recommendations so blogs with a stronger sense of community do better than larger, impersonal ones. Build up trust with your readers.

- Remind yourself why you chose to blog about your subject area (see Chapter 2) and ask what other people find interesting about this subject. If you know what your readers like, then you should be able to recommend products they could genuinely benefit from. If they see a product on your blog that they need, they'll buy it and you get the commission.

- Use the statistics provided by the affiliate network to be certain of what types of products your readers click on and what links they always ignore. In future, recommend more of the popular products and less of the poorly performing ones.

- Be completely honest when you review a product. If you list the negatives as well as the positives, then it makes the readers trust that you are not selling them a product purely to receive commission. They can then decide if the advantages outweigh the disadvantages, thus feeling involved in the sales process and so more likely to buy.

- Make it easy for the customer to find the product you recommend on a retailer's website by linking to the actual product rather than the retailer's homepage. If people can't find what they want to buy easily, they're likely to lose interest and log off without purchasing.

MAXIMISING YOUR REVENUE FROM ADVERTORIALS

When you're signed up to an agency like eBuzzing or PayPerPost, you can create as many sponsored posts as you like. In theory, there's no limit to how much you could earn. In practice, however, you need to have a long-term strategy. If you post too many advertorials then you're not focused on building up your blog's reputation as a leading resource in its subject field. Spending time writing something dictated by a brand means less time spent finding out something useful for your readers – and if readers don't find your site useful, they won't stick with you for long.

TIP

One advertorial a week is plenty. If in doubt, less is more!

CHECKLIST

Have you:

☐ Created an account with Google AdSense?

☐ Realised the importance of ad position and colour in growing Google AdSense revenue?

☐ Contacted a digital ad agency like Glam (glam.com) or Handpicked (handpickedmedia.co.uk)?

☐ Signed up for a Skimlinks account and looked around for other affiliate networks?

☐ Understood how to grow affiliate products by recommending products your readers may need?

☐ Registered for an account with an agency that looks after advertorials, such as eBuzzing (ebuzzing.com) and PayPerPost (payperpost.com)?

CHAPTER 9

IMPROVE YOUR INCOME – HOW TO BOOST ADVERTISING REVENUE

Are you happy with the amount of traffic your blog is getting? Are you sure? If you're reading through this book too quickly, stop now! Go back through Chapters 1 to 7, where I explain the foundations you need to establish before you start making money, and spend some time building up your community of readers. In the following pages of this chapter, I'll explain how you can go from a decent income to a fantastic income, but you need to be able to commit some time. At this stage of your blogging journey is your time best spent improving your blog and growing your traffic, or compiling a media package for advertisers and pitching to them?

If you're still with me, congratulations! You're obviously proud of what you've achieved so far and it is this confidence that you will need when approaching advertisers. I've learned from experience that selling anything depends on having a good attitude. The reason a lot of bloggers never realise their full money-making potential is because they are scared. A lot of us are frightened of rejection. I understand that – it's a horrible feeling – but if you don't start a task because you are afraid of the word 'no', then you will never hear the beautiful word 'yes'.

When it comes to selling advertising directly, every time you get a 'yes' remember that you will be twice as well off as when you were with an advertising agency. If you want to make serious money from your blog, then the only way is to sells ads yourself and cut out the middle man. When you rely on an ad agency they take 50 per cent. Now you can bank 100 per cent of all the takings!

Still not convinced? If you have a truly great blog then you have all the skills necessary to sell ads. To pitch successfully you'll need to write a clear and concise media package. Bloggers are writers. You'll need to start a conversation with some new people (the advertisers). Bloggers engage with new readers on a daily basis. You'll need to get across to advertisers some of the benefits they'll receive from buying into your blog. Bloggers know how to get the facts and detail at the top of a blog post. Trust me, you're a lot more amazing than you think.

If you follow my ten-step sales guide, which is tried, tested and used by me to monetise *Live Like A VIP*, I'm confident you'll have interest from at least one advertiser within a week of completing the email stage of the process. That's Step 6, so come on – hurry up! We have a lot to do between now and then.

THE *LIVE LIKE A VIP* TEN-STEP SALES MANUAL

PREPARATION: START WITH AN OPEN MIND

Often the subject of selling ads is more complicated than it needs to be. One person says one thing, another person says something else, and so you apply a bit of what each person tells you and end up with a weak and directionless approach. It's far better to follow one strategy – and to follow it well.

I may not be a professional ad sales manager, but I've found what works for me and I'm willing to share my technique. Not many people would do that but I believe demystifying the sales process makes it clearer for both bloggers and advertisers to work together.

I fully expect to be asked if putting together this manual will harm my chances of getting advertisers. On the contrary, I think it will only help both bloggers and advertisers to communicate. After reading this guide, bloggers will have more confidence to approach advertisers to tell them how many people read their blog. In turn advertisers will realise that blogging is a powerful medium and they will get a lot of 'bang for their buck' in taking out online advertising as opposed to print or TV advertising.

If, like me, you're getting upwards of 80,000 to 100,000 unique users a month, you need to know how to communicate this. You're not lying or tricking advertisers by following this guide – rather making life easier for them by getting in contact in a professional way and explaining that you reach a market of people they want to advertise to.

THE METHOD: TEN STEPS TO SUCCESS
Step 1: Believe you can do it. This is easier said than done, but it's vital. If you don't believe in your blog then you can't expect other people to spend money on it. When you're reading this chapter, is your attitude, 'I probably won't be able to sell ads

myself, I'm too shy'? Or is it, 'I'm really shy but I want to make money, so I'll give it a go'? If your attitude is right then you can do anything!

Imagine calling up a potential advertiser with a pitch that goes something like this: 'Hi, I have a blog. It's pretty good. It's not as good as so-and-so's blog and traffic levels still need to improve and I don't always have a budget to buy the best photos, but it's averagely good. You should advertise on it.' The chances are they'll hang up on you quite quickly. However, say you called up the same advertiser with this pitch: 'Hi, I have a blog that has won such and such an award. It gets 100,000 unique users a month and we have advertising opportunities available' – you'd probably get a chance to explain yourself further.

To build confidence in your abilities, simply look back over what you've achieved. If you're reading this chapter after thoroughly reading Chapters 1 to 7, then your blog should already have a good level of traffic. Now make a list of what other achievements you've had. Have you been endorsed by any key industry figures or magazines (here's the place to say that Kylie said you're her favourite fashion blog, or *Vogue* named you as 'one to watch')? Have you won an award or planned a big event? Has your blog led you to go on TV?

If you look over this list five times, then you should feel pretty proud of yourself.

Step 2: Put together a media sales package. This will be your calling card when approaching potential advertisers.

If you want to communicate how much traffic your blog gets, it helps to lay it down in black and white on paper. (Well, maybe use some colour to make your graphs and pie charts look pretty.)

If you get nervous or start to stutter when faced with a potential advertiser, you can pass them this document and it contains all the information they need. As a general rule, keep it concise and to the point. I've found you can sum up most of your information on one side of A4 paper.

All the information you need can be found in your Google Analytics account. If you designed your blog as I explained in Chapter 3, then you'll have started the account from day one, which means you can show off how your traffic has grown. Google Analytics automatically creates reports containing graphs to monitor traffic falls and spikes. Download one that best sums up your success. Then look out for:

• Number of unique users
• Number of page views
• Number of page impressions.

State these figures at the top of your sales package. These statistics communicate how many people you reach, and that's an advertiser's first question. Start with unique users and then give page views and page impressions in that order. The number of page views and page impressions will be higher than the number of unique users, but there is no point trying to hide it as advertisers will be looking out for all three figures.

The second question is what type of people read your blog – what are their ages, education levels and interests? For interests, you can use information found in Google Analytics that tells you what search terms your readers entered to discover your blog. For ages and interests, you may need to go directly to your readers and ask them. Put up a survey on your blog asking them five questions about their lifestyle and set a competition prize. Within a fortnight, you should have enough entries to enable you to complete this stage.

Finally, do you have any press cuttings or testimonials from authoritative figures that add to the overall purpose of indicating how fabulous you are? If so, summarise these at the bottom of the sales package and point out where the advertiser can go to read the full article. End with your contact details. If an advertiser is impressed, you want to make sure they know how to contact you!

> ### TIP
>
> If you want to learn from the best, check out some of the media kits made by the world's highest-earning blogs. *Perez Hilton* (perezhilton.com), *Techcrunch* (techcrunch.com) and *The Huffington Post* (huffingtonpost.com) all have media kits available to view online. You'll find them if you scroll down to the very bottom of their homepages and click on the small 'advertise' link, right at the end of the page.

Step 3: Define your pricing structure. When you visit a shop you will see that most of the products have price labels on the item or on the shelf where the item is stocked. This helps the customer to clearly see whether they can afford it and if not they walk out of the shop and don't waste anyone's time. Fixed prices also keep the business organised as the shop owner can see what items are left on the shelves and how much they could potentially earn if they sold them all.

Not preparing a package – with costs – before you speak to advertisers will only end in confusion. You can always change your prices and negotiate with businesses when you sit down and chat, but you need a realistic starting price in mind. If you don't give a business an estimated pricing point then they could end up wasting your time if you come in to chat only to find they can't afford it. Also, it's a lot easier for you to stay motivated if you set yourself a target of selling five ads for £200 each than haphazardly trying to pull in £1,000 from somewhere.

The best way to work out your initial starting price is to ask around and see if you can find out what other bloggers are charging. If advertisers can get a similar level of traffic for less money they won't come to you, so you need to make sure your prices are on a par with other bloggers in your field. Look at what size ads other bloggers offer and how much they charge in CPM.

If in doubt, it's best to start low and raise your prices as you become more in demand. If you started gently and offered a small 125 x 125 pixels ad in your sidebar for £1 CPM (£1 for every 1,000 page views) and found those ads were selling like hotcakes, then you could increase your prices when you spoke to the next lot of advertisers. A blog with 100,000 unique users a month would earn £100/month from a £1 CPM model, which seems good value all round. If you want to see what a 125 by 125 ad looks like, check out leading tech blogs *Read Write Web* (readwriteweb.com) and *Techcrunch* (techcrunch.com). *Read Write Web* displays 125 by 125 ads in the sidebar, while *Techcrunch*'s ads are in the main body of the blog, usually found after the first or second post towards the top of the page.

Step 4: Identify potential advertisers. Selling advertising space is a numbers game. If you have a long list of potential advertisers some will have a budget, some won't, and others still won't be convinced of the value of online advertising as opposed to print or TV. Put together a list and you can simply work your way through it, crossing off the no's and celebrating the yes's.

It's easier to stay positive with a long list of possible advertisers. If you do get a bad rejection then you'll see that there are lots of other potentials out there who may need you. Work your way through your list methodically and I guarantee you will find them. To make a list, you could:

• Install Google AdSense on your blog and monitor what companies' ads get displayed in your space. It's worth adding these companies to your list as they clearly have a budget and you could offer them a better deal.

• Look at other blogs in your niche and see what companies are advertising on them. If they're advertising on another blog they clearly value the importance of online advertising in principle.

• Visit industry events and trade fairs and look at the companies who have paid for display stands. If they're paying out for a stand at a trade fair, they're clearly trying to reach more people.

• Look back over some recent blog entries and work out what kind of products you have written about. Who makes these products? Add these brands to your list. Have you ever written about any venues (shops, restaurants, tourist attractions)? If so add these to your list too. It shows there's a good fit between your readers' interests and the brand's products.

Step 5: Analyse your hit list. Advertisers will always have different reasons for wanting to take out ads. If you can identify reasons specific to each then it means you can spell out exactly how an advertiser can benefit from your traffic when you contact them.

For example, if I was approaching an advertiser who had just launched a new business, I would give them my traffic figures and stress this could be useful in increasing exposure for their new business. However, if I was approaching an advertiser specifically targeting women with a new handbag, then my approach would focus on a fact about my readership profile, highlighting my female-to-male ratio skew, to indicate that advertising on my blog could help the brand reach more women.

It's simple common sense. Work your way through your long list methodically, each time asking why a company might need to advertise. Common reasons are:

- **To launch a brand-new product**.
- **To increase their online sales.** Some brands are only just starting to open an online shop and could benefit from an advert on your blog directing readers to their new venture.
- **To reach out to a specific group of people**.
- **To change the perception of their brand.** If a brand is commonly perceived to be old-fashioned and stuck in a rut, it may try to reinvent itself by advertising online and attempting to be more dynamic.

Step 6: Draft an email. With your list of potential advertisers and their needs in front of you, it's time to communicate how you can meet each business's needs.

Email is more convenient than phone. People choose when to open emails, but a phone call interrupts someone's daily routine and you never know what's happened to that person the moment before they take your call. Some recent news might have put them in a bad mood so they'll be feeling negative before you've even started your pitch.

All you need is a clearly written, short and concise email stating the key facts – who you are, what traffic you receive and what that means for their business.

The first two points will stay the same, no matter what advertiser you talk to, so save time by writing these down on a Word document and copying and pasting into each email. The third paragraph will change for each business, but you've got the advertiser's need written down on your original list. It will take you less than a minute to summarise it for the email. It's not as if each email requires a lot of effort. Copy, paste and summarise, send. Copy, paste and summarise, send. You can do it with the TV on in the background.

TIP

When sending emails to advertisers, it's vital to get the direct email address of the person in charge of advertising spend. Generic email addresses such as info@ or news@ will not do as there is a big chance they'll reach the wrong person and be deleted by them before they get to the right person. If you've spent a lot of time working on your media sales package, you may as well spend a bit more researching the people directly responsible for budgets to eliminate the risk of your email being ignored.

Step 7: Close the deal. If you send emails to enough people to communicate your impressive statistics, then you will receive emails back. At this stage, it's up to you to take a potential advertiser's drop of interest and whip it up so it becomes a huge bowl of excitement.

If you're well prepared, the whole process will flow smoothly. The first thing to do is to arrange a meeting because communication is better face to face. As you may have guessed by how often I am using this word, communication is vital.

Turn up on time and look professional. When an advertiser is buying a blog they are also buying a part of you, so you need to be a good ambassador for your blog.

Stay confident by reminding yourself of the levels of traffic you get. See, this advertiser really needs you! Have your media package printed off so you can hand it to the potential advertiser at the start of the meeting.

If your media package figures are good enough and you look like a sensible business person, this is normally enough to make advertisers willing to spend money on you. However, if they seem nervous about spending online – do remember it's a relatively new niche – then be ready to quote some of your other advertisers to them. If a small clothing boutique finds out that River Island has previously advertised on the same blog, they'll be more likely to want to do the same.

Step 8: Offer a discount for repeat bookings. It will make life a lot easier for you if you sell advertising space to one business for a long period of time rather than being forced to approach new advertisers each month. Therefore why not reward advertisers for repeat bookings? Give them the option of twelve-month, six-month, three-month and one-month packages. If you don't give them the option of twelve-month frames, then you'll never know if you could get it. And if you do get it, it'll make life a million times easier for you.

If an advertiser shows a slight interest in a twelve-month

package, then offer them a month's free trial so they can see exactly how much advertising will benefit their brand. If you're directing good traffic to their website after month one, they will be keen to keep this up for the next year.

Step 9: Offer add-ons to the package. Winning over a new customer is a big thing. It's a time-consuming process to get someone to buy something from you, so why not ask if they want another service while you're there? Trust me, it's a lot easier to sell two things to one customer than it is to sell two things to two separate customers.

A lot of successful retailers already use this tactic. For example, I buy my business cards at Vista Print (vistaprint.com). After I add the cards to my shopping basket, before I pay for them I'm asked if I want to add headed notepaper or stickers or envelopes to my order. Often these items are offered at 20 per cent less than their usual price to encourage impulse buying. When you visit a grocery store, often there are items like chewing gum and chocolates by the tills. This is to encourage shoppers to add more things to their basket while they're in the shop. When you visit a McDonald's, you're often asked if you'd like a Meal Deal or a Large Meal Deal instead of a single burger. Once a customer has made a decision to buy something, they won't walk out the shop if you ask them if they'd like to buy one more thing. Most of the time, people do say yes, resulting in more revenue for the business. If you sell twice as much to each customer then you're doubling your profits.

So what add-ons can you offer your customers? If your blog has a newsletter, ask all potential advertisers if they would like to buy ad space on the newsletter in addition to online space. If you have a marketing event like a fashion show, launch party or public speaking event planned, then ask if these companies are interested in paying to display branding at the event. If you don't ask, you don't get.

Step 10: Taking payment. After you've talked an advertiser through pricing options and lengths of commitment, they can start to imagine the ad going live and anticipate the benefits they will have on their traffic. They're excited and they realise the good things in life are never free, so they're prepared to pay your rates. Please make it easy for them to transfer the money!

Make sure you agree how the advertiser is going to pay you at the time you do the deal – BACS/PayPal/cheque. If you leave it and contact them a couple of weeks after your meeting, they will have lost some of their initial enthusiasm and you may have to go into your pitch all over again.

A couple of weeks after sealing the deal, it's a good idea to contact the advertiser to see how they are getting on. This level of personal care will mark you out from other media they advertise with, and they'll be more likely to deal with you again or recommend you to other advertisers.

CHECKLIST

Have you:

☐ Re-read your blog to congratulate yourself on how amazing you've made it? Believe that advertisers are privileged you're approaching them.

☐ Complied a media sales package to communicate your blog's traffic and audience reach?

☐ Worked out how much you're pricing your ad space?

GET RICH BLOGGING

☐ Made a list of potential advertisers for brands operating in your subject area?

☐ Compiled an email to introduce yourself to advertisers, communicating the advantages of advertising on your blog?

CHAPTER 10

BEYOND THE BLOG – OTHER REVENUE STREAMS

For most bloggers, direct advertising will never bring in more than 50 per cent of their income. A lot of the money earned by bloggers comes from freelance blogging for other sites, writing for newspapers and magazines, public speaking or getting involved with a 'special project'.

When your blog has decent levels of traffic, you will automatically become a 'name' in your niche. And the better known you are, the more people will want to work with you. What they ask you to do depends on your niche – fashion bloggers are more likely to be asked to co-design a handbag, while parenting bloggers may be invited to become involved with the preparation of a new range of baby food. This chapter gives an overview of what's out there so that you don't miss out on a potential opportunity if you haven't been asked to do anything yet. Here's how to get a piece of the action.

FREELANCE BLOGGING

Most businesses are starting to add a blog element to their websites as it boosts their SEO (search engine optimisation). In Chapter 1, I explained how one of the benefits of a blog over a static website is that Google and other search engines rank blogs highly, giving credit to how often they are updated and how many links it is possible to create with a blog. Therefore businesses who are trying to drive new traffic to their website through search engines need a blog element but quite often, they haven't got a clue about how to run one.

If you've built up decent levels of traffic to your blog and are well known in your niche, you've already shown you have a talent for blogging. Most businesses would rather hire someone with a proven track record than take a risk on someone new, so the fact that you already have a blog puts you head and shoulders above any other candidate in the field.

If no one has approached you yet, maybe it's because they don't realise you are available for hire. Sometimes the best bloggers are the most unapproachable as people assume they're far too busy with their own blog to do anything else. Therefore you need to use your blog as a showcase. Create a banner advert in the sidebar to direct readers through to a page containing examples of your freelance work and writing you've done for other blogs. Keep the advert simple – something like 'Check out my guest blogs' or 'Web watch: places I contribute'.

If you haven't done any guests blogs yet, then consider offering your services for free to some friendly bloggers to get something for your portfolio. You'll build relationships, get links back and have something for your showcase area – triple result!

Start talking about it. Sometimes you need to spell out you're available before it sinks in. Start a conversation with your friends and other bloggers and specifically say you're up for doing some more writing, and do they know of a website or blog that needs some copywriting? Even if the answer is no, they may hear of an opportunity at a later date and remember your conversation.

Be proactive and contact businesses operating in your niche. If you've spotted that a company's website could be improved, contact them and offer your services. The worst they could say is no thanks. If you keep looking and asking around, then you will find at least one business that needs your help. After all, let's look at it logically and consider how many new businesses start up every month. A business doesn't come equipped with its own fully functioning blog, so if you catch them at the right time there is a good chance they'll hire you to do their blog.

And it works! I've done guest blog posts for fashion retailers, beauty brands, hairdressing brands, a travel company and a coffee manufacturer. At the start, expect to earn £100 per article and increase your fee as you get more in-demand. Alternatively, you could offer a company a discount in exchange for providing a month's worth of content for them, as I do for the hair colour remover brand Colour B4 (Colourb4.com).

MAGAZINES AND NEWSPAPERS

Your blog is your personal online CV and cuttings library, showing you can write and that you have a lot of knowledge about a specific subject. This means that if you approach a magazine or a newspaper with a suggestion for an article, they're more likely to accept it because they can check out your blog to see if your piece will be well informed and well written.

Sometimes magazines and newspapers make it easy for bloggers and contact us directly because they enjoy reading our blogs. This does happen, trust me. If you have a lot of traffic, then there's a good likelihood some of your readers will have pretty interesting jobs. If, however, you're still waiting for that magic commission then you need to get to get out there and make it happen for yourself. Here's how:

Use your blog to communicate you're available for hire. Again, have a banner advert in a sidebar to direct people to examples of your published work.

Be realistic. If you ask for a column in a magazine straightaway you're bound to be disappointed. Start off slowly by pitching a short article. If that's published, make the next article longer. Suggest having a series of articles. Each time, be professional about it and hand your copy in on time and drive awareness to the article by pointing it out on your blog. Sometimes a magazine's website will benefit from a surge in popularity when a well-known blogger contributes an article, which is a sure-fire guarantee that the blogger will get commissioned again.

Spend time creating a great pitch. When I edited two pages in the *Sunday Mirror* newspaper, I received thousands of pitches from freelance journalists. The best ones were short, snappy and well structured. A killer pitch contains:

- **An appropriate idea.** Having an idea for a blog post is very different from having an idea for a newspaper or magazine. You can publish any idea you like on your blog, but you need to convince a printed title that your idea would look good inside their magazine. Magazines and newspapers are typically divided into sections such as news, features, fashion, health and beauty, and sport. If your idea won't slot into any of these sections then it won't get used. You may think it's a great idea to do a Top 10 Baby Names piece for your blog, but can you imagine a newspaper or magazine editor spending money hiring someone to write this sort of content?

- **A three-paragraph summary.** If you want a commissioning editor to take you seriously, then you need to communicate an idea concisely. Editors have hundreds of pitches landing on their desks every week, and one of their filtering tactics is to delete those that look too long and complicated. Start off with a short heading, written in bold capitals, to sum up the story. Paragraph one is the who, what, when, where and why of the idea, containing key facts and statistics. Paragraph two explains how you can flesh out the piece to make it a decent length and lists industry experts who you could approach for a quote. Finally, in paragraph three you may suggest which section of the magazine suits the idea, helping a commissioning editor to visualise it on one of their pages.

- **A short introductory email.** As a general rule, email is better than phone. Commissioning editors are busy people so if you add any more stress to their lives by telephoning at the wrong time you won't get heard.

Find out the editor's name and address, then email them directly. I think if someone uses Sir/Madam it looks lazy. Couldn't they be bothered to research the editor's name?

Also, find out if you have any connection with the editor as it's good to have something to make your pitch different to the hundreds of others on the pile. Have you worked with the editor before in any capacity? Do you have any mutual friends in common in a social capacity? Did you attend the same university? It doesn't matter how tenuous the connection is, use whatever fact it takes to stand out from the rest of the emails in an editor's inbox!

Copy and paste your three-paragraph summary into the main body of the email. Attachments take time to click on and you want to make it easy for an editor to read the idea that you've carefully thought up.

- **Confidence.** After you have sent your email, wait at least two weeks before contacting an editor again. If you bother them straightaway you will look desperate.

If they get back to you with a yes, be brave enough to reject a payment offer if you think it's too low. I know from experience that editors will try to offer the lowest price possible, often expecting to have to barter with a freelancer. If you accept the first price quoted, you may be missing out.

If you get rejected first time then try, try, and try again. Ask for feedback about your ideas and modify them in your next pitch. Through this process you will ultimately become a better writer. If you've ever failed a driving test you may have felt pretty terrible about it at first, but you will learn the error of your ways and do something differently for the next test. If you keep trying, you'll get there in the end.

And it works! I've written for *Company*, *Grazia*, *Love It*, *More*, *Heat*, *Look*, *Star*, *Now*, the *Mail On Sunday*, the *National Enquirer* and the *New York Post*. These articles have earned me between £200 and £500 for a short news article, £600 to £800 for a mid-length feature and between £1,000 and £3,000 for a longer feature or an exclusive news article.

CASE STUDY

Heckler Spray (hecklerspray.com) editor Stuart Heritage started writing for the *Guardian*'s film and TV section as a result of his blogging activity.

Q: Stuart, how did the *Guardian* spot you?

S: The blog was directly responsible for me working for the *Guardian*. A few years ago the *Guardian* did a list of the 50 most powerful blogs in the world, and for whatever reason my blog was included on the list. So I used my inclusion in the list to beg them for work, basically. Keeping a regularly updated blog is brilliant training if you want to write professionally, and that's especially useful if you don't have a formal journalistic background. I don't think I could ever give up blogging – I still have a blog (www.luvandhat.com), but it's just for fun. Also, the *Guardian* doesn't let me swear very much, so it's a good outlet for that!

Q: What tips would you give anyone wanting to get spotted?

S: Develop your voice. Don't be afraid to have opinions. Use Twitter as much as you can. Write about things that you're passionate about. Write as often as possible. If you're good, people will find you. Don't give up!

Q: Should a blogger be aware of any differences between blogging and writing for print publications?

S: The thing I love best about blogging is that a post is never a standalone piece – it's the start of a conversation. If I wrote a book and someone wanted to comment on it, they'd have to borrow it from a library, write 'You're rubbish' on the last page in biro and then put it back on the shelf. But with a blog post, you can have dozens of people telling you that you're rubbish in a matter of seconds. Traditional media is only just catching up with the fact that the boundary between writer and reader doesn't exist anymore. Bloggers have known this for years.

BOOKS AND E-BOOKS

A lot of bloggers make a very good living from books and e-books without spending too much time on it. Your content is already available on your blog, so you could collate your best articles and package it up with a few new stories.

Some bloggers are extremely lucky and get offered book deals by publishers who have spotted their blogs. This does not happen very often. If you sit around waiting to be spotted by a publisher, then you could be waiting a very long time. Be proactive.

- **Research.** Do you know of any bloggers in your subject field who already have book deals? Who publishes their books? If you can find some publishing companies that tend to commission a lot of bloggers, visit their websites to check out the submission guidelines. All major publishing houses have put together guidelines explaining how authors can submit book ideas.

- **Self-publish.** An author of a self-published e-book can sometimes earn as much as 70 per cent of the cover price, which is a lot more than they could expect to make from a book deal with a publishing house. The easiest way of self-publishing is to open up a free account with Create Space (createspace.com), which is part of Amazon. If you have the content, you could get your e-book published the same day and start making money!

And it works! The original blogger with a book deal was Belle Du Jour, whose diary of her secret life as a call girl has been made into several books and a TV show. Ker-ching! *Mumsnet* have released several books on pregnancy, babies and parenting, and most food bloggers have their own cookery books. Food blog *Julie/Julia* ended up being turned into a Hollywood movie starring Meryl Streep.

PUBLIC SPEAKING

Who likes going away and getting paid for it? If your blog is spotted by the right people you might end up being invited to speak at a seminar, a team-building day out, a conference or even a holiday on board a cruise ship. In whatever field you blog about, you'll find there are industry get-togethers and networking days, and the organisers of these events are constantly looking for ways to keep the schedule fresh and interesting.

If your blog is an authoritative resource on a certain subject and you haven't been approached yet, the only reason there can be is that people don't realise you are available for hire.

• **Sign up to a public speaking agency.** Look for an agency that specialises in representing media personalities. I recommend Celeb Agents (celebagents.co.uk) or Cassius Management (cassiusmanagement.com). The UK's leading public speaking agent JLA (jla.co.uk) has thousands of celebrities, business people and sports figures on their books, representing individuals who earn from £1,000 to £10,000 in fees. If you have credible qualifications and an interesting story to relate, they'll list you on their website and you'll be instantly seen by anyone searching the roster to plan a big event.

- **Look at what other bloggers in your field have done.** If you see that so-and-so has spoken at a specific place for a certain event, call up that place and call up the event organiser (they probably work for different companies) and put yourself forward. You're not stepping on the other speaker's toes because companies hire different speakers each time to keep things varied. If they hired someone similar before it shows they like the concept of having a blogger as a speaker. Even if they don't use you immediately, they'll have your details for future reference.

And it works! I've spoken at the Ideal Home Show at Earls Court, the Clothes Show Live at the Birmingham NEC, as well as being a guest host at a music festival in Pag, Croatia. Fashion bloggers get a lot of good gigs as there are often opportunities during international fashion weeks in Milan, Paris and New York as well as start-up festivals in places like Los Angeles, Sydney and Brazil. If you're a tech blogger you may be able to use the opportunities surrounding the big industry get-togethers such as the CES conference in Las Vegas or the IFA conference in Berlin. The fee you will receive for any gig varies greatly and is normally inversely proportional to the glamour of the assignment. For example, a team-building retreat in the Caribbean may just cover your flights, accommodation and basic expenses, while you'd get more money in your pocket speaking at a business centre in Slough.

SPECIAL PROJECTS

One of the things I love most about blogging is that no two days are ever the same. You constantly get the opportunity to try new things, and occasionally you are told about something new and get paid to play an active role in the start-up process.

For example, when fashion chain Forever 21 launched in the UK, it hired blogger Bip Ling (bipling.com) to be an ambassador for the brand. Hiring Bip meant that she wrote about it on her blog, telling all her followers about the new fashion brand on the block. Fashion brand Coach hired Emily Johnston of *Fashion Foie Gras* (fashionfoiegras.com) to design a limited edition handbag, knowing she would promote it to her readers. And surprisingly, when Peroni beer was looking to make their brand more fashionable, they hired fashion blogger Susie Bubble (stylebubble.typepad.net) as an ambassador for the project.

An order for a special project will normally come from a PR company, which a business has hired to help raise its profile. Therefore if you want a special project, you need to make sure you're known by all the PR companies that operate in your subject area. Contact the PR companies to explain who you are, what you do and how popular you are. I suggest going to your Google Analytics account and printing off the most recent monthly report to show unique monthly users, number of page impressions and an overview of which geographical regions your readers come from. The PR may not have a special project straightaway, but if they see you reach a lot of people they will remember you when they have a client who wants to reach a specific target market.

And it works! Since I started *Live Like A VIP*, I've said yes to a variety of interesting collaborations proposed by well-known brands. This has involved testing out a revolutionary new electronic toothbrush, dying my hair and removing the colour, comparing the differences between a Wi-Fi device and a dongle, and helping to design a new handbag. On average, I received between £1,000 and £5,000 for these projects.

SELLING THE BLOG

If you build up your traffic in the right way, bide your time and stay consistent, your blog will make you a multi-millionaire. Arianna Huffington, founder of the *Huffington Post*, made headlines in 2011 when she sold out to AOL for $315 million, and she's not the only one. In 2005 Michael Arrington started a blog called *Techcrunch*. Then in 2010 he sold it for $30 million to AOL. Topping this, Chris Sherman started his gaming blog UGO in 1997. In 2007 it sold to the Hearst Corporation for a record $100 million. But it's not just gadget blogs that are valuable. Celebrity blogger Nikki Finke sold *Deadline Hollywood* to the Mail Media Corporation for $14 million, while mummy blogger Danielle Friedland sold *Celebrity Baby Blog* (later renamed *Babyrazzi*) to Times Inc for $10 million.

Why are these blogs worth so much? The answer is a media company values a blog on how many millions of followers it has, as well as whether that number is consistently growing and the blog has a dynamic revenue stream. The growing and dynamic aspects are key here, as the media company is buying it for its potential. Right now, blogs with a large following earn lots in advertising, but if there is no potential to expand the following then the media buyer will not earn as much from his investment as from a blog where there is potential to diversify and expand.

Therefore, if you want to sell your blog one day you need to keep on growing. You can never sit back and get complacent or traffic will stick at a constant level – or even worse, drop – and your blog will decrease in value. Keep doing what led you to grow traffic in the first place: keep getting press coverage, keep your staff loyal, keep doing collaborations and projects with brands to raise your profile, make your website known by getting involved with events, and develop links with other bloggers to boost both your SEO and your reputation in the industry.

A word of warning when it comes to selling blogs: make sure you accept an offer at the right time. You want to grow the blog to make it as big as you possibly can on your own before selling out. If you can keep going without help then do so, because the higher you build up your traffic, the higher your next offer will be. Although Facebook is not a blog, it's a good illustration of the power of saying no to a sales offer. The online community thought Mark Zuckerberg was crazy when he declined an offer to sell Facebook to Viacom in 2005 for $75 million and then an offer of $1 billion from Yahoo in 2007. He eventually made the company public in 2012, and with share prices on the first day of trading valued at $38.23, Zuckerberg's persona share was worth $19 billion. If he'd sold in 2005, he'd have missed out on so much!

I'm hoping to sell *Live Like A VIP* eventually. I've followed the tactics outlined in Chapters 1 to 7 to build up my traffic and I can earn a six-figure income from direct advertising, collaborations and public speaking. This is much more than I earned working for newspapers. However, I'm realistic enough to appreciate that it's going to take a few years of going over the steps I outlined, trying new things to grow traffic and looking at other bloggers for inspiration before I get to the multimillion-dollar level. I set it up in 2009 and I've seen that most blogs take at least five years to reach those heights. As long as I see growth, I'll keep going. If you get bought out before me, congratulations! See you on the Forbes rich list in a few years' time.

CHECKLIST

Have you:

- ☐ Created an area in your blog to showcase your guest blogs and writing for other publications?
- ☐ Contacted newspapers and magazines with a pitch idea?
- ☐ Signed up to a public speaking agency?
- ☐ Signed up to the PR companies, making them aware you're available for special projects?
- ☐ Analysed your blog content to see how you could compile it into a book or an e-book?
- ☐ Got the motivation to keep standards high so you can eventually sell your blog and become a multi-millionaire?

PART II

'I'm not an expert in this, but I know someone who is…'

When businesses are starting out, they ask experts for advice. Often they pay consultants at the top of their game to share their tips and open up their contacts books. I'm qualified to talk with authority on how to earn money blogging about the entertainment industry, but you would not hire me to teach you how to make money through blogging about food or drink. (As a showbiz journalist, I'm often dancing at a gig at the time most people are sitting down to eat dinner.) Therefore I have sought out the superstar bloggers in each field and they've been generous enough to share their industry-specific advice – and it's all free!

In the following chapters, you'll discover how to contact PRs and agents operating in your field so that you keep on top of all the latest industry news. When you're just starting out you might feel a little lonely and a little unloved, but with a full contacts book it's up to you to tell people you've arrived and persuade them to give you some content. I've also asked the bloggers to reveal which social networks they use most often so you can fit right into a ready-made community and share the contents of your blog with other users of that network.

To keep it organised, I've drawn up a checklist at the start of each chapter telling you what you'll learn if you read on. I hope it's useful – I certainly wish someone had told me all this when I started out!

CHAPTER 11

TIPS FOR FASHION BLOGGERS

Hang on to your handbags, it's time to run through some essential information about the fashion industry! If you want to make money from sharing your style tips, predicting trends and telling us about beautiful things then this chapter contains everything you need to know to get started.

THE FASHION BLOGGER'S CHECKLIST

- **A list of friendly fashion bloggers.** It's vital to see what other people in your industry are writing about so you can make sure you offer up what they do… and a bit more. Also, for SEO (search engine optimisation) purposes you should reach out to these bloggers and start exchanging links.
- **A list of contacts at PR agencies.** This is how you get content… and party invites.
- **A list of fashion networking organisations.** When you

---

get stuck on a particular issue you need to ask for advice. Networking organisations are full of other bloggers who have probably experienced similar things to you. Join in and your contacts book will grow even more.

- **The top Facebook groups.** To target your social media campaign you need to reach out to where your target readers already like hanging out. You could post in a group that has 1,000 members but it would be more effective to get involved with a group that has more than 100,000 members.

- **Interviews with key bloggers.** Learn what bloggers go through to build up their brand and what they'd recommend to newbies in the industry.

FRIENDLY FASHION BLOGGERS

Bookmark these blogs and comment, comment, comment. I spoke to all of them while researching this book – they're lovely!

- *Bangs And A Bun* (bangsandabun.com)
- *Clothes On Film* (clothesonfilm.com)
- *Hit Bag* (hit-bag.com)
- *Fashion Editor At Large* (fashioneditoratlarge.blogspot.co.uk)
- *Fashion Fades, Style Stays* (fashionfadesstylestays.com)
- *Fashion Foie Gras* (fashionfoiegras.com)
- *Individualism* (individualism.co.uk)
- *Jay Strut* (jaystrut.com)
- *Katie Chutzpah* (katiechutzpah.blogspot.co.uk)
- *Menswear Style* (menswearstyle.co.uk)
- *Red Carpet Fashion Awards* (redcarpet-fashionawards.com)
- *Retro Chick* (retrochick.co.uk)

- *Sara Luxe* (saraluxe.com)
- *The Clothes Whisperer* (theclotheswhisperer.co.uk)
- *What Olivia Did* (whatoliviadid.com)

PR AGENCIES

If you want to know who's wearing what, or to get details of the next season's collections, you need to be on the mailing list. This requires a bit of detective work. Make a list of brands you think you will be writing about a lot. Find out the phone number for Head Office, or for Customer Services if you cannot locate Head Office, and ask the operator for the contact details of the company's PR. If they're big brands they will almost always have at least one person doing PR and most companies also hire an external PR agency.

Now contact the PR agency and ask them what other brands they represent. Add all this information to your list as getting PRs on side means getting more editorial opportunities and more invites to cool events.

When you start to attend launches organised by one PR company, talk to every other blogger at the event and ask if they know of any more events coming up and if they work with other PR companies. In this way, you'll be constantly adding to your list of PR contacts to ensure that you're on top of all the juiciest content to give your readers, thus growing your community and traffic. Don't underestimate the importance of doing all this as you should know by now that more traffic means more money!

If you're based in the UK or the USA then you could pay a small monthly fee for a subscription to a media contacts directory such as Fashion Monitor (fashionmonitor.com) or The

Media Eye (themediaeye.com). For a small charge of around £50 a month, you'll get access to a database of PRs meaning that if you need to find a specific PR quickly you just enter your search terms into the online database and immediately get the relevant contact details. These forward planning providers are a good investment if you're serious about fashion blogging, but if you're just starting out, you may want to limit your spending. Therefore, to save you some money and time, I've asked the established fashion bloggers to share their best UK-based PR contacts. Pay attention to the size of the list if you're based elsewhere in the world. If you start off with this number of contacts and attend all the events, you will quickly meet others and expand your network. Never be afraid to call up a PR company because they should be happy to hear from you. Remember, fashion PRs are paid to generate coverage so they're looking for blogs like yours to place stories about their clients.

The UK-based PR companies that you'll need if you plan to cover British fashion are:

- APR Communications (aprcommunications.com): luxury brands including Harvey Nichols, Bvlgari, David Morris and TAG Heuer
- Arcadia (arcadiagroup.co.uk): high street stores including Topshop, Miss Selfridge, Dorothy Perkins and Burton
- Brightlight PR (brightlightpr.co.uk): Damsel In A Dress, Jonathan Aston, Juju Shoes
- Chase PR (chasepr.co.uk): Miss Sixty, Energie, Gant, Simply Yours
- Brandnation (brandnation.co.uk): Kangol, Hudson Jeans, Aristoc

TIPS FOR FASHION BLOGGERS

- Boudoir PR (boudoir-pr.com): Goldsmiths, Lipsy, Junk Food Clothing
- Dee Vasili PR (deevesalipr.com): American Retro, Gianmarco Lorenzi, Zoe Tee's
- Eden Cancan (edencancan.com): Moda In Pelle, Spanx, Puma
- Eskimo PR (eskimopr.com): Prey of London, The Vestry, Fallow Denim
- Exposure PR (exposure-pr.com): Esprit, Hobbs, Levis, Dr Martens, Toy Watch
- Lee Publicity (leepublicity.co.uk): Littlewoods, George at Asda, Very.co.uk
- Lexis PR (Lexisagency.com): New Look
- Phil Hall Associates (pha-media.com): Ann Summers, Brand Alley, Goddiva.co.uk
- Purple PR (purplepr.com): DKNY, Roberto Cavalli, Lanvin, Karl by Karl Lagerfeld
- Push PR (pushpr.co.uk): Chamilia, Holistic Silk, Tara Starlet
- Relative MO (relativemo.com): Amanda Wakeley, Erdem, Giles
- Shine PR (shinecom.com): Forever 21, eBay boutique
- Slam PR (slampr.com): Boohoo
- Starworks PR (starworksgroup.com): Lacoste, Temperley, Kate Spade
- Surgery PR (surgerypr.com): best for trend-conscious labels including Lacoste, Fila, Police Eyewear, Superdry and Replay
- Talk PR (talkpr.com): Figleaves, Swarovski Crystallized, Stylistpick.com
- Yellow Door (yellow-door.com): Oasis Fashion, Swarovski, Radley, Acne, Louis Vuitton, Clarks, Westfield London

NETWORKING ORGANISATIONS

Feeling a little lonely in the blogosphere? If you submit your blog to these networks your news will appear on their homepage and increase the likelihood of others finding your blog, plus you can browse the network to find details of other fashion bloggers to befriend. The best fashion blogger networks are:

• *Fashion Industry Network* (fashionindustrynetwork.com)
• *Fashion Networks* (fashionnetworks.com)
• *Fashion United* (fashionunited.com)
• *Independent Fashion Bloggers* (heartifb.com)

FACEBOOK GROUPS

How do you choose which of the thousands of fashion-based Facebook groups to join? Pick the ones with the most members so you can reach as many people as possible. The fashion bloggers I've spoken to recommend searching Facebook for the following groups:

• *Independent Fashion Bloggers*
• *Superstar Fashion Network*
• *Who What Wear*
• *Fashion TV (FTV)*

INTERVIEWS

Need more motivation? Here are some interviews with the founders of my favourite fashion blogs. They may be successful now, but they all started from scratch. I asked them to share what they've learned. They've all achieved impressive things in the fashion blogging world, and I certainly learned more of what it's like to do their job through these interviews.

Case study

Melanie Rickey from *Fashion Editor At Large* (fashioneditoratlarge.blogspot.co.uk)

Melanie started her career by working for the *Independent*, writing for *Vogue*, *POP*, *Ponystep* and editing *Grazia*'s fashion features and news pages. She is a frequent judge at Graduate Fashion Week and has 26,668 Twitter followers.

Q: Do you have any advice for people starting out in the industry?

M: Have a strong belief in what you and your blog stand for, and stick to it. Don't be tacky, don't follow the crowd. Don't accept freebies, it only makes you look cheap. Be ambitious, and always charming!

Q: Are there any mistakes you made that you'd like to warn other bloggers not to make?

M: Learn as much as you can about HTML and how to design and make your blog look good; read up on the publishing laws that exist to serve online space.

Q: What's the best way to spread awareness of a fashion blog to get traffic up?

M: I find Twitter is the best way to promote the blog, using both my own feed and other people's retweets; also getting newspaper websites to pick up my stories, and of course recommendations from other respected bloggers.

Q: What's the biggest difficulty facing a fashion blogger today?

M: Making a decent income solely from a blog is very difficult unless you are extremely talented, driven and have a unique point of view online.

CASE STUDY

Muireann Carey-Campbell from *Bangs And A Bun* (bangsandabun.com)

***Cosmopolitan* magazine listed *Bangs And A Bun* in its top five UK fashion blogs. Muireann is a resident public speaker at the Tate Britain and a blogging consultant for a number of fashion brands. She has 7,635 Twitter followers and 1,352 Facebook fans.**

Q: Any advice for people starting out in the industry?

M: Be patient! While the Internet and social media is a fast-moving machine, the cogs can often move very slowly. You won't start a blog and be invited to red carpet events the week after! It takes time to build up a readership and a following. Find a mentor-type figure, a blogger you look up to maybe, who can offer you a little guidance, and write down your goals. Set yourself some targets so you're not just aimlessly flailing about on the Web.

Q: If a fashion blogger is starting from nowhere, how can they build up their social media followers?

M: It takes a lot of hard work – I don't think there's an easy way. Start talking to people online. Bear in mind that the audiences differ according to the social media platform, so vary content in accordance with that. At this stage I think it's safe to say you should be putting as much effort into creating and building your social media following as you do your blog. Also you need to be following and commenting on other people's blogs to get noticed!

Twitter and Facebook can act as a kind of extension of

your blog, a place to continue the conversation. The more you converse on those channels, the more visually present you are in people's timelines and they'll head to your blog to check out more.

Q: How long did it take you to make money from your fashion blog?

M: Well, for the first two years no one was reading my blog, really. Looking back, that was kind of ideal – it gave me a chance to work on my style and tone and figure out what works and what doesn't. I would say I was well into year three before I started to see financial reward from it.

CASE STUDY

Kristin Knox from *The Clothes Whisperer* (theclotheswhisperer.co.uk)

Kristin has written two books about design genius Alexander McQueen – *Alexander McQueen: Genius of a Generation* and *Culture to Catwalk: How World Cultures Influence Fashion*. *The Clothes Whisperer* has 10,492 Facebook fans.

Q: What advice would you give to an aspiring fashion blogger?

K: Stay true to yourself, as cheesy as it sounds. Don't try to position yourself against the 'superbloggers' or sites like *WWD*, *Style.com* or other fashion authorities. Leave the expertise to the experts, bring your own experience to the table and find a unique way of talking about fashion, be it fashion and food, fashion and babies, fashion and yoga... whatever!

Q: What's a typical daily routine for a fashion blogger?

K: There is no such thing as a 'typical' day, which is why I feel blessed to do what I do. I guess the quotidian consistencies would include checking of email, checking of Twitter, scheduling of posts (once to twice a week) and charging up lots of electronic devices. Other than that, just doing what journalists do, that is to say, going out, meeting people, seeing things and experiencing fashion life.

Q: How can a blogger spread the word?

K: I guess being mentioned in the press helped. I just grew steadily. I'd rather have quality readers over quantity.

CASE STUDY

Karen Hendry from *Katie Chutzpah* (katiechutzpah.blogspot.co.uk)

A resident blogger at Vogue.co.uk, Karen has previously worked as head of marketing and PR for Muubaa, Ann Summers and Ted Baker, and used her expertise to start her own blog about the fashion industry.

Q: Any advice for people starting out in the industry?

K: That depends on whether you mean solely blogging or fashion. Nothing succeeds without a lot of work and effort for both. You have to be committed, be open to learn, to socialise well and also to have respect for those in the industry you're applying yourself to.

I'd say that any good blog has a unique voice (a bit like a newspaper columnist), reveals the character of the writer and also shows their knowledge and experience. The latter two are pretty much vital. Anyone can write a blog with an opinion and I'd encourage that, but to actually give a balanced perspective and compare to what's gone before, you need knowledge and experience.

Q: Is there any mistake you made when you first started blogging that you think others could learn from?

K: I think you can be too eager to succeed and so too pushy. I see that happening a lot more today, to be honest, as more and more people start blogging and trying to stand out. You have to be prepared for the unexpected and to receive rejection. It takes time to build up a following and to gain respect from your peers and regular readers.

Q: Where do you get your images from?

K: My images are either taken on my trusty iPhone, or I receive PR imagery from the brands and PRs that I work with – particularly catwalk images. I prefer using professional photography as a lot of time, effort and money has already gone into producing it. I intersperse these with my own images, particularly at events, as it always gives a personal touch.

Q: How can bloggers get noticed by the media to get name-checked in magazines and newspapers?

K: I'm still working on that myself! Twitter is brilliant for getting a following, but again it's best used as a conversation and not solely to promote yourself. Followers (on Twitter and Blogger) want to see a person's personality. Some people try to be PC but the best tweeters give an honest and funny opinion on anything from fashion and beauty to reality TV and politics. It's also a great exchange of information. If a media-related person comes to know you as you engage well in conversation (just as in real life), they remember you and also sometimes seek out your blog.

There are also a lot of blog competitions and awards out there like the Cosmo Blog Awards, which promote new blogs and get them known. I have to say I'm not a fan of awards that simply have the bloggers promote the competition and request votes. Perhaps it's my nature, but I hate the 'please, please vote for me' requests – it's just not my bag.

Really it all depends on whether you start writing because you actually like writing or solely because you want to become famous. I'm not at all bothered about the latter. I'd rather entertain readers and enjoy what I do. If I get recognition along the way, fantastic. It's a bonus, not the aim of the blog.

Q: What spin-offs have resulted from your blog, and would you have had the opportunity to do them if you didn't have a blog?

K: I've been asked to guest edit sites, be a brand ambassador and been invited on some great press trips. Often I'm at events solely because my blog has become well known enough for me to be a semi-well-known blogging figure. It's really just the same as being a journalist on a title and being targeted by a brand or PR as they think your publication and your style of writing (and personal style) fit their brand.

Q: If someone approached you asking you to take a post down, what are the circumstances in which you would do it?

K: I always try to be very careful legally. In the above case, it would have to be because you were breaking a press embargo (I don't, and wouldn't as I've worked in the industry for a long time) or because you'd written something that was factually incorrect. Again, research, knowledge and fact checking are *vital* to be hailed as a good blogger.

I do, however, often get riled by pernickety brands or PRs who ask you to alter a small word or description on a post you've written. I refuse as I politely point out it is a blog and an opinion and not a free advertisement. Let's face it, often these very PRs and brands wouldn't ask this of a magazine or newspaper journalist. Bloggers are no different.

Q: Do you work with PRs? Any tips for dealing with PRs?

K: PR agencies and in-house PRs at brands are absolutely vital for a good blogger. There are a great many excellent PRs out there (as well as an awful lot of bad ones!). The PR's function is to promote their client or brand to whatever media they think will influence readers and appeal to their market (many of my readers are actually magazines as I can see from the URL feed). If they see you as an influencer or a good place that's right for their product, the PR will approach you with news and launches. The main advantage of a blogger is that they can write at any time and post a blog immediately, so it's very fast. Good PRs realise this and those who 'get' social media send out the correct information, in time for the launch and very importantly in a format you can use. (N.B. Tip for PRs and brands – PDFs are the bane of a blogger's life as they are nothing short of nice-looking junk mail as you can't cut and paste excerpts of information or lift imagery. Bloggers often write in chunks

– many bloggers hold down full-time jobs – so have to write when they can. PDFs make it difficult to do that as the blogger has to request information all over again.)

I have so much respect for PRs (I trained as one and it's still part of my work) as they often don't get thanked for all their hard work. Just saying thank you for the invitation to a launch, emailing your blog post when you publish about their client and also tweeting appreciation helps make these guys' lives easier. The more brands see you act professionally and deliver on your promises of coverage, the more you work with them and the wider your reputation becomes. Of course, you can't please everyone all the time and sometimes you won't think a product or story is right for your blog, or you simply don't like it or a designer's collection. Being honest about why this is so in your blog by being reasonable is perfectly acceptable. I work with lots and lots of PRs internationally as I cover fashion and beauty so I deal with New York, Milan, Paris and London-based PRs daily.

CASE STUDY

Craig Landale from *Menswear Style* (menswearstyle.co.uk) Craig has expanded his blog into an Internet business and is now an online marketing expert and director of The Online Marketing Consultancy.

Q: Do you recommend WordPress or Blogger, or designing your own custom-made blogging system?

C: There's no reason why you don't keep with a blog template using WordPress or Blogger if it fits the style you want. The trend for blogs is to keep them clean and simple so plenty of templates cater for this. If your website grows big enough, you could move onto your own platform with your own host servers, but it's really not necessary.

Q: Are there any mistakes you made when you first started blogging that you think others could learn from?

C: Blogging too much. People don't have time to read your posts if you're submitting 5+ per day. I post once a day – and not every day at that. I also make sure a blog is worth posting. Too often I see blogs post a picture with a single sentence or statement. This won't keep readers engaged.

Q: In terms of traffic to the blog, how did you spread the word when you first started?

C: I used Twitter, Facebook, Nuji and Pinterest to spread the word. I focused on building readership of my social accounts to promote the blog. My favourite forum called *Reddit* has a sub *Reddit* community called 'male fashion advice' and I will often take part in discussions and submit links too.

Q: How do you keep readers interested?

C: I follow the trends and the latest products to hit high street stores. Relevance and up-to-date blog posts will bring in the readers.

Q: How can bloggers use Twitter and Facebook to get web traffic up?

C: Follow brands you like; follow other blogs you like. Get active and participate with them. Hold a Facebook competition or a Twitter retweet competition so the entrants end up spreading news about the competition to all their followers. If they retweet the competition it will be seen by everyone that follows them. Make good use of the hash-tag such as #LFW during London Fashion Week, for example, and before you know it, you'll have a good number of followers.

Q: Who looks after the advertising on your site?

C: We have clear rates written on our website and we simply invoice the company for any advertising they choose.

CASE STUDY

Chris Laverty from *Clothes On Film* (clothesonfilm.com) The blog is endorsed by Ralph Lauren and won Channel 4's best fashion blog contest. Chris writes for *Mr Porter and Empire Magazine.*

Q: Why did you decide to set up a blog?

C: Two reasons: firstly writing gigs had dried up and I cannot stand wasting time, so it was a productive way to work for free. Secondly, I really did have a desperate need to talk about clothes in movies. I was not an expert on the subject, but I had a degree in theatre and film, some journalism experience, plus I knew fashion and I knew films. I had worked in film production before for Pinewood Studios so I did also have background in the industry, however distant.

Q: How can a blogger stand out from other blogs in the field?

C: The subject matter, I guess. There are not really any other blogs out there talking about costume in movies, certainly not to the level of detail that *Clothes On Film* does. That was always the intention. If I was going to do this I didn't want

to cut corners; I wanted it to be best costume/clothing/
fashion resource for film available. That is why I do not post
much. I'm only interested in the best article, not the
quickest, although that's not always the healthiest way to be
for hits. I do have some contributors to the site, for which
I'm very grateful as they really know their stuff. If I had any
advice for those starting out in the blogging world it is to
post regularly but with the very best work you can. You are
really only as good as the last thing you post in this game.

Q: Where do you get your images from?

C: PR companies provide me with shots for new films or
DVD/Blu-ray releases. All of the screengrabs I take myself. I
have never pilfered any screengrabs from someone else's
site, even in the early days, because that's just bad form. The
blogging community is just that; we should respect each
other's hard work and not be sneaky.

Q: How do you engage the readers through Twitter and
Facebook and maintain a conversation?

C: In a way that was easier when I had fewer followers on
Twitter. Now it can be difficult to chat to everybody, but I
will always respond to a polite request or question. I keep an
eye on new followers, and if I recognise someone or their
work I'll probably follow back straightaway. If I don't, then
I'll just wait for them to talk to me. If the chats are light and
fun I will most likely return the follow. You can't follow
everyone (and honestly read their tweets, anyway). I post
links to articles about costume or fashion in film, whether
they are on my site or not. I also chat about films on
television, maybe cocktails or the weather. I steer clear of

politics and religion because that can get a bit deep for a casual chat.

Q: If a blogger is starting from nowhere, how can they build up their social media followers?

C: It does not hurt to get some celebrity fans on Twitter and that means putting the time in to chat. You can relax a bit when you have built up followers, but until then you need to chat as often as possible. A bit of luck is involved too; you might just write an article that has caught a celebrity's eye and he/she will tweet about it. Do not under any circumstances beg them to follow – it never works and makes you look pathetic. As with everything related to blogging, the more interaction you have with your readership, the better. Patience is a virtue too. There is no quick route – building up a reputation, readers, likes and followers takes years, not months.

Q: In terms of traffic to the blog, how did you spread the word when you first started?

C: I was not on Twitter straightaway so I just spent as much time as possible on telling the press I existed. I emailed magazines about my blog posts and occasionally they picked up on things. In the first few months most of my referrals came from fan sites for articles like the Grace Kelly Paris dress from *Rear Window* or Cary Grant's grey suit from *North by Northwest*. That brought attention but also criticism, as I was beginning to rush posts out without properly researching. It took a while to grasp this, but I learned that I only had one shot at keeping readers once they had visited the site. No one was going to spread the word about an article that was pretty good; it had to be very good – the best. On a practical note I nagged PR companies for interviews with anyone related to clothes and/or film (I *never* strayed from the niche). A couple of big American sites eventually linked in to *Clothes On Film* and it all kind of snowballed from there. It took about nine months for anything serious to happen, though. Like I said, blogging is patience.

CASE STUDY

Sara Wilson from *Sara Luxe* (saraluxe/com)

Sara is a stylist and creative executive for an online fashion store. She has been featured in *Grazia, Company and Drapers*. She was the official *Company* magazine reporter for the Brit Awards 2011.

Q: Describe a typical working day.

S: I am a stylist and creative executive for an online fashion business so every day is slightly different for me. One day I will be working with our marketing team creating newsletters and content for the site, the next, casting models, styling outfits and planning campaigns shoots and then running style advice hours for the customers. Once I get home, I will shoot my outfit and write up a blog post, catch up on other blogs or attend any fashion events that I feel benefit myself and my blog content.

Q: How do you keep the conversation going with social media followers?

S: I try to answer every email and tweet I can. I do get a lot of emails asking me to do surveys for university work and I try 100 per cent to do them all – I was once a student and know how important it is – but I just don't have the time. I love having interaction with my followers on Twitter – they are so supportive – and I also try to meet as many as I can. It has given me an opportunity to make new friends all over the world.

Q: How long did it take for you to make money from your blog?

S: It took a while. Many opportunities have opened up for me since starting the blog– full-time job offers and so on. I think people have to prepare themselves for the long haul with blogging. It is not an instant way to make money – I had to wait at least a year and a half.

CASE STUDY

Aaron Christian from *Individualism* (individualism.co.uk) Aaron has collaborated with *Esquire*, Topman, Reiss and Aubin & Wills, shooting video content for their blogs. He is the video style editor for men's luxury fashion giant Mr Porter.

Q: What makes your fashion blog unique?

A: Firstly, we only create original content. Secondly, we don't try and take ourselves too seriously. We are trying to merge style with comedy a lot (check out our *Sins of Style* series) as we feel it's the best way to connect with men. I can't go a day without laughing.

Q: Were there any key moments that brought a lot of traffic, and how did they help?

A: Yes, we were on Radio 1 over the weekend. Getting

mentioned in the press and on the radio is the best way. Also, if you get a retweet from a celebrity on Twitter it can get a huge amount of traffic. Sometimes if a celebrity is featured in our blog's *Sins of Style* they will retweet. However, although it's good to get spikes, the key thing is to be consistent and produce work on a regular basis that is of a high quality and different.

Q: How can a fashion blogger keep readers interested?

A: We like to get our readers involved on Facebook, which we update all the time and use it to pick up inspiration. We also host style parties called Buttoned Up & Laced Up so we connect with them in real life.

Q: How can bloggers use Twitter and Facebook to get web traffic up?

A: With Twitter, you need to just engage and actually reply. With Facebook, you need to build it up and create ways to let your readers take part in something and ask questions and so on.

Q: Is it hard to blog and have a social life?

A: Yes and no. You need a balance – the real world will help you stay fresh. Nothing beats human connection. You have to have fun doing it. I see this as a long journey so I'm in no rush. I've learnt you have to live in the moment, as the present is the only thing we ever really have. Balance that with planning and prep, and you'll be fine.

CASE STUDY

Jay Strut from *Jay Strut* (jaystrut.com)
Jay is often seen at New York Fashion Week and is

regularly featured on fashion sites such as **The Fashion Spot. He has 30,477 Twitter followers.**

Q: If a blogger is starting from nowhere, how can they build up their social media followers?

J: Getting to give your readers up-close and personal access from the source is incomparable to just writing about it. Being there even if you aren't invited shows potential readers and followers that you are serious about this, which in turn makes them more intrigued. I think that travelling is one of the best investments you can make as a blogger, especially in the arts.

Q: How can bloggers use Twitter and Facebook to get web traffic up?

J: Keep people in the loop, even if you feel like you are overdoing it – just think that there are people doing it ten times more than you!

Q: How can bloggers get noticed by the media to get name-checked in magazines and newspapers?

J: Again, I think that just getting out there and doing what nobody else is doing is very important. You have to be there. You are given the power and the will to do anything you want with this world. Only you can work, save up your dollars, book your flight to New York Fashion Week and follow your dreams to success!

Q: Any advice for people starting out in the industry?

J: Serious advice: never give up, never look down and *always* strut your stuff!

Q: Is there any mistake you made when you first started blogging that you think others could learn from?

J: Do not ever compromise your brand. Stay true to yourself at all times!

Q: How long did it take you to make money from your blog?

J: Everything happens as a natural progression, income is generated more so from me being me and building relationships and working with brands.

CASE STUDY

Gemma Seager from *Retro Chick* (retrochick.co.uk)

Gemma's achievements include collaborations with the South Bank Centre, Very.co.uk, Boots No7 and Bravissimo.

Q: What do you think makes a blog successful?

G: I think it's 50 per cent luck and 50 per cent talent. Good writing is very important. If people can't decipher your meaning through poorly constructed sentences and terrible spelling then they'll switch off.

Q: Where do you get your images from?

G: I take most of them myself, or I use Creative Commons licensed images or images from websites when writing about clothes.

Q: What's the best bit about being a blogger?

G: Being your own boss.

CHAPTER 12

TIPS FOR BEAUTY BLOGGERS

To make your beauty blog look polished and pretty you need to learn from the experts. When you started to put on make-up, you probably watched someone who knew what they were doing. I've tracked down the leading beauty bloggers who have built up large communities around their written articles and videos and asked how they did it. If you want to attract readers to your beauty blog then you need some content, and this chapter explains exactly how to get going on a good note.

THE BEAUTY BLOGGER'S CHECKLIST

- **A list of brilliant beauty bloggers.** It's vital to see what others in your industry are writing about so you can make sure you offer up what they do… and a bit more. Also, for SEO (search engine optimisation) purposes you should reach out to these bloggers and start to exchange links.

- **A list of contacts at PR agencies.** This is how you get contents, products to review and party invites.
- **A list of beauty networking organisations.** When you get stuck on a particular issue you need to ask for advice.
- **The top Facebook groups.** To target your social media campaign you need to reach out to where your target readers already like hanging out and reach as many people as possible in the same place.
- **Interviews with key bloggers.** Learn what bloggers go through to build up their brand and what they recommend to newbies in the industry.

BRILLIANT BEAUTY BLOGGERS

The world's a more beautiful place when you have people to guide you along the way. If you're just starting out, then have a look at how these established beauty bloggers have built up their brand. Get in touch with them if you have any specific questions.

- *Amy Antoinette* (amyantoinette.com)
- *Beauty Fool* (beautyfool.com)
- *Be Beautiful Blog* (bebeautifulblog.org)
- *British Beauty Blogger* (britishbeautyblogger.com)
- *Cult Beauty* (cultbeauty.co.uk/blog)
- *Dolce Vanity* (dolcevanity.com)
- *London Beauty Queen* (londonbeautyqueen.com)
- *Perfectly Polished* (perfectly-polished-nails.com)
- *Pixi Woo* (pixiwoo.com)
- *The Sunday Girl Blog* (thesundaygirl.com)

PR AGENCIES

Liaising with PRs is an absolute must if you are a beauty blogger. As you will already know, buying new beauty products to review each week can get expensive and by subscribing to as many PR agencies as you can, you will be able to review products they send to you and you may even get paid for it. Not only this, establishing relationships with beauty PRs enables you to attend the best events and rub shoulders with the beauty elite.

If you're writing about beauty and make-up in the UK then I have gone through a long list of beauty PR agencies and include the best ones below. Start with these and you will pick up more by mingling with other bloggers. If you're writing on a global level then you need to use a bit of initiative to find the relevant PRs. I suggest making a list of beauty brands you think you'll cover and telephoning Head Office or Customer Service to ask for the contact details for their PR agency. Start by aiming for 15–20 PR agencies and you'll pick up more through attending industry events.

Everyone in the UK should sign up for the free beauty news alert service *Diary Directory* (diarydirectory.com) to learn about new product launches, industry news and product requests. The most important UK-based PR agencies to include on your list are:

- Beauty Seen PR (beautyseenpr.com): Revlon, Nars, Biore, Decleor
- Boudoir PR (boudoir-pr.com): Cialte, Invisible Zinc, Nail Rocks, Penhaligons
- Brandnation (brandnation.co.uk): Barry M, Charles Worthington
- Can Associates (canassociates.co.uk): Fake Bake, Fabulous Face and Body, Nouveau Beauty Group

- Focus PR (focuspr.co.uk): Elegant Touch, Eylure, Collection make-up
- Frank PR (frankpr.it): Body Shop, Garnier Nutrisse
- Get Touched (gettouched.com): Barefoot Doctor, Stargazer, Blinc
- Gloss Communications (glosscommunications.co.uk): Trevor Sorbie, Michael Barnes, Front Cover
- House PR (housepr.com): St Tropez
- Lexis PR (lexisagency.com): Arm and Hammer, Dove, Sure, Vaseline
- Mischief PR (mischiefpr.com): QVC, Radox, Sure, Lynx
- Monty PR (montypr.com): Soap And Glory, Bliss, Blink, VictoriaHealth.com
- No-Bull Communications (nobull-communications.co.uk): Adee Phelan, DGJ Organics, Colour B4
- Pegasus PR (pegasuspr.co.uk): Bio-Oil, Eau Thermale Avene, Holland & Barrett
- Phil Hall Associates (pha-media.com): Nicky Clarke Electricals, Neville Hair And Beauty, Nu Beginnings Boot Camp
- Shine PR (shinecom.com): GHD hair straighteners
- Talk PR (talkpr.com): Aussie Haircare, Wella Professional, Herbal Essences

NETWORKING ORGANISATIONS

You may be hot on your own but you could be sizzling if you teamed up with some other beauty bloggers. Your combined traffic could fill the entire beauty hall of a department store (trust me, it will do so eventually).

If you want to meet like-minded people on the Net and

check out what the competition is doing, then the top beauty bloggers have pointed me in the direction of the following networking groups:

- *iFabbo* (ifabbo.com)
- *Makeup Alley* (makeupalley.com)
- *Specktra* (specktra.net)
- *The Beauty Blog Network* (beautyblognetwork.com)
- *Total Beauty* (totalbeauty.com)

FACEBOOK GROUPS

Let's cut through the clutter on Facebook and join the groups where we'll meet the most people and the best-connected ones. The top beauty Facebook groups are:

- *Beauty Tips Network*
- *Bloggers Worldwide*
- *Jeddah Beauty Blog*
- *The Beauty And Make Up Blog*
- *The Beauty Blog Network*

INTERVIEWS

If you think you know everything you need to know about beauty then think again. There is always something new to learn, and these beauty bloggers have started from the bottom of the make-up bag and worked their way up. Follow their advice carefully and you may even become a bigger force to be reckoned with.

CASE STUDY

Jane Cunningham from *British Beauty Blogger* (britishbeautyblogger.com)

Jane had a column in the *Guardian* and regularly writes for the *Huffington Post* blog. She has written beauty books – *The Compact Book of Being Beautiful* and *101 Beauty Tips: The Modern Woman's Guide To Looking Good And Feeling Great*. Jane has 18,285 Twitter followers.

Q: If a blogger is starting from nowhere, how can they build up their followers?

J: The best advice I can give is to follow other bloggers and start a relationship with them. Comment on their posts and follow them on Facebook and Twitter. This will get you noticed by their followers and hopefully traffic will rise on your site. Comment, comment, comment! Basically, just shout the loudest.

Q: How do you engage the readers through Twitter and Facebook and maintain a conversation?

J: I get more tweets than I can possibly answer but I do really try and get back to everyone, even if it is only briefly, as it is important readers think we are a community.

Q: How can bloggers use Twitter and Facebook to get Web traffic up?

J: The more you interact with readers on Twitter, the more others pick up on it. I have also introduced giveaways on my page, which has increased my traffic by 31 per cent – which is massive when you think of it in thousands.

Q: How often should a beauty blogger update?

J: At least three times a week if you want to grow a community.

Q: How long did it take you to make money from your blog?

J: It has been a slow process. Blogging is still my second job as I work in a fashion retail head office, which is my main income. I am making money out of the blog now, but that is due to advertisers. I have also given some talks at several further education colleges as a beauty 'expert', which I get paid for.

CASE STUDY

Renee Lorentzen from *Beauty Fool* (beautyfool.com)
Beauty Fool* has been part of *Vogue* Italy's best beauty blogs, and been featured in publications such as *Harper's Bazaar*, *JUICE* and *Cosmopolitan.

Q: Beauty blogs are everywhere now – what advice would you give to someone starting out?

R: Probably the best thing to do is not to compete because it'll just make you go mad. There are *so* many blogs, thousands, millions even – search 'beauty blog' and in Google there's over 650 million results – so don't even bother. Just focus on making your blog the best it can be. As far as the competition between local blogs in your area (where the competition is probably much smaller), try to find a way to stand out and be different although, again, my advice would be not to compete. After all, people are allowed to read more than one blog at a time!

Q: Is there a typical working day for a beauty blogger?

R: I'm a full-time blogger so it's quite the freelancer's life, meaning every day is a little different. But most days include meetings, answering emails, perhaps attending an event or two, and of course writing, taking photos, editing and researching for my blog posts.

Q: Where can a beauty blogger get images from?

R: I mostly take them myself, but sometimes I use the press images sent by the PR professional, sometimes I see beautiful images online, but always make sure the original creator is mentioned so I can give them credit. No credit, no posting in my opinion but overall I try to take all my own images.

Q: In what way do you edit images before posting?

R: Other than cropping and resizing, I edit the 'look' of a lot of my photos. I love Polaroids and vintage-looking photos, so I like to edit them to make them look like that. I also like making collages and other fun things to keep it looking interesting!

Q: What are the benefits of blogging?

R: I love writing, and as a full-time blogger I get paid to do it full time. There aren't many jobs where you are paid to do what you love. I first found out about blogging in 2004 and have been hooked ever since.

CASE STUDY

Alexia Inge from *Cult Beauty* **(cultbeauty.co.uk/blog)**
Previously, Alexia has worked as a fashion assistant at the *Telegraph*, **been the PR co-ordinator at GAP and used her knowledge from being an account manager at Mission Media to form** *Cult Beauty*.

Q: What advice would you give a beauty blogger wanting to grow traffic?

A: Being the first to write about hot new product discoveries that really took off in popularity really worked well for us, plus some of our competitions once the affiliates got hold of them.

Q: What do you do to attract new readers?

A: PR around the *Cult Beauty* retail site seems to work well. When people read about interesting new launches for the shop, they look around to see what else we are talking about. Relationships with other bloggers, linking and tweeting them when they write great stuff is really good practice because they tend to do it back to you. The best thing, though is really good, relevant content. Nothing beats this.

Q: How do you keep readers coming back?

A: Keep the content fresh – it's really important to have integrity in our message, make sure we get back to comments quickly. Beautiful imagery.

Q: A lot of blogs write about new products, so what separates you from the rest?

A: Two things. You have to be the first. Also, we don't just stick to the UK. Our blog gives our readers first sight of all the brilliant cult products our expert panel are discovering from all over the world, from the top-selling mascara in Japan [DJV Fibrewig] to a perfume that melts with your pheromones, smells different on everyone and *amazing* on anyone [Molecule 01], great tips on how to use them to best effect and a slightly playful commentary on the latest beauty launches out there.

CASE STUDY

LaaLaa Monroe from *Dolce Vanity* (dolcevanity.com)
LaaLaa is a freelance make-up artist and has been twice nominated for the Cosmopolitan Blog Awards and has been featured in *Grazia* and *Cosmopolitan*.

Q: Were there any key moments that brought a lot of traffic, and how did they help?

L: Whenever there is a new collection or product being launched that's got an amazing buzz, you'll find if you're first to get details of the product there'll be an increase in hits as everyone wants to know!

Q: How can a beauty blogger keep readers interested?

L: Alongside keeping to what I know works with my blog, I experiment. Give back to the up-and-coming bloggers. As I know, it's hard when first starting out. Finding out first-hand what my readers want to see is important, as well as publishing content that I find interesting. Versatility is a good word when it comes to blogging.

Q: How often do you update the blog, and what is the reason for this?

L: Twice a day when possible. I like to keep my blog out there and relevant. I enjoy blogging and sharing as much as I can.

Q: Describe a typical working day.

L: I'll start off reading my emails and also reading other blog posts that have occurred during the night. I typically like to get a lot of reviews out, but mix up my posts with make-up looks when I can. Photography can take up a while as lighting has to be correct and the images as clear as possible. When it gets to writing up posts, research and honesty is key. I take a keen interest in what I'm putting out so the detail needs to be there for my readers. As I'm now qualified as a make-up artist, I've added networking with photographers and models to my hours to begin building up my portfolio.

Q: Do you work with PRs? Any tips for dealing with PRs?

L: I do, now. Initially I stayed away from them as I heard they can be a bit annoying and I wasn't writing my blog for PR. I only want to write about products and treatments that I believe in, not just to make money. I still have that opinion now, but I have learned to negotiate with them.

Q: How long did it take you to make money from your blog?

L: It took about a year or so, to be honest. It is a very long process, and trying to get advertisers on board was difficult, but as soon as I was winning awards and magazines like *Grazia* and *Marie Claire* were noticing me that's when the ads came – and the money.

CASE STUDY

Samantha Chapman from *Pixi Woo* (pixiwoo.com)
A full time make-up artist, Samantha has worked with photographers such as Tony McGee and Lord Snowdon and celebrities such as Myleene Klass, Sir Paul McCartney, Peaches Geldof, Ashley Tisdale and Charlotte Church. She runs the blog *Pixi Woo* with her sister Nicola and the girls post hair and make-up videos. The blog's been featured in *Harper's Bazaar*, *Cosmopolitan*, *Tatler*, *Elle*, *Company* and the *Sunday Times*. The girls have been able to develop and market their own product lines including cruelty-free make-up brushes called 'Real Techniques'. *Pixi Woo* gets 77,849 Twitter followers and has 117,191 Facebook fans.

Q: If a beauty blogger is starting from nowhere, how can they build up their followers?

S: It really helps to link all your media platforms. Twitter, Facebook, YouTube, Blogger, Instagram and so on can all be linked so that updates appear on all platforms. Most importantly, join in conversations and get chatting to people. It's not called social networking for nothing!

Q: What do you chat about?

S: You don't have to just chat about beauty, chat about everyday things that people relate to and be sure to engage with responses.

Q: How can bloggers get noticed by the media and get name-checked in magazines to increase followers?

S: I don't think there is a quick way to do this. It really comes down to posting regularly, hard work and networking to get your blog seen by as many people as possible. When people talk about you, others will hear via social media and before too long you can build up relationships with other blogs and magazines.

Q: What's the biggest difficulty facing a beauty blogger today?

S: Negative people [trolls]: these people try to ruin the user experience for everyone by belittling content or making deliberately obtuse comments. You need to have very thick skin to be a blogger, especially on YouTube, but the positives do outweigh the negatives. The best advice I can give is to *never* respond, as it just perpetuates the negative comments.

Q: What are some of the best things that have happened as a result of your beauty blog?

S: My sister and I run the blog together, and it's got us a weekly column in the *Mirror*. We have created content for Channel 4 and *Cosmopolitan* magazine. We are also part of the Avon UK make-up artist team, alongside Jackie Tyson and Liz Pugh. We have done some public speaking also. We appeared at London IMATS [International Make-up Artist Trade Show] this year and have a range of make-up brushes called Real Techniques that are available in Boots in the UK and Ulta in the US. We probably wouldn't have had the same opportunities had we not started blogging because we both worked as make-up artists behind the scenes before.

CASE STUDY

Hayley Carr from *London Beauty Queen* (londonbeautyqueen.com)

In 2012, Hayley won Rodial's Best Beauty Blogger. She has been a judge for the Beauty Club Awards 2011 and Tesco Magazine Your Beauty Awards 2011. *London Beauty Queen* also produced official videos for Rimmel at London Fashion Week 2011.

Q: How can beauty bloggers build up web traffic?

H: It's vital for bloggers to use social networks because that's where people are. You may forget to read a blog, but you're on Facebook and Twitter all the time so can easily click a link – most of my traffic comes from these sources. It's much easier to pick up a follower on Twitter than it is to have a new reader discover you from Google, plus that's where your personality really comes through if you optimise social media well.

Q: How did you pick a design for your blog?

H: It was an ever-evolving design from when I first launched it. I've been through about five redesigns and to start with just picked something I thought looked appealing. However, this soon changed as I realised blogs need to stand out and be different to make their place known in the 'bloggersphere', so I developed a strong branding around my blog's name. I was careful to stick to the red, white and blue colour scheme rather than going for something bland, neutral or 'samey'.

Q: What should a beauty blogger talk about on social networks like Twitter and Facebook to maintain a conversation?

H: I use Twitter religiously to talk about everything I'm doing, from my lunch to a running commentary of *EastEnders*. It's important for my readers, followers and fans to know I'm a real person with real opinions, even if they're about *X Factor*. It's important to make sure people know you're there and use you as a resource, to ask questions and to comment – the more approachable you are, the more engaged your readers become.

Q: How often should a blogger update the blog?

H: I update daily (within reason) because I like to give my readers a reason to return regularly. It's easy to fall off a Google reader or for another blog to take over – the more presence you have, the better. I also notice a huge drop in hits if I don't blog daily – the more I blog, the more people come to say hello.

Case study

Amy Parkin-Low from *Amy Antoinette* (amyantoinette.com) Amy has featured in publications such as *More!* magazine and *Cosmopolitan*. She was a judge for the UK Beauty Awards, which took place at the Clothes Show Live 2011. Q: What do you do to attract new readers?

A: High-quality content that is consistent and regularly updated. Good-quality photos are important as they're key in reviewing a product and showing how it really looks and performs in a real-life setting. Informative content and a friendly tone also help in making a blog successful, as well as having an aesthetically pleasing site.

Q: Are there any mistakes you made when you first started blogging that others could learn from?

A: Write and review what you think is interesting. I made the mistake of reviewing everything and anything, and I wasted so much time and lost followers. So I would advise you to write and review what you are passionate about.

Q: How often do you update your blog, and what is the reason for this?

A: I try to update as much as possible, but as it's so time-consuming realistically I manage to upload three or four times per week, which still keeps my site fresh and updated.

Q: Where do you get your images from?

A: I photograph them myself.

Q: How can bloggers use Twitter and Facebook to get web traffic up?

A: I mostly promote my site through Twitter. Regularly interacting with fellow bloggers and my readers helps in spreading the word about my site. When I tweet and use Facebook more I can see a real difference in my traffic.

CHAPTER 13

TIPS FOR PARENTING BLOGGERS

Are you sitting comfortably? You're about to step over the threshold of a new generation of world influencers. The new wave of 'mummy bloggers' are so powerful that they can bring down entire governments. When former British Prime Minister Gordon Brown was interviewed by *Mumsnet*, there was a scandal and outrage as he refused to answer one of the bloggers' questions about his favourite type of biscuit. By not answering the question, he was accused of being uptight and out of touch. Most people can easily pick their top biscuits, so Gordon Brown isolated himself from the population by failing to answer that question. As the interview was online, it was seen immediately by *Mumsnet*'s millions of readers around the world so there was no chance of covering up his indiscretions. In fact, the interview is still online, which means it has much more impact than a political interview in a newspaper that's often discarded soon after being read.

I've spoken to *Mumsnet* and to other bloggers who have travelled the world, collaborated with household names and sat on competition panels of major award ceremonies – all because they know how to engage with other women. If you want to draw on your experiences as a parent and start up a conversation with like-minded people, read on.

THE MUMMY, OR DADDY, BLOGGER CHECKLIST

- **A list of lovely lifestyle bloggers.** Check out what other people are covering and share links.
- **A list of contacts at PR agencies.** Contacting PR companies is how you get news and events relevant to you and your family.
- **A list of parenting networking organisations.** Find out about online groups where you can learn from others how to grow your business.
- **A list of the most popular Facebook groups about parenting.** Join the ones where you will reach the most people to get your brand established.
- **Interviews with key parenting bloggers.** Find out how others have earned money and created a great work/life balance.

LOVELY LIFESTYLE BLOGGERS

Mummy blogs have exploded onto the Internet scene in the past five years, and there's no sign of this slowing down. Whatever stage of motherhood – from pregnancy to teens – men and women are sharing their experiences of parenting and making money from it. I have spoken to the best of the best to give you an insight into being a parent and maintaining a useful and entertaining blog.

- *Frugal Family* (frugalfamily.co.uk)
- *A Modern Mother* (amodernmother.com)
- *A Mother's Ramblings* (amothersramblings.com)
- *Are We Nearly There Yet, Mummy?* (arewenearlythereyetmummy.com)
- *BritMums* (britmums.com)
- *Jessica Gottlieb* (jessicagottlieb.com)
- *Jo Beaufoix* (jobeaufoix.com)
- *Mari's World* (marisworld.co.uk)
- *Muddling Along Mummy* (muddlingalongmummy.com)
- *Mumsnet* (mumsnet.com)
- *Northern Mum* (northernmum.com)
- *Slugs On The Refrigerator* (slugsontherefrigerator.com)
- *Sticky Fingers* (stickyfingers1.blogspot.com)
- *Who's The Mummy* (whosthemummy.co.uk)

PR AGENCIES

As parenting blogs differ greatly in terms of the type of things they cover, from family days out to craft activities, you need to start by making a list of the areas you're covering most often. For each area, make a list of brands or businesses that operate in this field. For days out it might be Disneyland and for craft activities it could be a specific brand of colouring pencil or crayon. Use the Internet to find a telephone number for the Head Office and ask the switchboard operator to put you through to the brand's PR representative.

If you're writing about parenting issues in the UK, then the top

PR agencies to contact are:

- Beige (beigelondon.com): Virgin Active, Virgin Media, Zumba Fitness, Sony
- Brando (brando.com): Dr Oetker
- Brazen (brazenpr.com): The Blackpool Tower Dungeon, Makro, Trivial Pursuit, Dirt Devil
- Early Learning Centre (elc.co.uk): baby and toddler toys, outdoor toys and furniture, dolls' houses and toy houses, dressing up and pretend play, action figures and playsets, vehicles and construction, learning and books, creative play, puzzles and games
- EdenCancan (edencancan.com): Mamas and Papas, lastminute.com
- Focus PR (focuspr.co.uk): Cadbury
- Jackie Cooper (jcpr.com): Galaxy chocolate, Seven Seas Vitamins, Xbox
- Lexis PR (lexisagency.com): Arm and Hammer, Dove, Sure, Vaseline
- Kazoo (kazoo.co.uk): BT Vision, Cotswold Outdoor
- Mischief PR (mischiefpr.com): Jaffa Cakes, Radox, Lynx, Dulux, Ben & Jerry's
- Mothercare (mothercare.com): baby carriers, clothes, pushchairs, nursery and bedroom, feeding, baby and changing
- Mums Stuff (mumsstuff.co.uk): products for breastfeeding, changing bags, clothes, baby gadgets
- Neil Reading PR (neilreadingpr.com): *Dancing on Ice* tour, *X Factor* tour, *Walking With Dinosaurs*, *Sister Act: The Musical*
- Pegasus PR (pegasuspr.co.uk): Dr Organic, Bio Oil, Chemists Direct

- Shine (shinecom.com): Evian, Volvic, Sony, Tupperware, Clarks, eBay
- Slam PR (slampr.com): Food – from Propercorn popcorn and Lola's Cupcakes – to essentials for busy mums such as The Body Shop and Filofax
- The Lifestyle Agency (thelifestyle-agency.com): Pierre Marcolini, Planet Hollywood, Waitrose

NETWORKING ORGANISATIONS

As with fashion, mummy bloggers like to create a community where ideas can be shared, content may be posted and finding each other's blogs for hints, tips and – in many cases, friendship – is easy. Although there is a lot of competition out there, mummy networks are designed for parents to help each other and empower fellow parents. The best mummy networks are:

- *Cyber Mummy* (cybermummy.com)
- *Family Friendly Working* (familyfriendlyworking.co.uk)
- *Ladies Who Latte* (ladieswholatte.rsitez.com)
- *Mom Bloggers Club* (mombloggersclub.com)
- *Motivating Mum* (motivatingmum.co.uk)
- *Mums Business Club* (mumsbusinessclub.com)
- *Mums The Boss* (mumstheboss.co.uk)
- *Netmums* (netmums.com)

FACEBOOK GROUPS

There are many mummy groups on Facebook, but it is difficult to become part of them all. Some are better than others for various areas of parenting, and the bloggers I have spoken to have recommended me these:

- *I Love Being A Mom*
- *Parenting.com*
- *Modern Parenting*
- *Natural Parenting*
- *Peaceful Parenting*

INTERVIEWS

Have you ever wondered how these supermums juggle having a family and maintaining a work/life balance? They have a better organised diary than the Prime Minister – in fact they're more powerful than the Prime Minister! Thankfully they cleared time to talk me through the essentials of parenting blogging. Follow their wise advice and you too could become the next *Mumsnet*.

CASE STUDY

Elinor Shields, blogging editor of *Mumsnet* (mumsnet.com) Britain's most trafficked parenting website, *Mumsnet* has since spawned similar sites to cope with the mass of mummy bloggers. *Mumsnet* have published several parenting books, too – *Pregnancy: The Mumsnet Guide, Toddlers: The Mumsnet Guide, Babies: The Mumsnet Guide* and *The Mumsnet Rules*. *Mumsnet* has 29,194 Twitter followers and 19,838 Facebook fans.

Q: How do you decide what to cover on the *Mumsnet* blog?
E: Anyone who has a blog can apply to join, and we accept blogs on anything and everything of interest to our audience so we've got a broad mix of posts on parenting, politics and all the juice in between. Bloggers in the network remain free to write about and publish what they choose on

their blogs. We link out to all blogs and individual posts on our site and social media. It's pretty simple, really: the bloggers get the readers, and retain full control and ownership of their work.

Q: Where do you draw the line? Can you give away too much information?

E: Our policy is to keep intervention to a minimum and let the blogging flow. Blogs are a powerful way to talk about pain, release stress, gather and express your thoughts. And there are few places online where you have the freedom to say (almost) what you like. That said, we do not allow blogs in the *Mumsnet* bloggers' network that are obscene, racist, disablist, libellous, contain personal attacks or otherwise break the law.

Q: How do you monitor what is on the *Mumsnet* blogging network?

E: As we help our bloggers to reach more readers, we rely on them to keep a closer eye on whether their posts adhere to our editorial guidelines and terms of use – particularly with reference to libel and copyright. We are always dipping into our most recent posts, and our community is brilliant at bringing anything problematic to our attention.

Q: How does *Mumsnet* and the blogging network get noticed by important people?

E: Promotion on the UK's busiest parenting community of nearly two and a half million monthly unique visitors can get you quite a long way! We also make sure we spread the word on a great post to followers on Twitter [@MumsnetBloggers] and fans on Facebook [MumsnetBloggersNetwork]. Our bloggers are a vibrant mix of new voices and big names, with many politicians, journalists and writers. They help to raise our profile.

Q: Do you have any advice for people starting out in the industry?

E: Be yourself. The great thing about a blog is that it's your space – and you can be as formal or informal, as truthful or fictional, as you like. And read other blogs. Anyone who writes will know that you learn by reading others' work – and the same is true of blogging. Reading other blogs could give you inspiration or keep you up to date on the latest blogging trends. Commenting on others' blogs is a great way to build a web presence and be welcomed into the blogging community – and other bloggers need encouragement, too!

Q: Are there any mistakes you made that you'd like to warn other bloggers not to make?

E: Some of our newbie bloggers can go overboard with colours, fonts and masses of 'arty' pictures. In terms of great blog design, less is definitely more. And don't forget to update often! An untended blog is a very sad thing indeed.

Q: How important is it for a blogger to be aware of legal issues?

E: Very! A bigger audience brings more responsibility. As we help our bloggers to reach more readers, we rely on them to keep a closer eye on whether their posts adhere to our editorial guidelines and terms of use – particularly with reference to libel and copyright.

Q: If someone approached you asking you to take a post

down, what are the circumstances in which you would do it?

E: As I mentioned earlier, we aim to keep intervention to a minimum and let the blogging flow. And the circumstances for every post are unique. That said, we treat all reports seriously and take fast action on any posts that break our guidelines.

Q: And finally, what do you think the future is for mummy bloggers and perhaps the industry as a whole?

E: It's rosy! *Mumsnet* has long been home to loads of funny, provocative parents and we've been thrilled to give a similar platform to talented bloggers, many of whom haven't really been heard. New blogs are coming online every day because so many people have something to say. Now's the chance to voice your views and make yourself heard.

Case study

Pippa Wright from *A Mother's Ramblings* (amothersramblings.com)

Pippa has appeared on *Mumsnet* and *BritMum*'s Blog of the Year Awards list and has her own YouTube channel.

Q: What makes your blog unique from other blogs?

P: When people think of parent bloggers they think about parents blogging about their family and that is exactly what I do, so it doesn't sound unique but it is. I blog about my family and the fun we have, the stupid things we say and the silly things that we do, and there is no other family quite like ours. I'm not afraid to make a fool of myself – I've posted a video of me dancing in a lift, I've published a blog post where I told people how much I weigh (and the support I got was amazing), I've been open about my family dynamics, about our devastation when relatives have died. We like to have fun and that comes across in every post, as does the amount of love that we have for each other.

I guess what makes it unique is us – me and my family. I often joke that we wouldn't be out of place in a British sitcom, but it's true: we are a real family and we show that.

Q: How do you decide what to cover on your blog?

P: If it happens in our life then it happens on our blog. This past weekend, for example, we spent a day with our extended family and we went to London. Whilst I won't be blogging about every last conversation I had with my family, I will blog about us having spent time together if it was fun. The trip to London will be blogged in full as we went to the Science Museum, and it was fun. I think of the people who read my blog as friends and so if it is something I would share with a friend, it is something I would blog about.

Q: Where do you draw the line? Can you ever give away too much information?

P: If in doubt, I leave it out. I also use a few blogging friends and my husband as a back-up just to confirm I'm not daft in posting something. My husband asked if I wouldn't publish one particular blog post because it was too personal and he didn't feel comfortable, especially as the people he works with are all avid readers. As it is our life that I am putting out there he gets a say, as do the children (and when they have done something that is funny but they are embarrassed by, I haven't posted).

You can give away too much information without meaning to, and it was only when I met an online friend that I realised how much she knew about me and my children and our routine that I realised I probably give away a lot more than I thought. I do take some steps to 'protect' us – I don't quite live where people think I do, our real names are not mentioned and if something is private, that is how it stays!

Q: Have your kids had any bad experiences as a result of you sharing things?

P: No, I'm lucky that the sort of things I share are about our life as a family rather than individual experiences.

Q: How do you fit blogging into your busy life?

P: It's because I have a busy life that I blog, but I don't think it's that busy. I guess that I'm good at multi-tasking as I will blog whilst I'm working (I work from home) or watching TV, and I keep a notebook with me at all times so I can write, and I keep ideas on my phone too. For me it is just one other thing that I like to do so I make time. Right now, for example, dinner is cooking, I'm listening to my daughter practise her violin, my son is playing with a toy we're reviewing, and I'm speaking with you. It's just normal life for me.

Q: What's the best thing you've done as a result of your blog?

P: There is so much! I've been a judge for a national competition (twice), I've got to cook with famous chefs and bakers, I've made best friends, I've got a job, I've had experiences and been able to give my children experiences that they wouldn't have had access to otherwise, I've won awards, I've spoken at events – but I think that the best thing is that I've been able to see how fantastic my family is, and spend time with them.

CASE STUDY

Cass Bailey from *Frugal Family* (frugalfamily.co.uk)
Cass has been nominated for Parentdish Blog of the Year several times and contributes her frugal and child-friendly recipes to other blogging sites such as *BritMums*. She has 3,990 Twitter followers and 852 Facebook fans.

Q: Why did you decide to set up a blog?

C: Basically my brother died of cancer and left his young son behind. I wanted to make sure that if anything ever happened to me my children would have something to remember me by and would have a record of all of our happy times in one place. I decided to add a bit of a money-saving angle to it as I was trying to reduce my hours at work to spend more time with the children.

Q: How did you come up with the name for your blog?

C: I thought for ages about what I wanted to call my blog. I don't really like the word 'frugal', but *The Diary of a Frugal Family* has a nice ring to it, I think (hope!). I knew that I didn't want to have mum or mummy in the title as I didn't want the blog to only be about the children or me as a mum.

Q: How did you pick a design for your blog?

C: Initially I used a free template – I just Googled 'free template' and found lots of sites, but as I got more serious about blogging, I used a designer to give my blog a custom makeover. I'd really recommend this to anyone who wants to make their blog a success – it helps give you a bit more individuality, and you can use your logo consistently throughout your Twitter/Facebook avatars. I wanted to go for the cupcake image because I like cupcakes, no other reason really. I think it's important that the look of a blog represents the blogger, and mine definitely does.

Q: Do you recommend WordPress or Blogger, or designing your own custom-made blogging system?

C: I started off with Blogger but again, as my blog developed I decided to go self-hosted with WordPress. Ultimately, I think that WordPress is much more flexible, and with Blogger there is always the danger that they own your blog and can decide to delete it. This way my blog is mine and no one but me has control over it.

Q: How do you decide what to cover on your blog?

C: I try and have a good mix of family and money-saving posts, and I have a little notebook that I carry with me in case I think of something while I'm out. I really should have one on my bedside cabinet as well, as I always think of things in the night and can never remember them in the morning.

The family posts include anecdotes about the family, the things we bake and craft, days out we've had – anything, really. When I have a problem, I blog about it (to a certain extent) and always get some great advice because whatever problem I'm going through, there are always people who've already been in that position.

The money-saving posts include what we've done to save

money, ways to make money and special offers that I think would save my readers money. I write posts on how to use cash-back websites or how to sell on eBay to help people make a bit extra.

I join in with a few of the regular blogging link-ups as they're a good way to get new readers and sometimes can be a bit of a prompt to write something I possibly wouldn't have done before.

One thing I won't do is blog about blogging – I hate reading posts where bloggers are writing about what others should or shouldn't be doing on their blog – a blog is your own space, and if people don't want to read something you've written they have the choice to click on the cross in the corner of their screen.

Q: Where do you draw the line? Can you give away too much information?

C: I always try and keep at the front of my mind that if I put something out there, I can't ever fully take it back. I absolutely think you can give too much information away and my general rule is that if I wouldn't tell one of the other mums at the school gate a story, I won't write it on my blog. I won't write anything really embarrassing about the children, and I rarely write about my husband. I did once write something that I thought had crossed the line – not in a controversial way, just something I wasn't sure I wanted people to know – and I deleted the post after I'd thought about it. I know people will have read it and it wasn't all that important in the grand scheme of things, but I felt better knowing I'd deleted it.

Q: Have your kids have any bad experiences as a result of you sharing things?

C: No, I blog semi-anonymously so not many people know that I blog, and I don't really use my full name on my blog or on Facebook. I also refer to the children as Miss and Master Frugal, which is a bit corny but better than using their real names in my opinion. I do use photos of them on the blog, though.

Q: Is there any benefit to your kids from seeing you have a successful blog?

C: Not necessarily a benefit to having a successful blog, but they love looking through my posts with me and remembering things we've done together. I plan to print out all the family posts one day and make them up into a memory book for them. To me my blog isn't successful because of the visitors I get every day, or because of my position in the monthly blog rankings, it's a success because I enjoy doing it and I can look back at what I've written and feel proud. It took me a while to get to this point, though if I'm honest I did go through a bit of a star-obsessed phase where I checked my visitor numbers every day and was gutted if someone unfollowed me on Twitter.

Q: What's the best thing you've done as a result of your blog?

C: Last year we were invited to go and see *Glee Live* in one of the executive boxes at the 02 Arena in London, which was an amazing, amazing night. We've just come back from a weekend in Dublin, where we were literally treated like VIPs for the whole weekend. Our room in the hotel was so big it had three balconies – which amazed the children! We regularly get offered tickets to theme parks, festivals and all sorts of great days out, and I love the fact that the children are included too. We've had some great 'money can't buy' experiences that the children will remember for ever.

I've also made some lovely friends, some of which I consider to be my extremely good friends now.

Q: How do you fit blogging into your busy life?

C: I work part time and go straight from work to picking the children up from school. I check my emails on the walk from the car to the playground and reply to any urgents when I get home, but I do try not to have the laptop on until 7pm when I settle the children down. It's not always possible if I have a deadline, or if something urgent comes up, but that's my general rule. I do get more time now than I did because the children are often playing, so I sneak on the iPad while they're out.

Q: How did you get noticed by the media?

C: I think it just happens naturally. I'm usually in or around the top 10 of the Tots 100 and Foodies 100 blogging charts each month, so I think it comes from that mainly. I'm not a 'put myself out there' kind of person so I just wait for it to come to me. I think blogging starts off slowly but if you stick at it, people will find you and then more people will find you, and then the PRs and media will find you, too.

CASE STUDY

Jessica Gottlieb from *Jessica Gottlieb, A Los Angeles Mom* (jessicagottlieb.com)

Jessica was one of the first women to write a parenting blog; some say she pioneered the term 'mummy blogger'. Her expertise has been used on American television shows such as *Dr Phil* and in 2012 she was listed in *Forbes* magazine as one of the most powerful women on Twitter. Jessica is currently involved in the video blog *Momversation*, which focuses on issues related to her blog. She has 22,046 Twitter followers and 415 Facebook fans.

Q: Where do you draw the line? Can you give away too much information?

J: There are very clear lines – I don't share images of my kids, their real names or my husband's first name. There's nothing about having a blogger as a parent that's helpful for kids. When mine go for their first jobs and HR Googles them there will be no links to me. Also, I talk about parenting. That does not mean that I need to talk about my kids. Those are two very different things.

Q: Is there any benefit to your kids from seeing you have a successful blog?

J: The kids have enjoyed some incredible vacations as a result of the blog and my son (who loves cars as much as I do) gets a real kick out of the extended drives.

Q: What's the best thing you've done as a result of your blog?

J: I've introduced my neighbourhood to epicchange.com and they've supported the Shepherds Jr middle school in Tanzania.

Q: How do you fit blogging into your busy life?

J: Blogging is my day job. After I drop the kids off at school,

I sit down and get to work. It's a two-hour commitment every morning.

Q: How did you get noticed by the media?

J: It's been many years of building relationships. Responding to reporter queries from HARO [Help A Reporter Out] is a great beginning.

CASE STUDY

Jo Beaufoix from *Jo Beaufoix* (jobeaufoix.com)
Jo won Made for Mums Best Blogger and was a finalist in the BMB Inspirational Blogger finalist in 2010. She has 1,510 Twitter followers and 493 Facebook fans.

Q: How can a mums' blogger get readers interested?

J: I write about stuff that interests me and am very honest so hopefully that's what keeps people coming back. I try to write with humour, and if I do product reviews I keep them short and sweet, or use a daft or quirky angle to make people smile. If I'm honest, I write for me really. My blog is snippets of my and my family's lives. It's helped me through nappies, toddlerhood, the break up of my marriage, two house moves, illness, several pet deaths, loss and all the mini crises that are part of life, as well as the fun bits. I suppose because of that there's a lot there that people can identify with. I also have moments of complete random silliness, so I hope that kind of stuff makes people come back too.

Q: What do you do to attract new readers?

J: When I started out I read tons of other blogs religiously, joined in blogger meet-ups and took part in networking events I found on Facebook all over the place in the hope of meeting new people and gaining new readers. That's the way to make real friends out there if you are a newbie. When Susanna started the fab *BritMums* I was one of the founding members and now it's huge, so that's another fab way to make friends and attract readers. These days I tweet posts, Google+ them if I remember, and all my posts automatically feed through to Facebook. As a single parent I have a lot less time now I'm back at work so my blogging has had to slow down as life is so much busier now. I can't read as much as I used too, but just stop by every now and then to catch up on what's going on out there. I can't see myself ever stopping, though – I love it! It's a creative outlet, an escape and at times a bit of a lifesaver.

Q: Where do you get your images from?

J: I use my own photographs or stock.xchng. If ever I find an image elsewhere I always give credit and link to the site where I found it.

Q: Any tips for dealing with PRs?

J: My girls and I have had some amazing experiences, thanks to PRs so I do work with them but in my own way. I only take on reviews that will benefit me and my children in some way, such as a trip, an exciting product or something we can learn from. Be open and honest with the people you are dealing with and remember, you're doing them a favour. Your blog is worth something; your time and effort is worth something – it's up to you to decide what.

One thing I would say is that working with PRs has changed my blog in some ways that aren't so good. It's lovely to get products to review and so on, but my blog is less my own now. The writing that I enjoyed has played second fiddle to reviews at times, and I hope to get back to my more creative stuff in the future. As a mum on a budget though, I can't deny that free children's shoes, school uniform, holidays and other treats make a difference, so there will always be a place in my heart for PRs.

CASE STUDY

Marianne Whooley from *Mari's World* (marisworld.co.uk) Mari is an official Butlins Mum Ambassador and editor of *BritMums*, with 1,519 Twitter followers and 399 Facebook followers.

Q: How do you decide what to cover on your blog?

M: The million-dollar question! A thought comes into mind along with another few thoughts and the most exciting one wins. Basically all other thoughts are filed away for a rainy day.

Q: Where do you draw the line? Can you give away too much information?

M: Yes, you can, and I have gone back and cancelled various posts that on reflection maybe were too open.

Q: Have your kids had any bad experiences as a result of you sharing things?

M: Not yet and I hope they never will – it's one of those things you just don't know.

Q: Is there any benefit to your kids from seeing you have a successful blog?

M: I have two older children who live in Italy, a country which could be classed as being 'behind' in social media. It's impressive to them to see their mum so 'forward thinking' and hopefully I can help drag them into this new online era.

Q: What's the best thing you've done as a result of your blog?

M: So many things: working with P&G on their Olympic campaign, meeting Charlie Webster at the Women's Aid/Avon event, being asked by *BritMums* to edit their blog – that is a massive result for me!

Q: How do you fit blogging into your busy life?

M: It's continuous multi-tasking. Whenever I have a few minutes I squeeze something in, a tweet, a Facebook update, a blog post and sometimes the ironing doesn't get done on time – oops!

Q: Do you work with PRs? Any tips for dealing with PRs?

M: I do, and the best tip I can give is to work up a relationship. When people know you and trust you, and can rely on your work they are more inclined to work with you.

Q: Is there any mistake you made when you first started blogging that you think others could learn from?

M: Do not mention your friends in posts. I never named anyone, but some people could see themselves in my writing and were very unhappy with it. Sadly they never spoke out. If they told me otherwise I would have acted immediately, but instead I ended up losing those friends.

CHAPTER 14

TIPS FOR TECHNOLOGY AND BUSINESS BLOGGERS

Are you ready to sync you iMac, brush up on your Java, devour your Apple, charge up a BlackBerry and get the most from being with Orange? If you like to know what technological gadgets are big and tasty, and get a thrill from buying a new piece of kit then technology blogging is clearly for you. It's all very well buying gadgets and reviewing them but if you want to turn it into a business, here's how:

THE TECHNOLOGY BLOGGER'S CHECKLIST

- **A list of terrific tech bloggers.** It's important to keep up to date with what others are reviewing.
- **A list of contacts at PR agencies.** This is how you can learn about upcoming releases and get opportunities to test new items.
- **A list of technology networking organisations.** There's

---

no need to be lonely when lots of people can solve your geeky questions.

- **A list of the most popular Facebook groups.** Join the most useful group to network and you'll have more time to spend on other things.
- **Technology industry tips, tricks and interviews with key bloggers.** Get secrets from the top titles in tech, including *Tech Week* and *Tech Radar*.

TERRIFIC TECHNOLOGY BLOGGERS

These bloggers are your go-to guys for any technology, gadget and industry advice. There isn't an app they don't know about, or a technology advancement they cannot advise you on. Plus some of them have a day job in SEO or Internet marketing, so see what they have to say about link exchanges.

- *All About Symbian* (allaboutsymbian.com)
- *Breakthrough Business Strategies* (blogtalkradio.com/breakthroughbusiness)
- *Engadget* (endgadget.com)
- *Electric Pig* (electricpig.co.uk)
- *Geek* (geek.com)
- *Giga Om* (gigaom.com)
- *Gizmodo* (gizmodo.com)
- *Mashable* (mashable.com)
- *Read Write Web* (readwriteweb.com)
- *Redmond Pie* (redmondpie.com)
- *Tech Bubbles* (techbubbles.co.uk)
- *Tech Crunch* (techcrunch.com)
- *Tech Dirt* (techdirt.com)

- *Tech Radar* (techradar.com)
- *Tech Week* (techweek.com)
- *Ubergizmo* (ubergizmo.com)

PR AGENCIES

It's vital for a technology blogger to sign up to some well-established PR agencies. Not only will this build relations in your field, but you will also be able to access to the information from technology companies as it is made available, attend functions designed to showcase new creations and perhaps receive some product to review. Without the assistance of a good PR then you can kiss goodbye to trialling new software before anyone else and beating your competitors to the story.

All of the global technology brands have regional PR agencies, so whether you're based in the United States, Asia or Europe, you'll need to spend time locating the right one for you. Sadly, there's no easy James Bond style gadget to do it quickly so you'll need a computer connected to the Internet and a phone. Make a list of the companies you believe you will feature most often and browse their websites to find details of their PR contacts. It's not always easy to find this information so you could also call Head Office and ask the switchboard operator to be put through to the relevant PR contact in your region.

If you're based in the UK, I have listed the top PR companies for your technological needs:

- Beige PR (beigelondon.com): Virgin Media, 505 Games
- Citizen Brando (bbpr.com): Three.co.uk, Sony Ericsson
- Clifford French (cliffordfrench.co.uk): EA Sports

TIPS FOR TECHNOLOGY AND BUSINESS BLOGGERS

- Fever (feverpr.com): Toshiba, Canon, HTC, Smart Car, Mercedes-Benz
- Frank PR (frankpr.it): BlackBerry, Activision video games including Call of Duty
- Golin Harris (golinharris.co.uk): Orange Mobile
- Hill & Knowlton (hkstrategies.co.uk): Intel
- Itspr (itspr.co.uk): Hyundai cars
- Kazoo (kazoo.co.uk): Samsung, BT, Plusnet
- Mission PR (thisismission.com): Nokia
- PFPR Communications (pfpr.com): automative brands including Nissan and Mini
- Phil Hall Associates (pha-media.com): GAME
- Red (theredconsulatncy.com): Nintendo, Samsung mobile phones, McAfee

NETWORKING ORGANISATIONS

Feeling overwhelmed by the number of different technology bloggers out there? Why not join a network? If you join up with other bloggers you will find details of other like-minded individuals who are perhaps more knowledgeable in a different area of technology. That way, you won't miss out on anything and will increase the likelihood of other masterminds in your field following your thoughts. The best technology networks are:

- *Network World* (networkworld.com)
- *SMB Technology Network* (community.smbtn.org)
- *Techie Apps* (techieapps.com)
- *Technology Networks* (technologynetworks.com)

FACEBOOK GROUPS

We know Facebook is a force of technology in itself, but have you ever thought of becoming part of a technology-based group on the social networking site? There are hundreds to choose from, but to find the best is like searching for an MP3 in a haystack. The technology bloggers I have spoken to use the following groups:

- *Blogger and SEO Technology*
- *Cheapest Gadgets In The World*
- *Information Technology*
- *Oracle Technology Network*
- *Sapphire Technology Club*
- *Seagate Technology*
- *Technology*
- *Technology Guide*
- *Technology Today*

TWITTER

I know all you technology enthusiasts love using the latest apps and software, and with the help of Twitter you can combine your knowledge with the fastest form of technology. You tech guys rave about Twitter so I had to include a guide to the best tech people to follow in order to grow your blog.

The best way to use Twitter for business is to use the Twitter lists function. This involves subscribing to someone else's list and keeping that stream of people separate to those whom you follow for personal reasons. You can see people's lists underneath their photos on the left-hand side of their profile pages. Sign up to the following lists and you'll always be ahead of the crowd with the greatest gadget news:

- CIO (find this on profile @abbielundberg)
- Cloud (find this on profile @georgereese)
- Developers (find this on profile @latenitecoder)
- Digital and Social Media (find this on profile @courtnaybird)
- Legal Tech Thinkers (find this on profile @nikiblack)
- Mobile (find this on profile @tgruber)
- Most Influential in Tech (find this on profile @scobleizer)
- Tech News Brands (find this on profile @scobleizer)
- Top Tech Bloggers (find this on profile @louisgray)

INTERVIEWS

Does technology jargon sometimes scramble your brain? In the following interviews some of the world's best technology bloggers explain what they have learnt and how they overcome obstacles along the way. Technology is a tool, which is not only fast moving but also powerful. As a tech writer you have masses of tools at your fingertips, so perhaps a little advice wouldn't go amiss?

CASE STUDY

Paul Douglas from *Tech Radar* (techradar.com)

Tech Radar **reaches out to millions of people worldwide, with offices in London, Bath and San Francisco. The site won the Hitwise Award for the UK's Biggest IT Media Site in 2010 and brings you the best technology and gadget news.** *Tech Radar* **has 25,016 Facebook fans and 7,248 Twitter followers.**

Q: What makes your blog unique from other blogs?

P: We're the UK's largest consumer technology news and reviews site, and the place that people come to when they want to research phones, laptops, cameras and other technology items before they buy.

Q: Any advice for people starting out in the industry?

P: It's a competitive environment, so if you're to succeed you'll need to find a unique angle for your chosen subject and work tirelessly to attract visitors – so you'd better make sure it's a subject that you're deeply passionate about.

Q: If a blogger is starting from nowhere, how can they build up their social media followers?

P: Reach out to other blogs and tell them what you're doing. If they like it, they'll link to you.

Q: In terms of traffic to the blog, how did you spread the word when you first started?

P: By sending press releases to the media and talking to PR agencies and manufacturers to explain our mission. To spread the word to web users, we commissioned articles that we felt other blogs and aggregators would find interesting and want to link to.

Q: Would you recommend a new blogger uses video, and why/why not?

P: It depends on the subject of your blog. Does video give you something unique to offer your readers, and is it worth the time it takes to shoot and edit it? Is creating video content something you enjoy? You need to think about why you are creating video and how it can complement and enhance the rest of your content. Alternatively, perhaps video 'is' your content.

Q: How can bloggers use Twitter and Facebook to get web traffic up?

P: Engage with your followers on Twitter and Facebook. Ask questions and listen to feedback. Don't see social media as somewhere for you to spam with links to get quick and easy traffic. Treat it as a two-way conversation, not a one-way advertising medium.

Q: What do you think the future holds for tech bloggers?

P: It's really bright – it will only become cheaper and easier to create rich content as the tools improve. Of course, this means that competition for your audience's time will become tougher, so you need to continually look at the product you offer and honestly ask yourself whether it meets your readers' needs. Don't be afraid to experiment and innovate – it's much more fun, and more rewarding, than mimicking other blogs in your field.

CASE STUDY

Peter Judge from *Tech Week* (techweek.com)

***Tech Week* is one of the largest technology websites in the world and even hosts its own awards show: Tech Success Awards. The site has a vast amount of knowledge in everything from mobile phones to Internet security. *Tech Week* has 1,507 Facebook fans and 2,282 Twitter followers.**

Q: How is *Tech Week* unique?

P: We try to post better and quicker, and we definitely want to be more interactive with our own community. We are aiming to make interaction with our readers, the professional users of tech, a really strong feature. So we are profiling IT managers in our IT Life feature and running the Tech Success Awards to recognise great IT projects.

Q: How did you pick a design for your blog?

P: *Tech Week Europe* is published by Net Media Europe and the design is unified to a large extent, across all the publications in Europe. Within the corporate design for our UK site, we chose elements which allowed us to select which content appears at the top of the site, and to foreground good images, to be as visual as possible.

Q: How often do you update the blog, and what is the reason for this?

P: It's updated all day long on weekdays – that's because it's a business blog. We have an editorial staff of four in the office.

Q: Any advice for people starting out in the industry?

P: Get advice from someone who knows what to do, don't listen to bullshit!

Q: Is there any mistake you made when you first started blogging that you think others could learn from?

P: Not really. Things were so different when I first started; my experience then is not relevant.

Q: In terms of traffic to the blog, how did you spread the word when you first started?

P: We had a press launch, invited PRs to a hotel in London and inflicted a corporate video on them. I don't know if it helped, but as a long-time journalist who has suffered these things from the other side, I enjoyed the feeling of getting my own back.

Q: What do you do to attract new readers?

P: Pimp our stuff on the usual social media sites and on sites like Slashdot, where our kind of reader hangs out.

Q: Would you recommend a new bloggers uses video, and why/why not?

P: Video is more time-consuming than you think, harder to get traction with and definitely harder to make good-quality content out of than you expect. Also, if you are monetising with ads and page views, a five-minute video is still only one page view.

CASE STUDY

James Holland, editor at large at *Electric Pig* (electricpig.co.uk)

Electric Pig **hosts everything from reviews and videos to the newest technology from unknown brands, priding itself on giving you technology news which takes a unique position.** *Electric Pig* **gets 5,198 Twitter followers and 4,616 Facebook fans.**

Q: Why did you decide to set up a blog?

J: A group of us had worked for men's magazines and technology titles, mostly as staff at large publishers. We knew we could do something better, quicker and more fun under our own steam, free from the yoke of corporate red tape and without needing to conform to the working practices of a primarily print organisation.

Q: How did you come up with the name for your blog?

J: It's old American slang for a waste disposal unit. We saw that as being *Electric Pig*'s prime role: getting rid of the crap, and leaving you with just the best tech news every single day.

Q: How important is it for a blogger to be aware of legal issues?

J: Incredibly. You're publishing, which means you're liable, and most of the time you're writing with an opinion, which means you need to know how to position it and stay on the right side of the relevant legislation. If you don't take the law seriously it's only a matter of time before you hit difficulties. Often, the first mistake you make will be an expensive one.

Q: How important is it to engage with the readers via comments?

J: It's essential. Nobody likes to feel they're not being listened to, and when you first start out, while you're building an audience, you'll be faced with 'empty pub syndrome'. Nobody likes being the first one to strike up a conversation, so when one of your readers is brave enough to pipe up you should welcome them with open arms (or at least a friendly word or two in response).

Q: How do you engage the readers through Twitter and Facebook and maintain a conversation?

J: There aren't any rules, but if I could give you one piece of advice: don't automate your Twitter or Facebook output. Put a real human behind them, one who's approachable, with a good sense of humour. Someone your audience will want to talk to. Before you know it, they'll be doing that in droves.

Q: If a blogger is starting from nowhere, how can they build up their social media followers?

J: Write, tweet and post interesting things! If your output is sufficiently mind-tingling people will want to share it. From there, it'll snowball. But first, you need that interesting idea.

Q: Who looks after the advertising on your site?

J: We have a partner who handles ad sales. You could do it in-house, but it's time-consuming and needs significant expertise, not to mention significant financial outlay to begin with.

CASE STUDY

Rafe Blandford from *All About Symbian* (allaboutsymbian.com)

The man behind the 'All About' sites, Rafe has been running them for over a decade now. *All About Symbian* is the go-to site for anyone wanting mobile phone advice. The site gets 9,736 Twitter followers and 3,757 Facebook fans.

Q: What makes your blog unique?

R: We have a greater accuracy and depth of content than other technology blogs who try to spread themselves too thin. It is important to me that my team are well educated in this sector as the readers implicitly trust that what is written is 100 per cent accurate. I like to think the blog takes the approach of a broadsheet newspaper rather than a tabloid – its content is stronger and much more reliable.

Q: How often do you update the blog, and what is the reason for this?

R: It is largely dictated by the workflow of news. We usually update ten times a day, sometimes more or less, depending on resources.

Q: Any advice for people starting out in the industry?

R: Blogging is not a get-rich-quick scheme. There can be money to be made but that will always come later: it's about passion. You cannot force a blog from thin air. If you don't enjoy what you are talking about then a good life/work balance will never be achieved. If money is what you crave then at the beginning you need to start implementing certain things for fast success, like SEO and so on. The most important aspect is to enjoy it. If you don't, your readers will know and the site will be a failure. It is essential to to build a rapport with your audience.

Q: Is there any mistake you made when you first started blogging that you think others could learn from?

R: Commercially, I think I could have done a lot more. When I first ventured into it I didn't know I could make money and I wanted to do it because I felt passionate. I do look back and wish I'd had my business hat on and got involved with consultancy work and advertisers sooner. I also think many bloggers, including me, criticise themselves too much. Maintaining a blog or website is tough, and bloggers should give themselves more credit.

Q: How important is it for a blogger to be aware of legal issues?

R: It is important, as I understand that these types of issues occur whatever genre of blog you have. We had a couple of incidents when the site first launched as we promoted illegal software without realising it was illegal. Needless to say I removed it immediately. Sometimes we get threatened with legal action from massive tech companies, as they don't like what we have written. To be honest, as long as we haven't written anything illegal that's tough, as it is our opinion.

Q: If a blogger is starting from nowhere, how can they build up their social media followers?

R: Distribution of stories. It is vital for people to see snippets of your work on social networking sites to give them a taster. Initially we posted our work on other tech forums to drum up interest, but as Twitter and Facebook have become successful, there is no need for the forums as no one looks at them as much anymore. It is important to engage with the reader, as our reader wants to converse with us as we 'have the knowledge'. So reply to tweets and Facebook messages, as that's very important in gaining and keeping followers. Competitions are also important as they get readers actively involved with the site and its social networks. Although it is a massive traffic driver, it is difficult to update constantly if there isn't the manpower.

Q: How can bloggers get noticed by the media to get name-checked in magazines and newspapers?

R: Quality of content. PRs, journalists and writers trawl the Internet looking for sites like ours, so if your content is to a high standard you will get press interested. It is also key to get yourself a newsworthy story. People don't want to hear what another twenty sites are talking about. They want something fresh – this is a sure-fire way to get media attention (it worked for us). We have a lot of interest from *Wired* and broadsheets this way.

Q: How long did it take you to make money from your blog?

R: It did take a while, but once we started making the money it just kept (and keeps!) coming in. As I said earlier, I wish had been more corporate in the early stages as we would have made a lot more money by now.

Q: What spin-offs have resulted from your blog – books, public speaking and so on? Would you have had the opportunity to do them if you didn't have a blog?

R: I do a lot of tech consultancy work, which has cropped up because of the site and the attention we have got from it.

Q: What do you think the future holds for tech bloggers?

R: I do think blogs will become very much like print media. Magazines are becoming few and far between and only the strongest will survive. I believe this for blogs. Only the big blogs will make it, and the smaller ones will still be there – but just to fill Internet space.

CASE STUDY

Michele Price from *Breakthrough Business Strategies* (whoismicheleprice.com)

Michele Price is a bold and courageous entrepreneur who focuses on solutions and how to find opportunities inside challenges. She travels around the United States and internationally to help build online communities and her vision has not only created her blog – *Blog Talk Radio* – but other businesses too. Michele is a public speaker at business conferences and universities and an amazing literary agent too. She has 32,330 Twitter followers.

Q: Why did you decide to set up a blog?

M: Google has made more changes in what they give weight to for showing up in search engines – more and more folks are finding they cannot SEO their way to the top. A blog lets you show up online in ways to answer questions for your potential clients and be your SEO driver with content.

Q: How did you come up with the name for your blog?

M: I have multiple blogs; the radio show was not named until a year later so I used my name and because my name is common, I added 'Who is' in front of it. It took me about a year before I was able to practically wipe the other Michele Price off the first page of Google because of the depth of content I created and published.

Q: What makes your blog unique from other blogs?

M: What makes my blog unique from other blogs is my voice! Having been an entrepreneur first, I know what it is like to be making decisions from a start-up business's perspective so I like to feel I know how to give my readers what they want. I show them that I started out from nowhere and using the tips I'm sharing, I achieved a level of success. I broke through to the top! I am also a no-nonsense kinda gal, so my readers appreciate getting direct answers from me. I also focus on creating information that provokes them to ask their own questions – giving them better data to make informed decisions for their businesses.

Q: Any advice for people starting out in the industry?

M: Know these answers: what is your voice? Who are you talking to and why do they benefit from your perspective? Create a strategy first, and then develop your execution plan. When you are *very* clear on your purpose and your *why*, the rest falls into place. Be patient! It takes time.

Q: Is there any mistake you made when you first started blogging that you think others could learn from?

M: Having a landing page that directs them to different ways to engage with you. With multiple ways to work with me, one page that allows them to choose keeps things simple. The other is trying to be liked by everyone. Having a distinctive voice and being willing to take a stand separates me from all the wannabes. A copy is never as powerful as the 'real deal'.

Q: In terms of traffic to the blog, how did you spread the word when you first started?

M: When I first started it was a different space. I was big in Twitter and we had real conversations there nightly. You have to be so much more strategic and in multiple places to receive adequate attention today. I have shifted more time to LinkedIn and Google+ now as I am going after more business-oriented people, and the influencers have shifted to Google+.

Q: What is the biggest difficulty facing bloggers in general in America and across the pond to the UK?

M: We warned people not to wait too long to climb up the hill to be noticed and listened to, or the ability to build an audience would take more work. Did they listen? Many didn't. Now it takes far more effort and determination.

CHAPTER 15

TIPS FOR FOOD AND DRINK BLOGGERS

Food, glorious food! As our waistlines get bigger, so do the number of food and drink blogs. Have you ever wondered how to get those soufflés to rise perfectly? Or made one too many mistakes in the kitchen that you and the fire brigade would not care to remember? These food bloggers are at the top of their game, and this type of blogging is set to get bigger and bigger, with food becoming more than just a resource and more of a passion. And it's not just food, as wine lovers are taking to the Net to tell us all about the perfect tipple. How tasty!

THE FOOD, OR DRINK, BLOGGER'S CHECKLIST

- **A list of fabulous food bloggers.** Swap recipes and links to boost your cookbook and your profile in search engines.
- **A list of contacts at PR agencies.** This is how you're most likely to get restaurant reviews… and sometimes even free wine.

- **A list of food networking organisations.** Cooking for one is as lonely as blogging for one. Reach out to fellow foodies and you'll learn lots.
- **A list of delicious food-related Facebook groups.** You need to discover the most popular groups because you'd probably rather be baking than contacting every single food-related Facebook group.
- **Food industry tips, tricks from key bloggers.** Learn the secret ingredients to success from the crème de la crème of food bloggers, including the writers of *Love Food Love Drink* and *Maison Cupcake*.

FABULOUS BLOGGERS

Food and drink is not only something we consume, now it is also an art. With the likes of Heston Blumenthal creating original dishes such as bacon and egg ice cream, it has given rise to a host of foodies experimenting and sharing their tips on different ways to cook and eat and drink with the world. There are so many brilliant blogs to choose from, but I chose the following people as I know they all make money from their blogs, which is the ideal goal.

- *Bar Chick* (barchick.com)
- *Bakerella* (bakerella.com)
- *Eat Like A Girl* (eatlikeagirl.com)
- *Fuss Free Flavours* (fussfreeflavours.com)
- *Gourmet Chick* (gourmet-chick.com)
- *Greedy Gourmet* (greedygourmet.com)
- *Kavey Eats* (kaveyeats.com)
- *Love Food Love Drink* (lovefoodlovedrink.com)
- *Maison Cupcake* (blog.maisoncupcake.com)

- *Marmite Lover* (marmitelover.blogspot.co.uk)
- *Peach Trees and Bumblebees* (peachtreesandbumblebees.com)
- *Recipe Girl* (recipegirl.com)
- *Serious Eats* (seriouseats.com)
- *Tamarind And Thyme* (tamarindandthyme.com)
- *Two Peas And Their Pod* (twopeasandtheirpod.com)
- *Vinography* (vinography.com)
- *Young And Foodish* (youngandfoodish.com)

PR AGENCIES

Getting in touch with the right food PRs is almost as important as writing your blog. As a foodie, you are bound to review products and restaurants, write recipes and provide tips for fellow food lovers. It is possible to do without a press agency, but life will be much more fun (and cheaper) if you are sent the goodies and review restaurants for free. To be in touch with the best in the business, contact the list below:

- Beige PR (beigelondon.com): Wispa
- Brompton Brands (bromptonbrands.com): Mahiki, Whisky Mist, Brompton Club
- Exposure PR (Europe.exposure.net): Coca-Cola, Vitamin Water, Jameson Whisky, Bombay Sapphire Gin, Tiger Beer
- Focus PR (focuspr.co.uk): Godiva Chocolates, Lavazza Coffee, Courvoisier, Jim Beam, Maker's Mark, Stoli
- House PR (housepr.com): Cointreau, Disaronno, Sailor Jerry
- Jori White (joriwhitepr.co.uk): Franca Manca Pizza, Bubble Foods, GBK
- KK Communications (kkcom.co.uk): Shaka Zulu, Supper Club, Bunga Bunga

- Lexis PR (lexisagency.com): Diet Coke, Kraft Food, Oasis Drinks, Fanta
- Luchford APM (luchfordapm.com): Grosvenor Hotel, Lanesborough Hotel, Me Hotel, Thomas Cubitt
- Mason Williams (mason-williams.com): Marriot Hotels (including the Mayfair Hotel)
- Nudge PR (nudgepr.co.uk): chocolate specialists including Paul A. Young
- Phil Hall Associates (pha-media.com): Innocent Smoothies, Tasty Little Numbers
- Pretty Green (itsprettygreen.com): Red Bull, Nando's, Cadbury's
- Richmond Towers Communications (rt-com.com): food and drink products including Jus Roll pastry, Pink Lady apples, Havana Club rum
- Shine Communications (shinecom.com): Martini, Evian, Echo Falls, Bacardi
- Splendid Communications (splendidcomms.com): Smirnoff, Guinness, Marmite, Pepperami, Lucozade
- Weber Shandwick (webershandwick.co.uk): Jacobs Creek, Aldi supermarkets, Intercontinental Hotels

NETWORKING ORGANISATIONS

To ensure you are influencing and being influenced by the right people I strongly advise you join a food network. Like the other blogging genres, this provides unlimited resources to rival blogs, PR contacts and knowledge about other areas of your niche that perhaps you wouldn't normally have. If you're not in a network it's easy to get lost in the myriad of ideas of what you could potentially cover, but keeping an eye on what other people are doing helps you focus. The best food networks are:

- *Food Blogger Network* (foodbloggernetwork.com)
- *Food Buzz* (foodbuzz.com)
- *Martha's Circle* (marthascircle.marthastewart.com)
- *UK Food Bloggers Association* (ukfba.co.uk)

FACEBOOK GROUPS

How do you pick a useful food group? Well, unlike the other groups described so far, it might not be the one with the most numbers. Foodies are notoriously fussy when it comes to joining groups like these, so the lure of big numbers may not sway the best bloggers. After talking food to bloggers hotter than a tandoori oven, I have established the best foodie groups for you to join:

- *Food.com*
- *Food Gawker*
- *Food Network*

INTERVIEWS

Listening to other bloggers is one of the best tips I can give you. Everyone makes mistakes while blogging, but learning by them is what makes you better at what you do. These food and drink bloggers are the best in their category and can tell you a thing or two about the saturated food-blogging network.

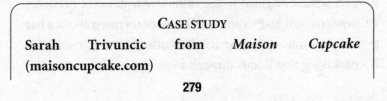

CASE STUDY

Sarah   Trivuncic   from   *Maison   Cupcake* (maisoncupcake.com)

Sarah is the author of *Bake Me I'm Yours: Sweet Bitesize Bakes*. **She has 5,608 Twitter followers and 2,605 Facebook fans.**

Q: How did you come up with the name for your blog?

S: I came back to setting up a blog seriously in 2009 when my son was two. Initially I was thinking of starting two sites, one celebrating French holidays and lifestyle, the other about baking. Then I decided one site was enough so it had to have a French-inspired name. Although I made a lot of cupcakes that summer, I only called the site *Maison Cupcake* because I thought a lot of people would be looking for cupcakes. I was very naïve in the beginning – I knew nothing about SEO or social media and actually thought the only way anyone would find my site was by clicking the 'next' button in Blogger. The name has in some ways become an albatross – I go months and months without featuring cupcakes on the site and yet a lot of people assume I'm a cupcake bakery. I've agonised about changing the name but in the absence of anything better, I've left it as it is. My French site is still in the pipeline but may emerge soon!

Q: Describe a typical working day.

S: My favourite type of day is to make two or three things in the kitchen, do some cake decorating, have lots of sunshine to take nice pictures, then trot off to a fun event or a review dinner in the evening. The reality is that there are far more days when I'm glued to the computer with email overload, being nagged by PRs about why I've not written about a bag of crisps and struggling to dismantle the sea of cardboard packaging that floods through the door.

Q: Who is the target market?

S: According to Facebook insights, my readers are 85 per cent female and aged between 25 and 55. I try to keep my material accessible and down-to-earth, although I'm very aspirational when it comes to cake.

Q: Any advice for people starting out in the industry?

S: Is blogging an industry? It's industrious certainly, so be prepared to work very hard getting very little back for a long time. My first advice is not to overvalue yourself – I hear ridiculous stories of people ringing up PRs saying they've just started a site and can they have X expensive product sent to them. You need to spend at least six months proving yourself and building up a following. I didn't get approached by a single brand for nearly a year even though I'm based in London [bloggers in London are more likely to get invites to events or products couriered to them]. I also spent the first 12 months leaving about 30 comments a day on other sites so other bloggers would find me – that's not something you can keep up forever, but it does explain why some small sites get treble the number of comments of well-known sites: it's all the reciprocal commenting. I'd rather have 200+ people read a new post and fewer comments than 20 comments from 20 readers. On the same token, I would hate to be thought of as someone who thinks they're 'above' commenting (which certain bloggers seem to) – my way round this is to tweet people's posts if I don't have time to comment, which is generally appreciated.

My other advice would be not to undervalue yourself – I never promote brands' Facebook campaigns or Twitter accounts unless they're paying me. It's natural to want to please the first brand who approaches you (this is why brands like new bloggers – they'll do a lot for free) but quickly you realise that the PR person emailing you is salaried and yet they're expecting you to create publicity for them for nothing. I am very careful now and only to agree to do things I get something out of. In the US, food bloggers charge hundreds of dollars to feature a named food brand on their site, yet here we think it's enough to be sent a few jars of sauce. You need to bear in mind that the company sends you goods at cost price, so a £50 product only costs them just over a tenner – the exchange isn't very balanced when you think about how much your time is worth.

Q: Is there any mistake you made when you first started blogging that you think others could learn from?

S: Well, apart from not having a clue about how to get people to find your site, I was fairly lucky. I joined Twitter at the same time as starting the blog and within a couple of months went to a blog conference with a lot of established European bloggers and so I had a more international and more ambitious outlook from the start. When I say that I mean that UK blogging has been a long way behind the US. Until recently here it was the norm to just have a basic Blogger template and everyone's sites looked the same. One of the earliest things I did was study all my favourite blogs and write a list of the features I wanted to install on mine. My other recommendation would be if you are serious about the future success of your site then invest in a domain and your own hosting space – WordPress.org is still way ahead of what Blogger can offer, and you have more flexibility to make your site individual.

Q: There are so many food blogs out there, how do you keep yours fresh?

S: I'm always tweaking my site, trying new designs and new ways of publishing stuff. This week I did a 'cook-along' via Instagram purely off the cuff, but I enjoyed it so much I am going to do it again and maybe others will join in! I guess the short answer is I never keep things the same for very long, and if I notice too many other people are doing something that previously was unusual, I try to move on to something new. Part of me thinks if another social media platform comes along I'll explode, but it's important to keep an eye out for what's going to be the next big thing and what's going to disappear, like Myspace.

Case study

Kenji Lopez-Alt from *Serious Eats* (seriouseats.com)
The blog combines the element of community and content to bring together food bloggers worldwide and was one of the first to do so. Not only this, but the website was also featured in *Time* magazine's most influential websites. *Serious Eats* has 149,907 Twitter followers and 42,472 Facebook fans.

Q: Why did you decide to set up a blog?

K: The blog was started by Ed Levine, who at the time was a writer for *The New York Times*. Essentially, he noticed that there was a lot going on in the food world on the Internet, but that much of it lacked the integrity of real reporting work done for magazines and newspapers. The goal with *Ed Levine Eats* (as *Serious Eats* was called before he changed the name) was to bring real food writing to an online audience. *Serious Eats* became one of the first legitimate large-scale, multi-writer food blogs.

Q: How did he come up with the name for the blog?

K: Ed used to use the word 'serious' when he was describing certain foods. 'That's a serious slice of pizza' or 'that's a serious hamburger'. It's at once serious, yet also quite tongue-in-cheek. What *Serious Eats* really does differently is that as long as you are serious about your food, whether it's a $50-a-plate fancy restaurant meal or a $1 hot dog, we'll cover it with the same passion and integrity.

Q: What makes this blog unique from other blogs?

K: We have three core values: to be passionate, discerning and inclusive. We're the home base for passionate food lovers across the country and around the world. As long as you love food, you are among friends here. At the same time, we're discerning: we know what is delicious and what's not. We don't care about the latest trends or celebrity chef gossip – we're here for the food, and that's what we write about. Finally, we are not judgemental at all – we love low-end burgers as much as we love fancy food.

We are a community more than any other site. Our comments and interactions with readers are unparalleled in the food blog world, and we're very proud of both our online and offline communities.

Finally, our recipe and techniques program is more intense and well developed than any other site. We take great care in finding recipe writers who not only know their stuff, but also understand how real home cooks cook so that our recipes are guaranteed to work and be tasty.

Q: How do you engage the readers through Twitter and Facebook and maintain a conversation?

K: Only way we know how: we're online all the time. Every tweet, Facebook post and email comes from a real person, who really cares about the site.

Q: If a blogger is starting from nowhere, how can they build up their social media followers?

K: Slow and steady. Gaining trust and building relationships online is exactly the same as in real life – you need to prove yourself trustworthy and interesting, and eventually people will come to you.

Q: In terms of traffic to the blog, how did you spread the word when you first started?

K: We didn't. All of our traffic is 100 per cent organic. *Serious Eats* has never advertised, bought email addresses, and so on. All our readership comes from word of mouth and social media. It's the quality of our content that brings people to the site, not our marketing.

Q: How can bloggers use Twitter and Facebook to get web traffic up?

K: People think social media is a shortcut to improving traffic. It's not. It's a tool by which you can spread the word about your great content, but content is what matters, first and foremost. If you have something unique to offer, people will come, and people will tell their friends about it.

CASE STUDY

Pritesh Mody from *Love Food Love Drink* (lovefoodlovedrink.com)

This site is more of an e-magazine, which combines food and drink tips with reviews. Pritesh is also the founder of Outln Consulting. *Love Food Love Drink* has 9,972 Twitter followers.

Q: How did you come up with the name for your blog?

P: I wanted a name that truly represented what the website was about. To be honest, I was surprised that such a catchy name was still available!

Q: What makes your blog unique from other blogs?

P: Content, personality and format. The best blogs are those that allow the writer's personality to come through, thus allowing the blog to develop a regular audience that identifies with the writer. We were one of the first foodie blogs to use an e-newsletter as the main form of communicating with our audience; the website is merely an archive of our posts.

Q: How do you decide what to cover on your blog?

P: Going back to my point on personality, it's purely based on the kind of restaurants, events and products that I would enjoy experiencing myself.

Q: Any tips for dealing with PRs?

P: PRs are an essential source of information for our content and we deal with a large number. There's no real secret to dealing with them; just be polite and be concise with the type of information you require.

Q: How long did it take you to make money from your blog?

P: Advertisers started taking notice of *Love Food Love Drink* about a year after its birth.

Q: Who looks after the advertising on your site?

P: A lot of brands come directly to me and I work with Handpicked Media, who come to me occasionally with interesting opportunities.

Q: Do you think it's possible for a blogger to write and sell ads at the same time? Have you ever tried this?

P: It's a fine balance but again, it comes down to how much you value the integrity of your blog and your reasons for creating the blog in the first place. Whilst I have had the opportunity to do so, it's not something that I have taken part in.

Q: What do you think the future is for food blogs, considering the industry is saturated?

P: The beauty of blogs is that anyone can wake up and decide to start one, although this also means that the food-blogging arena has become a little crowded. However, like the media industry in general, the success of a blog is made on the number and quality of its readers; create content that attracts a regular readership and you will become established.

CASE STUDY

Ashley Fryer from *Peach Trees and Bumble Bees* (peachtreesandbumblebees.com)

Ashley has written for other foodie publications such as *Delicious* and has over 50 contributors writing for her blog. Describing it as more of a community, she says the aim of the site is to bring foodies together. The site gets 146 Facebook fans and has 3,207 Twitter followers.

Q: Why did you decide to set up a blog?

A: I decided to set up *Peach Trees and Bumblebees* because I wanted a place to put all my recipes. I was forever ringing my mother to get old family recipes, and I was hopeless at writing down new inventions, so it just made sense to transfer the archives online. I cook for people a lot and am always being asked for recipes, so I thought it would be lovely to have a little online home where all my recipes could be enjoyed by other people.

Q: How did you come up with the name for your blog?

A: I wanted a name that conjured up the image of my dream kitchen: something light and quirky, with a country-esque feel to it. I pictured warm yellows and a big orchard, and eventually settled on *Peach Trees and Bumblebees*! It just felt nice and summery. I think it sums up the personality of the site nicely.

Q: What makes your blog unique from other blogs?

A: It's a community blog – it's not just my recipes on there, it's the best of the online foodie community. We have about 50–60 contributing writers, some of whom post recipes regularly, and others who post every few months. It offers a place for even the most novice of foodies to share their ideas. It's lots of fun.

Q: How do you make money from your blog?

A: Through advertising and product placement. I am careful to avoid making *Peach Trees* look too ad-heavy – it's essential for me to protect the integrity of the site. But yes, we do make a little bit of money through advertising, plus I get a fair few freebies, which is very nice!

Q: Any advice for people starting out in the industry?

A: Pick a unique selling point if you can, and go with it. Don't be afraid to experiment and try new things but most of all enjoy it. *Peach Trees* is hard work, but I love it. You have to love it to make it work.

Q: Is there any mistake you made when you first started blogging that you think others could learn from?

A: I sometimes wish I hadn't committed to posting a brand-new recipe every day – it's a fair bit of pressure! But thankfully we have a very active community and new recipes are appearing in the inbox all the time. I would say don't put too much pressure on things straightaway – blogs take time to get going and you won't get an instant following. Don't worry about the analytics or the user stats, just enjoy it and it will grow organically.

Q: How can bloggers use Twitter and Facebook to get web traffic up?

A: Both are essential for blogs these days. Most people get their content via their social media feeds, so it's the most natural thing to post updates to Facebook, Twitter, Pinterest and so on. Engage with your audience and talk to them – you will gather a loyal following if you can keep them entertained!

Q: How can bloggers get noticed by the media to get name-checked in magazines and newspapers?

A: I don't think that should be a goal straightaway but if you can build a loyal following and offer some high-quality content, it can be a natural by-product.

Q: What spin-offs have come out as a result of your blog – books, public speaking and so on? Would you have had the opportunity to do them if you didn't have a blog?

A: I've had more opportunities come my way because of *Peach Trees*. I've met some incredible people, and been to lots of exciting foodie events because of it. I've talked about doing a book, which could happen in a couple of years. At the moment, between my other blogs and my other commitments, I don't have time. *Peach Trees and Bumblebees* has definitely opened many more doors for me than I expected.

Q: Food blogging is becoming more and more popular. What do you think the future holds for this genre?

A: I think the future is bright for food blogging – especially for people who need special diets. The Internet is a haven for specialist diets such as gluten free, or vegan lifestyles. It opens up food to a whole new group of people. I hope that the industry continues to thrive – I *love* reading other foodie blogs, and if it means we're getting more people into the kitchen and cooking for themselves, then that's just brilliant!

CASE STUDY

The Secretive Founder and Editor of *Bar Chick* (barchick.com)

Bar Chick was one of the first blogs to write about the niche subject. She has a column in the *London Evening Standard* and writes for *Grazia*. *Bar Chick* has 4,595 followers and 2,536 Facebook fans.

Q: Why did you decide to set up a blog?

BC: Well, I used to go to a lot of bars and I am very passionate about bars, pubs and places to hang out so a couple of years ago, I decided to quit my job and continue to build the site.

Q: What makes your blog unique from other blogs?

BC: It specialises in a subject. When I first started there were not many websites doing what I do, and there still aren't now. I think as well it helps that there is 'one' voice. Although I have staff and people who contribute, I edit everything before it goes live, so the tone is constant.

Q: How did you pick a design for your blog?

BC: I saw a design of an American website and liked it, so I did something similar. An artist drew the Bar Chick sign, which makes it look unique.

Q: Any advice for people starting out in the industry?

BC: Specialise. There are thousands of blogs out and you need to make yours unique. There are loads of fashion bloggers, for example – if that is your passion, you need to figure out a way to give it that special edge that no one else has thought of.

Q: How important is it for a blogger to be aware of legal issues?

BC: I had a bit of a nightmare at the beginning with buying the domain name and trade marking the website, which is vital. My advice would be to seek legal advice before starting your site.

Q: How important is social media to your site, and how has it raised your traffic?

BC: I think you have to have a catchy name to get noticed on sites like Twitter and Facebook. There are so many Twitter and Facebook accounts that if yours sounds boring no one will follow it. I think what helps my site is that there is a 24/7 find-a-bar Twitter service. No matter where you are in the world, if you want to find a cool pub or bar we will tweet back an option – it's part of our service. The site gets a big following due to word of mouth too. So people may retweet or advise someone to go on the website and then they will follow us on Twitter, and vice versa.

Q: How can bloggers get noticed by the media to get name-checked in magazines and newspapers?

BC: The content has to be of a high standard otherwise any readers you get won't come back or recommend you. As I have said, it helps if your site is about a specialised subject as the information you are providing is going to be of a higher standard than any other freelance writer who doesn't have the same depth of knowledge.

CASE STUDY

Alder Yarrow from *Vinography* (vinography.com)
Alder was the first person ever to write a wine blog, which now means he is the most qualified person to talk to about wines. He writes for several drink publications in the US and has 11,615 Twitter followers and 273 Facebook fans.
Q: Why did you decide to set up a blog?
A: By 2003, I had become the 'go-to' guy for all my friends when it came to wine and dining. You know, the one who everyone automatically hands the wine list to when you're

all out eating together. I kept getting the same questions over and over again – what is your favourite merlot under $20? What's a new wine I should try? – and figured there had to be a better way of answering them. Blogs were starting to become a little more mainstream, and I knew I needed to learn a bit about what they were and how they worked (my day job is in the Internet and design space) so I thought I'd set up a wine blog and kill two birds with one stone.

Q: How did you come up with the name for your blog?

A: I'm trained as a photographer and know the Greek etymology of the word 'photography', and thought I could modify it to be 'writing with wine' instead of 'writing with light'. I typed the word 'vinography' into Google and got zero results. I should have taken a screen shot of that, as it's sort of hard to believe now.

Q: If someone approached you asking you to take a post down, what are the circumstances in which you would do it?

A: I've never taken a post down that I can recall. If I've made errors I always correct them. I will take comments down, especially those that are slanderous or offensive.

Q: Any tips for dealing with PRs?

A: I'm in the habit of writing posts now and again that are specifically targeted to the PR community. Wine PR is in a pretty dismal state of affairs – so many people's jobs seem to consist only of sending out press releases and horribly uninteresting, generic pitches to a bcc [blind carbon copy] line of 200 bloggers. The number of good PR people who really try to understand what I care about, build a relationship and work with me as a human being, I can count on the fingers of both hands. I'm constantly deleting emails, clicking 'unsubscribe' and reminding people that just because I gave you my business card that doesn't mean I asked to be on all your mailing lists.

Q: What makes your blog unique from other blogs?

A: My approach to wine is to tell stories about the people, places and histories behind wines. When I review a wine, the tasting note and score are the least important part, and smallest part of the wine review. The real meat of it is storytelling. Apart from that approach, I take my blogging quite seriously, and post as often as I can. I've also had partnerships with professional photographers for years, so that my readers can experience wine and wine country through images as well as words.

Q: Food and drink blogs are becoming popular very quickly. How do you plan to stay at the top of your game?

A: I don't look at what I do particularly competitively, particularly because I don't have to make a living at it (thank heavens!). In terms of my popularity, you can't underestimate the value of being one of the first wine blogs on the Internet, which my page rank reflects. Staying at the top of my game for me is really just about making sure I enjoy what I write, which has always been how I orient to blogging. I'm writing the kind of stuff I want to read, simple as that.

CHAPTER 16

TIPS FOR FILM, MUSIC AND CELEBRITY NEWS BLOGGERS

These are the subjects I know most about. Therefore, the information in this chapter is more detailed. Not only do I know exactly where to find enough content to fill a fast-paced entertainment blog, I know what it's like when you're first starting out.

I had a lot of questions when I was dipping my toes into the blogging waters and I wish I'd had someone to help me along my path. These questions come up time and time again, and they're bound to be asked by anyone who meets me for the first time and discovers that I earn enough money from my blog to make it my full-time job. It's time for me to answer the FAQs – once and for all!

In addition to this, I've asked the same questions of other bloggers who make in excess of six-figure salaries. My friend Perez Hilton is on a lot more, as he takes home a six-figure amount every single month through banner ads and endorsements, while the *I'm Not Obsessed* blog is valued at £10 million!

This chapter starts with my answers to the FAQs and also includes:

- **A list of the most inspiring music, film and gossip bloggers.** You need this to stay up to date with what everyone else is covering. Also, reach out to those whose blogs you like, add them to your blogroll and it will boost your SEO.
- **A list of groups entertainment industry bloggers should join.** We're a fun crowd – we should help each other out more often.
- **A list of PR companies every showbiz blogger should contact.** This is vital if you want gig tickets, screening passes, news about upcoming film and music releases and general news about the ups and downs of the showbiz world.
- **Answers to the FAQs from leading music, film and celebrity news bloggers.**

FREQUENTLY ASKED QUESTIONS

Q: How do you find out about all the parties?

A: 'Partying' is my business so I am super-organised. I wish I could say that invites constantly arrived through the post and in my email inbox, but a lot of the time I proactively find out what's on and ask if I can attend.

I subscribe to a diary-planning service, which lists exactly what events are coming up. It's called the Media Eye (themediaeye.com) and it's used by every major journalist, PR company and event organiser in the UK. If you're serious about staying on top of the latest entertainment news and you're based in the UK, you need a subscription. However, my top tip for all aspiring celebrity bloggers, wherever they may be around the world, is to make friends with photographers as they always receive tip-offs about events. No matter where you operate in the world, always make time to chat to a photographer on the way into an event as you never know what they'll tell you later down the line. Keep in regular contact with them, as they won't tell if you don't ask.

My final piece of advice is to contact every PR company you can think of when you first start out. You can only be invited to things if the PR knows you exist.

Q: How can I get free tickets to gigs/film screenings?

A: First of all, contact all the record labels and film studios and tell them what you do. Each has a dedicated press office and will be interested to hear about another outlet where they can get coverage for their clients. However, at the start you may find that you get more press releases than fun things like CDs and screening invites. For these, you may have to be patient. Build up your blog, create a following and the PR companies will be desperate to impress you so that you can pass on the news to your following. If you have to spend a bit of money at the start to build up a readership, put up with it as your free stuff will start to follow very soon.

Q: Are you allowed to take your friends to gigs/film premieres/festivals?

A: I wouldn't advise taking a friend to a work event, unless there were very special circumstances. Would a teacher take a friend to the classroom? Would a surgeon take a friend to the operating theatre? If you're writing about an event, then treat it as your job.

Friends have a habit of distracting you, especially if there is a free bar and they don't have to write about it the next day! Also, one of the benefits of attending an evening event is the opportunity to network. Trust me, you're a lot less likely to do this if you have a friend in tow.

Q: How do you decide what to wear?

A: I am always very strategic with my outfits. If I have an affiliate deal with a certain brand like H&M or Topshop or Uniqlo then I'll wear one of the new-season collection, take lots of photographs and give my readers a good incentive to want to buy a similar item. As an affiliate, I'll earn up to 10 per cent of what they spend.

Q: How do you get the balance right between work and social life?

A: This is the hardest thing for any self-employed person. At the start, I felt that if I was not blogging then I was wasting time. I was used to putting in long hours as a newspaper journalist and I thought it'd be a good idea to do the same when I set up *Live Like A VIP*. I quickly realised that I was equally stressed out as a blogger as when I was a journalist, which defeated the point of quitting my job. After all, I became a blogger to have a better life! Now I schedule breaks into my diary and make sure I have some time to do nothing. If possible, I try to take Sundays off as all work and no play will make anyone ill.

Q: What's the first thing I should do if I want to be a full-time blogger?

A: I think there are two things that all start-up bloggers need to do. Firstly, work out what you want to write about and ask yourself how much you love that subject and whether it will still interest you in five or ten years' time. Secondly, ask yourself where you want to be in ten years' time and plan backwards to achieve it. If you don't have a plan, then you won't last very long as a blogger.

Q: What's the daily routine like? Can you lie in, then go to a party and write about it?

A: Theoretically you can set your own hours, but you need to work hard at the start if you want your blog to take off. Coverage of an event is an important part of your day as the more you apply yourself at the event, the more likely you are to get exclusive content that will bring someone to your blog. However, once you have the content you have to write about it. Once you've written about it, you have to make sure you've told as many people as possible through Facebook, Twitter, a newsletter and directly contacting the celebrity agents and people you met at the event. After that, you need to keep up to date with what events are coming up so you can cover those in the future and make sure you're invited.

It's not just about events, either. In a typical day I'll get opportunities to do freelance blogging, magazine articles or special projects, and a PR might ask to meet me to show me the company's latest products or fashion collection. These PRs will also flood my inbox with press releases and I will skim read them all to see if anything will benefit the blog.

I try to switch off by midnight, unless there is a really lively showbiz party, but I am always awake at 6am. I want all last night's celebrity news to be on *Live Like A VIP* by 9am so that people can start the working day with their breakfast and my blog.

Q: How do you stay motivated?

A: I have both selfish and altruistic reasons for what I do. Hopefully, I am making a difference to people's lives by entertaining them, which is supremely satisfying, If someone laughs, smiles or starts a conversation with a friend as a result of something I've written, then I've done my job. People take life too seriously and there is too much depressing news in the world – I want to make everyone feel more fabulous!

I also find the job is a huge adrenalin rush and I thrive on adrenalin – I've run the London Marathon twice, I've flown a stunt plane, I've skydived, I love to scuba dive and I've done some pretty dangerous white-water rafting. When you turn up to an event or start an interview, you never know what will happen. You have the pressure of getting something fabulous to satisfy your readers and you know that if you don't get anything juicy, you will be disappointing a lot of people. Therefore, if you do get something there is a huge surge of excitement and you can't wait to tell everyone about it.

Q: How can I get a celebrity to follow me on Twitter or Facebook?

A: Celebrities are real people so if you want them to follow you, you have to do exactly what you do to make other people follow you – say something interesting! If you constantly repeat what others are saying or spam people by posting lots of links to your blog, you'll never get any followers. Instead it's all about saying things nobody else is saying, so following you will add something new to their lives.

Also, if you desperately want a certain celebrity to follow you then try to meet them in person and ask. I interview a lot of celebrities and sometimes I ask them to follow me on Twitter at the end of the interview. If you don't ask, you won't get. Tell them you'll tweet a link to the article when it's out so they have to follow you to see the interview!

Q: Do you have to know a lot about websites and HTML to run a blog?

A: I knew nothing about websites when I first started! I found WordPress very easy to use – simply write a blog post, hit the publish button and it's online. However, as I got more involved with the industry, I attended bloggers' networking events and met people who knew more than I did as I wanted to learn more. If you want to take blogging seriously, then eventually you'll need some technical knowledge as it will be invaluable if your blog breaks and you can fix it yourself. However, don't worry too much at the start.

Q: I'd love to set up a blog but is there room for a new one about music/film/celebrity gossip?

A: As long as you can contribute something different from what the other blogs are doing, there will be room for you. Just remember, you have to be unique if you want followers. If you do the same as everyone else then there's no point.

Q: What are the coolest things you've done?

A: I've been to the Cannes Film Festival, where I partied with George Clooney, Brad Pitt and Matt Damon and then attended a party on Bruce Willis's rented yacht. I've had corporate hospitality at some great gigs, including Beyoncé and Britney Spears and I DJed at the V Festival, which was a huge adrenalin rush.

Q: Do you run the blog completely alone?

A: At the start I did. However, once you grow a following people start asking if they can contribute in exchange for a byline and I say the more content, the better. Also, now the site makes money, I am able to afford to pay a full-time chief reporter, who is excellent.

Q: How do you decide what's worth writing about?

A: I put myself in the shoes of my readers. I ask myself if I could find out anything about the world of celebrity, then what would it be and why? Every time I think of covering an event, I ask myself: would the average reader actually care about this? If I wasn't personally involved in the story, then would I still write about it?

Q: Where do you get your images from?

A: You have to be so careful with images – as a general rule it's best to take them yourself so you know you have copyright. If you're not careful you can get into a lawsuit, as Perez Hilton experienced when he was involved in a dispute over copyright with the American photographic agency X17.

Q: What's your best advice?

A: Set yourself targets so you can work towards something concrete or you'll find it very easy to get distracted or disheartened. Also, show your readers that you care about them by interacting on Facebook, Twitter and by giving them rewards. Without your readers you would be nowhere, so it's important to keep them feeling valued and keep them coming back.

COOL CELEBRITY BLOGGERS

- *Cinevue* (cinevue.co.uk)
- *Deadline Hollywood* (deadlinehollywood.co.uk)
- *Gawker* (gawker.com)

TIPS FOR FILM, MUSIC AND CELEBRITY NEWS BLOGGERS

- *Go Fug Yourself* (gofugyourself.com)
- *Heckler Spray* (hecklerspray.com)
- *Hey U Guys* (heyuguys.co.uk)
- *I'm Not Obsessed – INO* (imnotobsessed.com)
- *Just Jared* (justjared.buzznet.com)
- *Lainey Gossip* (laineygossip.com)
- *Music News* (musicnews.com)
- *Perez Hilton* (perezhilton.com)
- *Pink Is The New Blog* (pinkisthenewblog.co.uk)
- *Popjustice* (popjustice.co.uk)
- *Popsugar* (popsugar.com)
- *Flickering Myth* (flickeringmyth.co.uk)
- *The 405* (fourohfive.co.uk)
- *TMZ* (TMZ.com)

PR AGENCIES

If you want to get on the guest list then you need to get in touch with record labels and film studios like Universal, Fox and Disney. These major labels and studios all have regional offices and details can be found on their websites. If in doubt, call the Head Office and ask for the PR department in your area. If there's a specific event for which you want to get press accreditation so that you can blog about it without having to buy a ticket then you need to visit that event or festival's website and look for the Contact Us section to find PR details. If no PR details are listed, call the switchboard number there and ask.

If you're thinking of covering British related celebrity events and news stories then your contacts book must contain the following PR agencies:

- Avalon (avalonuk.com): celebrity representation – comedians, event organisation
- Beige (beigelondon.com): Virgin Media, Virgin Active, Sony
- Cake (cakegroup.com): V Festival, Carling Beer
- Concorde Media (concordemedia.com): events including gala film screenings
- DawBell (dawbell.com): The Brit Awards, celebrity representation for music clients
- DDA Publicity (ddapr.com): brand launches and shop openings
- Eden Cancan (edencancan.com): fashion parties for their clients Spanx, Puma and Lipsy
- Freud Communications (freud.com): BAFTA Awards, UK film premieres, Soho House Group
- House PR (housepr.com): MOBO Awards, T4 On The Beach, London Freeze Festival, Thorpe Park
- LD Communications (ldcommunications.co.uk): Wireless Festival, Hyde Park Calling Festival
- Outside Organisation (outside-org.co.uk): events including Q Awards, Cosmopolitan Ultimate Woman Of The Year Awards, management including Katie Price
- Premier PR (premierpr.com): UK film premieres and West End theatre openings
- Pretty Green (itsprettygreen.com): events sponsored by their clients, e.g. Nando's Gignics, Red Bull Hunger Games
- Purple PR (purplepr.com): parties for their fashion clients DKNY and Cavalli
- Taylor Herring (taylorherring.com): Ivor Novello Awards, Lovebox Festival

• Way To Blue (uk.waytoblue.com): specialist in digital PR for films – Paramount, Lionsgate, 20th Century Fox

FACEBOOK

Celebrity bloggers use Facebook in a very different way to other bloggers. As yet there are no dedicated groups catering to bloggers. The only way to engage is to post your articles on the Facebook fan page related to the celebrity you're blogging about. For example, if I wrote a blog post about Madonna, I'd post a link to it on some Madonna fan pages.

If you generally love writing about celebs then you'll like the fact that there is no 'bloggers' community. We need to have some motivation to talk to the fans rather than talk to each other all the time. If you have a specific question for other bloggers you can normally find their contact details on their blogs.

TWITTER

Celebrity Tweets (celebritytweets.com) is my top tip for anyone wanting to get all the best celebrity Twitter action in one place. You don't need to follow the stars individually – just visit one website to see all the latest tweet gossip.

OTHER BLOGGERS ANSWER THE FAQS

Q: How do you find out about all the parties?

Cinevue: We partner with a website called Film Dates, which lists new releases week by week. We also have our own personalised widget.

Q: How do you get the balance right between work and social life?

Perez Hilton: Be prepared to not have a social life for the first two years!

INO: Sometimes it's very difficult. There are truly not enough hours in most days but you just have to commit to doing it, there's no way around it. Yes, you have to be on top of the work and be diligent, but you can't neglect your personal life, family, friends, yourself. You will 100 per cent burn out, which I have a couple of times. You can't just sit and work at the computer all day long, it's not healthy. Figure out how to maximise your work and play time, make sure you force yourself to have fun – life is short.

Flickering Myth: It can be hard to manage your schedule, particularly if you blog part-time and have to manage this alongside work and family commitments. As any dedicated blogger will tell you, it can be extremely addictive and time-consuming, and before you know it, you're spending hour upon hour sitting at your computer working on every aspect of your site. So if you're seriously considering taking up blogging, expect your social life to suffer!

Q: What's the first thing I should do if I wanted to be a full-time blogger?

Popjustice: TV, radio and print mentions don't help as much as you might think – it's really down to decent content. I notice it now, still: if I write something amazing, there's a traffic spike. If I don't, there's not. Actually, at the height of his fame I once registered justintimberlake.co.uk and pointed it at *Popjustice* – that helped quite a lot, although I'm not sure if it was for the right reasons.

Q: What's the daily routine like? Can you just go to a party then write about it?

TIPS FOR FILM, MUSIC AND CELEBRITY NEWS BLOGGERS

Go Fug Yourself: We bottom out at seven times per day – too early and we're not awake yet in California to troubleshoot; too late, and the other time zones drop off from their work days and might miss posts when they check in the next day. So we tend to go hourly, 8am to 2pm California time. If it's a major event, we go every half hour, and often start an hour earlier and end two or three hours later. It's about volume. We are so centred around what people wear that it's hard to generate content if nobody is leaving the house so we don't want to post fifteen times a day on Monday or Tuesday and then only have four things for Thursday, you know? We aim for balance, but on weeks after huge events where we know the material is in massive supply, we really push it and post a ton.

INO: I have a few sites, but for *I'm Not Obsessed* it's typically in the morning for a few hours. It used to be all day, but I just had to slow it down, especially since launching *LadyandtheBlog.com* and acquiring *Babyrazz.com*. Now, I have a bunch of wonderful writers who cover the news in shifts all day long. There's coverage from 7am until midnight or so.

Q: How do you stay motivated?

Perez Hilton: I have lots of fun – that's motivation!

Q: How can I get a celebrity to follow me on Twitter?

Popjustice: Blogs, like bands, need to use social media, but they need to use it carefully and cleverly. If all you do is post links to your blog on Twitter, I'm not going to want to follow you – there needs to be something more to what you do.

Q: It sounds like you have a great life. Are there any downsides to the job?

Go Fug Yourself: There have been times where I've written

something and regretted it, or gotten hate mail for something that actually made a good point about why I shouldn't have written it. Those days suck, because you get paranoid that everyone feels that way and that you've let the entire readership down. But there was one time really early on, in 2005, when we wrote about a lady from MADtv who looked kind of insane, and I concluded with, 'Where is her mother?' And another TV comedian who is friends with that lady wrote to us and was like, 'I am sure you had no idea, but her mother is actually recently dead, and I just thought you might want to know that.' I felt awful – I edited it immediately. And oddly, I saw that lady at my local post office last week and I still had a feeling of wanting to go give her a hug and apologise.

Q: Is there any advice that you can pass on to me?

INO: Try to build link exchanges with similar sites – the more the merrier. Sure, it's a business and it's competition, but a rising tide raises all ships, I think.

Q: How can I get free tickets to gigs/film screenings?

Popjustice: There are so many start-up bloggers that the chances of getting free tickets or CDs, or at least the ones you might want to actually listen to or attend, are fairly slim. Mind you, if you're only getting into it for free stuff, you're doing it for the wrong reasons. The best advice is to start reviewing stuff that's already within reach.

The 405: It took a while before people started sending us CDs and putting us on the guest list for shows, but not a super-long time. Initially it was whatever we were listening to (that we bought) that we covered.

Hey U Guys: We randomly received an email from Substance PR, who saw our site and liked it so they started inviting us to premieres and events. The first premiere we did was *Star Trek* and since then the phone hasn't stopped calling with event offers.

I really advise anyone who wants to start a film blog to start going to the cinema and reviewing. That's what we did and got recognised. If you have contacts that's great – use them. If not, just carry on what you're doing and you will get recognised. PRs are always on the lookout for new film blogs so if you are good and update regularly you will get noticed.

Q: Do you have to know a lot about websites and HTML to run a blog?

INO: About a year and a half ago we moved to WordPress and really like it. It's stable and there are constant updates, but updating themes and adding widgets [functionality] is really pretty easy. Sure, there are a fair amount of things you need to hire developers to do, but starting out, it's really great. A lot of people are developing cool apps/designs for WordPress.

Q: I'd love to set up a blog but is there room for a new one about music/film/celebrity gossip?

Hey U Guys: Competition is fierce, but also keeping on top of news and trends is vital. It's very easy to get left behind if you rest on your laurels. We support the little guys. Most film blogs these days are very corporate. Although we do cover all the mainstream movies – as we get invited to all the premieres now – we do like to give the independent films a chance at being covered. We try to act as professionally as possible and we always see the positive side of the film industry. Too many blogs concentrate on what is negative about film and we don't so much, so I think that's why we have become popular. We are truthful, but offer constructive criticism.

Go Fug Yourself: At the time we started, nobody's blog was as laser-focused on celebrity fashion in the way that we were. Now, I think the best thing we offer that's different is ourselves. You're not going to our site to see breaking news on what outfits people are wearing, you're coming to hear our point of view and then chat with us about it. We are not news-focused so much as personality-focused, and I think that's been what our readers respond to – we've created this community of regulars who feel like we are their friends, and we feel they are our friends, so every day it's like checking in to see if your buddies watched the Oscars and what the hell they thought of Kate Winslet's dress. We're an online water cooler, in a way.

Q: What are the coolest things you've done?

Popjustice: There have been *Popjustice* club nights, live nights, books, albums, even a record label, as well as things like consultancy and public speaking. The website is what it's all about still, though.

Q: Do you run the blog completely alone?

Popjustice: I have a freelance features editor who's in the office most days, as well as a small team of contributors who help with news. These are all people who've applied to *Popjustice* and who share my ideas about what makes pop brilliant and what makes pop bad.

Hey U Guys: The best decision I made was to have a partner, or deputy editor. Even if you have to bribe them, having John around was the best decision I ever made. I think otherwise I would have had a nervous breakdown by now. Also, it's important to have people work for you who have the same passion as you. This means they will get what you are trying to achieve and being on the same page helps – a lot.

Q: How do you decide what's worth writing about?

Popjustice: If it's amazing, it goes in. That's still the main editorial rule.

I want to end this book by saying how impressive it is to witness how much passion all the bloggers I interviewed had for their subject matter, which backs up one of the points I made at the start. If you want to succeed in blogging then you need to blog about the issue or topic that interests you more than anything else in the world, or you won't be able to keep up the work needed to get you to the top.

The time it will take you to make a name for yourself in your field depends on how much time you dedicate to your blog. The more hours you devote to interacting with your readers and refining your content, the quicker you will build up a community and develop it. However, don't be tempted to skip any of the steps outlined in chapters 1 to 7. These are vital to growing an audience and without a loyal readership, your blog is worthless. It doesn't matter how much effort has gone into writing a post if nobody is reading it. Start off slowly, test the waters, find out what people like and keep giving them more of it.

If I can get rich from my blog you can, too!

FURTHER READING

Blogging For Dummies (Third Edition). S. Gardner& S. Birley, 2010. Wiley Publishing

Blogging For Fame and Fortune. J.R. Rich, 2009. Entrepreneur Press

Blogging: The Essential Guide. A. Chitty, 2012. Need2Know

The Huffington Post Complete Guide To Blogging. A. Huffington, 2009. Simon and Schuster

ProBlogger: Secrets To Blogging Your Way To A Six Figure Income (Third Edition). D. Rowse & C. Garrett, 2012. Josh Wiley & Son